Two Types of Faith

.

The Martin Buber Library

First Syracuse University Press Edition 2003

10 11 12 13 14   6 5 4 3 2

This volume, without the Afterword, was first published in the United States
by the Macmillan Company, New York, in 1951.

The paper used in this publication meets the minimum requirements of
American National Standard for Information Sciences—Permanence of
Paper for Printed Library Materials, ANSI Z39.48–1984.∞™

Library of Congress Cataloging-in-Publication Data

Buber, Martin, 1878–1965.
[Zwei Glaubensweisen. English]
Two types of faith / Martin Buber ; translated by Norman P. Goldhawk
with an afterword by David Flusser.— 1st Syracuse University Press ed.
p. cm.—(The Martin Buber library)
Includes bibliographical references and index.
Translation of: Zwei Glaubensweisen.
ISBN 0–8156–3034–4
1. Judaism—Relations—Christianity. 2. Christianity and other religions—
Judaism. 3. Jesus Christ—Jewish interpretations. 4. Faith. I. Goldhawk,
Norman P. (Norman Panter) II. Flusser, David, 1917–
III. Title.
BM535 .B813 2003
296.3'96—dc21   2003012224

Manufactured in the United States of America

CONTENTS

Translator's Foreword
6

Foreword by Martin Buber
7

Two Types of Faith
17

Afterword by David Flusser
175

Index to the Principal Subjects and Names
237

FOREWORD

THE subject with which I am concerned in this book is the twofold meaning of faith.

There are two, and in the end only two, types of faith. To be sure there are very many contents of faith, but we only know faith itself in two basic forms. Both can be understood from the simple data of our life: the one from the fact that I trust someone, without being able to offer sufficient reasons for my trust in him; the other from the fact that, likewise without being able to give a sufficient reason, I acknowledge a thing to be true. In both cases my not being able to give a sufficient reason is not a matter of a defectiveness in my ability to think, but of a real peculiarity in my relationship to the one whom I trust or to that which I acknowledge to be true. It is a relationship which by its nature does not rest upon 'reasons', just as it does not grow from such; reasons of course can be urged for it, but they are never sufficient to account for my faith. The 'Why?' is here always subsequent, even when it already appears in the early stages of the process; it appears, that is to say, with the signs of having been added. This does not at all mean that it

7

is a matter of 'irrational phenomena'. My rationality, my rational power of thought, is merely a part, a particular function of my nature; when however I 'believe' in either sense, my entire being is engaged, the totality of my nature enters into the process, indeed this becomes possible only because the relationship of faith is a relationship of my entire being. But personal totality in this sense can only be involved if the whole function of thought, without being impaired, enters into it and may work within it, as properly disposed to it and determined by it. To be sure we are not allowed to substitute 'feeling' for this personal totality; feeling is by no means 'everything', as Faust thinks, but is at best only an indication of the fact that the being of the man is about to unite and become whole, and in other cases it is an illusion of becoming a whole without its being actually effected.

The relationship of trust depends upon a state of contact, a contact of my entire being with the one in whom I trust, the relationship of acknowledging depends upon an act of acceptance, an acceptance by my entire being of that which I acknowledge to be true. They depend upon this, but they are not this itself. The contact in trust leads naturally to the acceptance of that which proceeds from the one whom I trust. The acceptance of the truth acknowledged by me can lead to contact with the one whom it proclaims. But in the former instance it is the existent contact which is primary, in the latter the acceptance accomplished. It is obvious that trust also has a beginning in time, but the one who trusts does not know when: he identifies it of necessity with the beginning of the contact; on the other hand the one who acknowledges truth stands to that which he acknowledges as true, not as to something new, only now appearing and making its claim, but as to something eternal which has only now become actual; therefore for the first the status is the decisive thing, for the second the act.

8

Faith in the religious sense is one or the other of these two types in the sphere of the unconditioned, that is, the relationship of faith is here no longer one towards a person conditioned in himself or a fact conditioned in itself and only unconditioned for me, but to one which in itself is unconditioned. So here the two types of faith face each other. In one the man 'finds himself' in the relationship of faith, in the other he is 'converted' to it. The man who finds himself in it is primarily the member of a community whose covenant with the Unconditioned includes and determines him within it; the man who is converted to it is primarily an individual, one who has become an isolated individual, and the community arises as the joining together of the converted individuals. We must beware however of simplifying this twofoldness antithetically. This involves, above what has already been said, the consideration of a fact of supreme importance in the history of faith. The status in which the man finds himself is to be sure that of a contact with a partner—it is nearness; but in everything which grows out of it an ultimate distance persists which is not to be overcome. And on the other hand the act by which man acknowledges truth presumes the distance between a subject and its object; but the relationship which arises from it with the being indicated by the acknowledged fact can develop into the most intimate nearness, and indeed into the feeling of union.

The first of the two types of faith has its classic example in the early period of Israel, the people of faith—a community of faith which took its birth as a nation, a nation which took its birth as a community of faith; the second in the early period of Christianity that arose in the decay of ancient settled Israel and the nations and faith-communities of the Ancient East as a new formation, from the death of a great son of Israel and the subsequent belief in his resurrection, a

9

new formation which first, in prospect of the approaching End, intended to replace the decaying nations by the Community of God, and afterwards, in view of the newly-beginning history, to span the new nations by the super-nation of the Church, the true Israel. Israel on the other hand had arisen from the re-uniting of more or less disinte-grated family-tribes and of their faith-traditions—in Biblical language, from the conclusion of a covenant between them and the conclusion of a covenant between them all and their common God as their covenant-God. This faith in God was itself born—if one may, as I assume, rely at this point upon the Biblical narratives—from the tribe-forging and nation-forging migrations which were experienced as guided by God. The individual finds himself within the objective race-memory of such guidance and of such a covenant: his faith is a perseverance in trust in the guiding and covenant-ing Lord, trusting perseverance in the contact with Him. This type of faith was modified only during the time of the Diaspora permeated by Hellenism, the time when the mission was adapting itself to those who were sought, but hardly ever has it been changed in its inmost nature. Christi-anity *begins* as diaspora and mission. The mission means in this case not just diffusion; it is the life-breath of the com-munity and accordingly the basis of the new People of God. The summons of Jesus to turn into the Kingship of God which has 'come near' was transformed into the act of conversion. To the man needing salvation in the despon-dent hour, salvation is offered if only he will believe that it has happened and has happened in this way. This is not a matter of persisting-in but its opposite, the facing-about. To the one to be converted comes the demand and instruc-tion to believe that which he is not able to believe as a con-tinuation of his former beliefs, but only in a leap. To be sure the inner precinct of faith is not understood as a mere believing that something is true, but as a constitution of existence; but the fore-court is the holding true of that which has hitherto been considered not true, indeed quite absurd, and there is no other entrance.

That the faith-principle of acknowledgment and acceptance in the sense of a holding henceforth that so-and-so is true is of Greek origin requires no discussion. It was made possible only through the comprehension reached by Greek thought of an act which acknowledges the truth. The non-noetic elements, which were combined with it in the primitive Christian mission, originate essentially from the Hellenistic atmosphere.

In the comparison of the two types of faith which I have attempted in this book I confine myself principally to the primitive and early days of Christianity, and for that almost exclusively to the New Testament records on the one hand, and on the other side in the main to the sayings of the Talmud and the Midrashim, originating from the core of Pharisaism, which was to be sure influenced by Hellenism but which did not surrender to it; I draw on Hellenistic Judaism only for purposes of clarification. (The after-effects of the Old Testament always lead on to the problem of its interpretation.) It becomes evident that Jesus and central Pharisaism belong essentially to one another, just as early Christianity and Hellenistic Judaism do.

When I treat the two types of faith frequently as that of the Jews and that of the Christians I do not mean to imply that Jews in general and Christians in general believed thus and still believe, but only that the one faith has found its representative actuality among Jews and the other among Christians. Each of the two has extended its roots into the other camp also, the 'Jewish' into the Christian, but the 'Christian' also into the Jewish and even into pre-Christian Judaism as it arose from 'Hellenistic' religiosity, which was formed from the Oriental decay by the late-Greek *eidos*, a religiosity which penetrated into Judaism before it helped to found Christianity; but only in early Christianity was this faith fully developed and became in the strict sense the faith of believers. By the 'Christian' type of faith therefore is meant here a principle which was joined in the early history of Christianity with the genuine Jewish one; but it must be borne in mind, as I have pointed out, that in the teaching of Jesus himself, as we know it from the early texts of the gospels, the genuine Jewish principle is manifest. When later on Christians desired to return to the pure teaching of Jesus there often sprang up, in this as in other points also, an as it were unconscious colloquy with genuine Judaism.

The consideration of the difference in the types of faith leads to the consideration of the difference in the contents of their faith, in so far as they are intrinsically bound up with those. To draw attention to these connexions is a fundamental aim of this book. The apparent digressions also serve this aim.

There is scarcely any need to say that every apologetic tendency is far from my purpose.

For nearly fifty years the New Testament has been a main concern in my studies, and I think I am a good reader who listens impartially to what is said.

From my youth onwards I have found in Jesus my great brother. That Christianity has regarded and does regard him as God and Saviour has always appeared to me a fact of the highest importance which, for his sake and my own, I must endeavour to understand. A small part of the results of this desire to understand is recorded here. My own fraternally open relationship to him has grown ever stronger and clearer, and to-day I see him more strongly and clearly than ever before.

I am more than ever certain that a great place belongs to him in Israel's history of faith and that this place cannot be described by any of the usual categories. Under history of faith I understand the history of the human part, as far as known to us, in that which has taken place between God and man. Under Israel's history of faith I understand accordingly the history of Israel's part as far as known to us, in that which has taken place between God and Israel. There is a something in Israel's history of faith which is only to be understood from Israel, just as there is a something in the Christian history of faith which is only to be understood from Christianity. The latter I have touched only with the unbiased respect of one who hears the Word.

That in this book I have more than once corrected erroneous representations of the Jewish history of faith rests upon the fact that these have found their way into works of important Christian theologians of our day who are in other respects authoritative for me. Without sufficient clarification of that which has to be clarified men will continue to speak to each other at cross-purposes.

In particular I have to thank from the point of view of this book four Christian theologians, two living and two dead.

I am obliged to Rudolf Bultmann for fundamental instruction in the field of New Testament exegesis. I do not only remember with gratitude his works but also a memorandum on John iii which he wrote for me many years ago in answer to a question: this model colleague action of a German scholar in the highest sense has had a clarifying and stimulating influence upon my understanding of the passage, which deviates from his (as seen in Chapter XI of this book).

I thank Albert Schweitzer for that which he gave me to know immediately through his person and his life, the openness towards the world and through this the peculiar nearness to Israel, which are possible to the Christian and also to the Christian theologian (which Schweitzer has never ceased to be). I still treasure in my heart, never to be forgotten, the hours of a walk we took together through the scenery of Koenigsfeld and through that of the Spirit, and not less the day when we, so to speak hand in hand, opened the session of a philosophical society in Frankfurt-am-Main with two rather unphilosophical lectures on religious reality. He has expanded his lecture into the book on the Mysticism of the Apostle Paul. In the dedication, which he sent me twenty years ago, Schweitzer says that he establishes that Paul 'has his roots in the Jewish world of thought, not in the Greek'; I however can connect the Pauline doctrine of faith, which I treat in this book, only with a peripheral Judaism, which was actually 'Hellenistic'. On the other hand his renewed emphatic reference to the meaning of the servant of God in Deutero-Isaiah for Jesus has remained fruitful; already by as early as 1901 Schweitzer had given me a strong incentive for my studies on this subject.

I retain a thankful memory of Rudolf Otto for his profound understanding of the divine majesty in the Hebrew Bible and for a series of richly realistic insights in his work on eschatology, the importance of which far outweighs its errors; but even more for the noble frankness with which he opened to me his believing heart in our peripatetic conversations. The most impressive of these for me was the first, because first I had to drive a breach through the psychologist's wall which he had erected around himself, and then not merely an important religious individuality was revealed but in the actuality between two men, the Presence.

I give thanks to the spirit of Leonhard Ragaz for a friendship in which his genuine friendship towards Israel was expressed. He saw the true countenance of Israel, even when the political entanglements had begun to hide it from the world, and he loved Israel. He looked forward to a future understanding between the nucleal community of Israel and a true community of Jesus, an understanding, although as yet inconceivable, which would arise on neither a Jewish nor a Christian basis, but rather on that of the common message of Jesus and the prophets of the turning of man and of the Kingship of God. His ever fresh dialogue with me by word of mouth, by letter, and in the silent existence, was for him the preparatory dialogue between these two.

To my Jerusalem friends Hugo Bergmann, Isaak Heinemann and Ernst Simon, who have read the manuscripts, I offer thanks for valuable references.

I wrote this book in Jerusalem during the days of its so-called siege, or rather in the chaos of destruction which broke out within it. I began it without a plan, purely under the feeling of a commission, and in this way chapter after chapter has come into being. The work involved has helped me to endure in faith this war, for me the most grievous of the three.

MARTIN BUBER

Jerusalem-Talbiyeh, January 1950

I

I N one of the Gospel narratives (Mark ix. 14–29) it is reported that a boy possessed by a demon is brought by his father, first to the disciples of Jesus, and then, because they 'were not able' to cure him, to Jesus himself, in order to see whether he 'might be able' to help. Jesus seizes upon the father's word, 'if thou art able to do anything'. 'If thou art able!'[1] he replies, 'all things are possible to him that believeth'. The whole narrative is based, in accordance with the Old Testament pattern, on the two key-words[2] 'to believe' and 'to be able', and both are most expressively repeated time and again in order to impress upon the reader that he is to be definitely instructed in this instance about the relationship between the human condition of 'believing' and that of 'being able'. But what is to be understood in this

[1] The usual rendering, 'If thou canst believe', according to which Jesus is speaking about the faith of the father and not about his own, does not correspond, as is well known, with the authentic text.

[2] Concerning the key-words or governing-words in the Old Testament, cf. Buber and Rosenzweig, *Die Schrift und ihre Verdeutschung* (1936) 55 ff., 211 ff., 239 ff., 262 ff.

17

case by the designation 'he who believes'? It had actually been said that the cure was not possible to the disciples; if that is so, according to the words of Jesus they are not to be reckoned as believers. What is it then which generically distinguishes the faith of Jesus from their faith? It is a difference in kind because the question here is not about the degree in the strength of the faith, but rather a difference which extends to the ultimate depths of the reality concerned in such a way that only the faith which Jesus knows as his own may be called faith in the strict sense. The narrative which follows proves that there is such a difference, that it is not a question in this instance of a gradation in the intensity of an attitude and conviction, but rather of the polar distinction 'belief or unbelief'. 'I believe,' the father implores Jesus, 'help my unbelief!' Viewed from the standpoint of the event itself this statement is strange, for Jesus had not expressly alluded to the father's attitude of faith,[1] and one may suppose that the father mistakenly understood the declaration as referring to himself instead of to Jesus. But the evangelist is not so much concerned with a report which is consistent in itself as with instruction about a fundamental fact. He makes the father say what the disciples would have had to say to Jesus, who in his verdict traced their inability to heal the boy back to their unbelief. Indeed, the man who is referred to in the judgement of Jesus recognizes that it is unbelief; but, he pleads, I believe nevertheless! From his perception and understanding of himself he knows about a state of the soul which must indeed be described as 'faith'; but he does not in any way set this subjective fact over against the statement of Jesus about the objective reality and effect of the 'one who believes', as if it claimed equal

[1] Torrey to be sure translates in v. 23: 'if you are able' (he removes the τό as an addition by the Greek translator): but it is not to be supposed that Jesus attributes the cure to the father, provided that he only believes.

right—it is, as the narrator emphatically observes, a cry from the heart of the human creature, who nevertheless feels as he does and learns about faith what is to be learned about it by feeling; the world of the heart is not allowed to claim equal right, but it is also a world. Information about the authority and the limit of the feeling is imparted. The confession of the heart is valid; but it does not suffice to constitute the believer as an objective and objectively effective reality. What is it which does so constitute him?

In one of the most important works on the text of the Gospels[1] the saying of Jesus about the one who believes is interpreted in the following way: 'The sentence reads: to me, Jesus, all things are possible, because I believe I am able to heal the boy'; this being, according to the Greek text, the 'only possible meaning'. But that is an obvious contradiction. For 'I believe that I am able to heal him' asserts an inner certainty, like every use of the verb 'to believe' construed with 'that'. That this certainty is sufficient to produce the 'to be able' runs contrary to the experience of mankind; that is made quite clear in the story of Simon Magus from a circle which touches that of the New Testament; in the consciousness of faith in himself as 'the great power of God', he is certain that he is able to fly, and, on undertaking the flight from the Capitol before Nero and his court, breaks his neck; a naïve modern poet, Bjoernson, even wished to demonstrate by a dramatic example that a cure can go 'beyond our power' without going beyond our certainty. If however one refers the declaration of Jesus to himself only and not to man in general, then the 'because I believe' becomes quite absurd; for if the action belongs to Jesus alone, Jesus as Jesus, then it springs from his being Jesus and not from his certainty that he is able to heal. But

[1] Merx, *Die vier kanonischen Evangelien nach ihrem aeltesten bekannten Texte*, II Teil, 2 Haelfte (1905), 102.

in addition to this, Jesus and his whole purpose is brought perilously near to that of the magician. Are not magicians people who believe that *they* are able to heal?

But that Jesus did not only mean himself when he referred to 'one who believes', at any rate not fundamentally himself alone, is proved by the parallel version in Matthew's Gospel (xvii. 14–21), which sets forth with complete clarity the motif that it is not fundamentally an affair between Jesus and the people (represented by the father of the boy)—although in this case also they are referred to as 'unbelieving'—but one between himself and the disciples. The problem of the relationship between believing and 'being able' comes out here immediately in the disciples' question as to why they could not cast out the demon, and the reply of Jesus which opens with the definite 'because of your unbelief'; it is actually the disciples to whom is ascribed (not, as modified versions desire, a 'little faith'—which appears nowhere else) but that unbelief which is in kind opposed to faith. In the sequence the answer sets forth even more forcibly the fact that in this case it is not a question of a difference in degree, in intensity, in quantity: as little as 'a grain of mustard-seed' of the real stuff of faith is sufficient 'and nothing shall be impossible to you'. At the same time it is equally clearly stated that true faith is not the prerogative of Jesus but it is accessible to man as such, and provided it is true faith, they have sufficient, no matter how little they have of it. Therefore even more strongly than before there is forced upon us the question as to what this faith is and in what it differs so decisively from that state of soul which bears the same name.

'All things are possible to him that believes.' Elsewhere (Mark x. 27; Matt. xix. 26), it reads, in conjunction with the Old Testament: with God all things are possible. When the two sentences are taken together we come nearer the meaning of what is said about the man who has faith. Not to be sure if one means[1] that what is asserted there of God may apply to one who believes, that he has the power of God. The words 'possible with God' and 'possible to him that believes' do not really coincide. 'With God all things are possible' does not mean what the disciples who heard it knew very well, that God is able to do all things, however much this is also associated with it, but, transcending this, that with God, in His realm, in His nearness and fellowship,[2] there exists a universal possibility, that therefore all things otherwise impossible become and are possible here. This applies also to the person who has entered into His realm: the 'one who believes'. But it only applies to him in virtue of his having been taken into the realm of God. He does not possess the power of God; rather the power possesses him, if and when he has given himself to it and is given to it.

This idea of the man who has faith did not spring from Hellenistic soil. That which appears to be similar in pre-Christian Greek literature already in the tragedy always refers to a mere condition of the soul, not to an actual relationship which essentially transcends the world of the person. So far as I am aware, the only pre-Christian writing in which it is found is the Old Testament. Only from there are we able to learn to understand it more precisely.

In Isaiah xxviii. 16—which, to be sure, is generally misunderstood—God proclaims that He is 'to found in Zion the precious corner-stone of a founded foundation' (the threefold repetition is to direct attention in the highest degree to the character of decisiveness which here belongs to the verb). But in order to guard against false interpretation of the present-form, as if now the revelation of the corner-stone is to be expected, and so those now living

[1] Thus Lohmeyer, *Das Evangelium des Markus* (1937), 188.
[2] Cf. Matt. vi. 1; John viii. 38, xvii. 5.

21

might look forward confidently to the coming time, he adds: 'He that believeth will not make haste', which includes the thought: 'he will not wish to make haste'. (In conformity with this the words of God about His action which follow have a future form.) Here seemingly an aspect of the man who believes is given which is precisely opposite to the assertion of Jesus: instead of the working of miracles a strong reserve against them is attributed to him. But of course his connexion with the possibility of doing all things is thereby set forth: only if and because the 'hastening' is possible to him in itself can it be explained that he, the man who believes, will not exercise it, that is, will not ask for it with the power of prayer of his soul, while the unbelievers, mocking, scornfully demand (v. 19) that God may 'hasten' His promised work, so that they may come to 'see' it. Straightway however we notice that we have not yet arrived at the correct understanding. For what is possible to the man who believes, therefore also hastening, is here likewise possible to him only as to one who believes; but all through the Old Testament to believe means to follow in the will of God, even in regard to the temporal realization of His will: the man who believes acts in God's tempo. (We only grasp the full vitality of this fundamental Biblical insight when we realize the fact of human mortality over against God's eternity.) So the 'passive' in Isaiah and the 'active' in the Gospels are combined. This person acts because God's time commands him to act, the fact that illness meets him on his way indicates the Divine call to heal; even he can only act in God's tempo. The power of God has both, it ordains both, it authorizes both, even him who is apparently powerless. For his apparent powerlessness is the outward form of his participation in the power and its tempo. How he himself at times came to recognize this later on, the posthumous disciple of Isaiah has represented in

22

the figure of the passive arrow concealed in the quiver and its late understanding of itself (xlix. 2 ff.).

Both passages have also this in common, that the substantive participle, meaning 'he who believes', is used absolutely in both. As has already been shown, the fact that nothing is added to what the man of faith believes has a strong meaning and reason. It is not by any means an abbreviated terminus, arising from the permissible omission of 'in God'. Indeed the addition of this takes from the idea its essential character, or at least weakens it. The absolute construction conveys to us in both passages the absoluteness of what is meant. By which it shall not and cannot be said that 'faith in general' is meant, a thing which neither the Old nor the New Testament knows, but solely that every addition, because usual for the characterization of a condition of the soul, might tend to miss the fullness and power of what is signified, of the reality of the relationship which by its very nature transcends the world of the person.

II

ACCORDING to the report in Matthew's Gospel, the fundamental point in the earliest preaching of Jesus in Galilee was identical with that which, according to the same Gospel, the Baptist had earlier begun to use for the inauguration of each of his baptisms in the Judaean desert, and probably for the baptism of Jesus also: 'Turn, for the kingly rule of God has come near'. But in Mark, where the Baptist's words are missing, the word of Jesus, in which we perceive now a pneumatic and stormy rhythm in the place of the challenging and substantiating style of preaching, runs: 'The appointed time is fulfilled and God's rule has come near. Turn and believe in the message.'[1] (The verb at the end, which corresponds to the construction of the Greek translation of a verse in the Psalms,[2] can be rendered as there: 'trust the message!') The fact that the hearer is desired here to believe 'the gospel', which is only just now being announced to him, has raised a doubt in the minds of many expositors: 'Jesus will not have

[1] On the meaning of the word cf. Dalman, *Die Worte Jesu* (1898), 84 f.
[2] 106 (105) 12.

said this'.[1] But we ought not to go so far as to conclude that the verb itself is an addition. 'Turn and trust' does not alone sound quite genuine, but the conclusion does gain a peculiar force and completeness hardly to be obtained otherwise. Here too then the verb appears in the absolute sense. The preacher does not invite his hearers to believe his word: he aims after the intrinsic value of the message itself. The hour that has been predetermined for aeons has arrived, the kingly rule of God which existed from the beginning, but which was hidden until now, draws near to the world, in order to realize itself when apprehended by it: that ye may be able to apprehend it, turn, ye who hear, from your erring ways to the way of God, come into fellowship with Him, with Whom all things are possible, and surrender to His power.

Of the three principles of the message—realization of the kingship, the effecting of turning to God, a relationship of faith towards Him—the first is of historical and super-historical, cosmic and super-cosmic proportions; the second concerns the man of Israel who is addressed, in whom the being of Man as addressed has its concrete reality, and through him Israel as such, in which the intended humanity has its concrete reality; the third is concerned with the person alone—there is indeed a turning which the nation as such can accomplish in history, but the reality of the relationship has, according to its essence, its exclusive abode in personal life and cannot elsewhere take effect. The first of these principles, which concerns the existence of all that exists, is most strictly combined with the other two, which are confined to the actual life of those addressed. The world-governing *dynamis*, which has indeed been constantly and directly at work, but which as such is not yet apparent in itself, has now, in its coming from heaven to earth, so drawn

[1] E. Klostermann, *Das Markusevangelium*, 2. ed. (1926), 14.

near that the human race, that Israel, that the Jew who is addressed, can lay hold of it by the turning about of their life; since the message of the *kairos* which is fulfilled was proclaimed by the Baptist, 'everybody'—as a much-debated saying of Jesus (Luke xvi. 16 cf. Matt. xi. 12)[1] indicates—that is, everybody who fulfils the required turning, forces his way 'with power' into the *Basileia* which already touches his own sphere of existence, so that it can increasingly become an actual reality in the world. Nevertheless the individual as an individual cannot perceive this event in its course; he must 'believe', more correctly, 'trust'. But this is not merely an attitude of soul, which is required for the accomplishment of turning; the most decisive turning does not yet achieve sufficient human reality, but still requires something which is effective not only in the soul but in the whole corporeality of life; it requires Pistis, more correctly, Emunah. Since the *kairos* is fulfilled, the man who achieves turning into the way of God penetrates into the *dynamis*, but he would remain an intruder, charged with power but unfit for the world of God, unless he completes the surrender of the 'man who believes'. *Teshuvah*, turning of the whole person,[2] in the sphere of the world, which has been reduced unavoidably to a 'change of mind', to *metanoia*, by the Greek translator—and *Emunah*, trust, resulting from an original relationship to the Godhead, which has been likewise modified in the translation to 'belief', as the recognition that something is true, i.e. rendered by *pistis:* these two demand and condition one another.

[1] Cf. below in chap 9. I incline towards the view that in both parallel references fragments of a reading which cannot be restored have been mixed up with secondary elements of a different kind.

[2] It must nevertheless be noticed that the Old Testament does not yet know the noun in this meaning, but merely the verb; turning to God is still conceived exclusively as something concrete and actual.

The three principles of the message, an heirloom of the religiosity of Israel, are referred here to the time of the speaker as to that of fulfilment, and thereby to one another. That which was called the 'Old Testament' by men who became followers of Jesus after his death, the 'Reading', properly speaking, the 'Exposition', in whose living tradition Jesus had grown up, had developed them from scanty but pregnant beginnings. The kingship of God was announced from below as the rule over the people in the Song of the Red Sea, whilst the Sinai-revelation, introduced by the 'eagle's speech' (Exod. xix. 16), was proclaimed from above;[1] the prophets had shown the intended rule over the people as intended to become the manifest rule over the world in the future, in which the King of Israel will unite them all as 'King of the Nations' (Jer. x. 7); and the Psalmists had sung of His ascending the throne as a cosmic and earthly event, both eternal and imminent. The call to turn back 'to God' or 'up to God' is the primary word of the prophets of Israel; from it proceed, even when not expressed, promise and curse. The full meaning of this summons is only made known to him who realizes how the demanded 'turning-back' of the people corresponds to a 'turning-away' by God from the sphere of His anger or of His 'returning' to Israel (this 'turning' and 'returning' are sometimes emphasized together). Yet this conjunction does not correspond to the relationship between a supposition and a conclusion, but turning and returning are related to one another as two corresponding parts in a conversation between two partners, in which the one who is infinitely subordinate preserves also his mode of freedom. We understand this dialogicism as a whole when we consider that previous to the word of God which was proclaimed in its

[1] Cf. Buber, *Koenigtum Gottes*, 2. ed. (1936), 111 ff.; *Moses* (1948), 74 ff.; 101 ff.

full rigour in the period after the collapse (Zech. i. 3; Mal. iii. 7) 'Turn back to me and I will turn again to you' the cry from below rings out even before the collapse (Jer., xxxi. 18): 'Let me return and I will turn to Thee', and after the collapse it appears again, at the end of the Lamentations (v. 21), refined and purified: 'Let us return to Thee and we will turn.' The individuals who had projected this turning-back 'with their whole heart and with their whole soul' (1 Kings viii. 48) know and acknowledge that they need the grace of their King for its execution. And now to these two —the acknowledgment of the kingship and loyalty to the King which is fulfilled in the complete faithfulness to Him— there is joined Emunah, as the third principle of the message.

We find the imperative 'have faith' ('trust') at a later place in the Old Testament, in a record in Chronicles (2 Chron. xx. 20). In a connexion which is historically very doubtful Jehoshaphat of Judah addresses his army before the battle, and says: 'trust (*haaminu*) in the Lord your God and you will remain entrusted (*teamenu*)'. The sentence is a much-weakened imitation of Isaiah's word to Ahaz of Judah (Isa. vii. 9): 'If you do not trust you will not remain entrusted.' Here too a deeper stratum of the meaning is brought out by the absolute use of the verb. We are not here presented with a mere play upon words in the relating of the two verbal-forms to each other; as nearly always in old Hebraic texts this is the way for something to be inferred by the hearer or reader. The two different meanings of the verb in the passage go back to one original: stand firm. The prophet is saying (to put it into our language): only if you stand firm in the fundamental relationship of your life do you have an essential stability. The true permanence of the foundations of a person's being derive from true per-manence in the fundamental relationship of this person to the Power in which his being originates. This 'existential' characteristic of Emunah is not sufficiently expressed in the translation 'faith', although the verb often does mean to believe (to believe someone, to believe a thing). It must further be noticed that the conception includes the two aspects of a reciprocity of permanence: the active, 'fidelity', and the receptive, 'trust'. If we wish to do justice to the intention of the spirit of the language which is so expressed, then we ought not to understand 'trust' merely in a psychical sense, as we do not with 'fidelity'. The soul is as fundamentally concerned in the one as in the other, but it is decisive for both that the disposition of the soul should become an attitude of life. Both, fidelity and trust, exist in the actual realm of relationship between two persons. Only in the full actuality of such a relationship can one be both loyal and trusting.

Both the word of Isaiah and the word of Jesus demand in a similar way, not a faith 'in God', which faith the listeners of both possessed as something innate and as a matter of course, but its realization in the totality of life, and especially when the promise arises from amidst catastrophe, and so particularly points towards the drawing near of God's kingdom. The only difference is that Isaiah looks to it as to a still indefinite future and Jesus as to the present. Therefore for Isaiah the principles are apportioned to three moments which closely follow one another in his 'I'-narrative about the beginnings of his effective work (chap. vi–viii): when he sees 'the King' (Isa. vi. 5), when he gives his son the name 'a remnant remains' (implicit in vii. 3), and when he calls upon the unfaithful viceroy of God to trust (vii. 9); for Jesus they are blended in the first proclamation of his preaching in Galilee.

III

As part of the narrative of the acts of Jesus in Galilee, Mark relates (viii. 27 ff.) how, while journeying with his disciples, he asks them first whom he is considered to be by the people, and then what they think, and how the second question is answered by Peter that he is 'the Anointed-One'. Critical research inclines to the opinion that this is a 'faith-legend', transmitted presumably in a fragmentary form,[1] in which the Church put its confession of faith in the Messiah into the apostle's mouth; for the question about the opinion of the disciples could not have been understood, according to the character of the saying and the situation, either as a Socratic question or as a real one, given that Jesus 'was of course as well-informed as the disciples' about the circumstances. My impression is that the narrative may well contain the preserved nucleus of an authentic tradition of a conversation which once took place

---

[1] Bultmann, *Die Geschichte der synoptischen Tradition*, 2. ed. (1931), 276; cf. Bultmann, *Die Frage nach dem messianischem Bewusstsein Jesu, ZNW* 19 (1920), 156 ff.; *Theologie des Neuen Testaments* (1949), 2 f. ('an Easter story projected by Mark into the life of Jesus').

'on the way'. The question is certainly not of a pedagogic nature; but I can quite well imagine it being asked in all seriousness. I offer no opinion as to whether one may suppose that Jesus 'did not attain to complete certainty about his appointment to the Messianic office until the end';[1] this is not to be decided, and the arguments for and against will presumably continue to be discussed as heretofore. But it is to be expected of anyone who thinks of Jesus neither as a god only apparently clothed in human form, nor as a paranoiac, that they will not regard his human certainty about himself as an unbroken continuity. The certainty a person has about his nature is *human* only in virtue of the shocks to this certainty; for in them the mean between the existence of God and the demonic delusion of being God, the region reserved for that which is authentically human, becomes evident. One may consider that other question of Jesus, which was his last, the 'Why?' addressed to 'his' God in the words of the Psalmist about the abandonment which had befallen him, to be a later interpretation of the wordless cry of death; that both Mark and Matthew accepted it, however, witnesses to the fact that even so great a shock to the Messianic consciousness, as this expression of 'unfathomable despair'[2] shows, was not felt by the conviction of the Church to contradict the Messianic status. Whatever may be the case with the much-debated problem of the 'Messianic consciousness' of Jesus, if it is to be understood as human, we must admit lapses in the history of this consciousness, as must have been the case on the occasion which was followed by the conversation with the disciples—assuming

[1] Brandt, *Die evangelische Geschichte* (1893), 476.

[2] Lohmeyer, loc. cit., 345. M. Dibelius, *Gospel Criticism and Christology* (1935) p. 59, supposes to be sure 'that the words of this Psalm on the lips of Jesus signified that he was resigned to God's will', but I cannot agree with this.

that one is inclined to take this conversation seriously, as I do. A teacher, whose teaching depends entirely upon the effect produced by his person and therefore by his nature, has a presentiment of the cross-road of his fate and his fateful work, and is seized with uncertainty as to 'who' he is. The attack of uncertainty belongs inevitably to the essence of this moment, as the 'temptation' does to that of an earlier one.[1] The situation breaks through the limits of the psychical process; it presses on to the real question. To whom else shall a teacher, who not only no longer has a teacher himself but evidently neither a friend who really knows him, direct the question than to his pupils? If anybody could answer him, they could; for from the unique contact which such a relationship produces they have acquired the experience from which alone the answer could be made.

These considerations were necessary in order to lead up to the problem which has to occupy us: how a section of a similar nature in John's Gospel is related to the account in the Synoptics about the conception of faith. Each time in the Synoptics Peter answers with a simple declaration which begins with 'Thou art' (Thou art the Anointed-One, or God's Anointed, or the son of the Living God). Both question and answer are absent from John—it could not have been otherwise, since his Jesus belongs to a spiritual realm rather than to our human one, and he is not open to attacks of self-questioning; instead Peter gives expression here to his word in connexion with another conversation. In his reply to the question of Jesus to the disciples as to whether they too would go away from him, he says (vi. 69): 'We have believed and known (more exactly, we have

---

[1] Bultmann explains this too as a mere legend (*Theologie des Neuen Testaments*, 22); I can only consider the Synoptic stories of the temptation as the legendary elaboration of the encounter with the demoniacal which determines a definite stage in the life of the 'holy' man.

attained the faith and knowledge) that thou art the Holy One of God.' In Mark and Luke the demoniacs invoke their master with this title, which is derived from the Old Testament and means there one consecrated to God, be it priest or Nazirite; in the New Testament texts the generic term turns naturally into an emphatically singular one, which John elsewhere defines with precision (x. 36): it is God Himself Who has sanctified him, His 'only-begotten Son' (iii. 16), when sending him into the world. They 'believe' and 'know' that Jesus is the Holy One of God. The direct statements about the master in the Synoptics have in this case become one about the disciples. In the Synoptics, Peter in answer to the question as to 'who' Jesus is in the opinion of the disciples, makes a declaration about this nature, but in this case he confesses his faith in an asserting sentence (that . . .). This faith, joined with the knowledge that is condensing it (see also x. 38, xvii. 8), but almost identical with it, is the 'work of God' demanded of men (vi. 29); the one who does not believe 'in' him whom He has sanctified and sent, falls, instead of 'having' 'eternal life', under God's wrath 'which abides on him' (iii. 36). It is not as if this way of expressing faith were itself foreign to the Synoptics; but where it occurs it concerns predominantly, or at least in the main, trust. On the other hand, of course, a 'believing that' does appear also in the Old Testament (so Exod. iv. 5), in order to say that belief is accorded to an account received about some event, without there being attributed to this act of faith any of that fateful meaning such as we find in the statements of John. The boundary line is drawn again in such a way that, having regard to the type of faith, Israel and the original Christian Community, in so far as we know about it from the Synoptics, stand on one side, and Hellenistic Christianity on the other (whereas Hellenistic Judaism, with its effacements of the boundaries,

33

has only rarely been equal to the earnestness of the religious process; compare the vacillations in the conception of faith in Josephus and even Philo, who it is true does rise in a few places to a genuine philosophic expression of Israel's life of faith).[1]

If we consider the Synoptic and Johannine dialogues with the disciples as two stages along one road, we immediately see what was gained and lost in the course of it. The gain was the most sublime of all theologies; it was procured at the expense of the plain, concrete and situation-bound dialogicism of the original man of the Bible, who found eternity, not in the super-temporal spirit, but in the depth of the actual moment. The Jesus of the genuine tradition still belongs to that, but the Jesus of theology does so no longer.

We have taken our stand at that point in the midst of the events reported in the New Testament where the 'Christian' branches off from the 'Jewish'. That Judaism in its way of faith itself subsequently turned aside to dogmatically 'believing that', until its Credo in the Middle Ages reached a form not less rigid than that of the Christian Church—except that its formulae were never set in the centre—this fact belongs to another connexion. In the period at the beginning of Christianity there was still no other form of confession than the proclamation, be it in the Biblical form of the summons to the people, 'Hear, O Israel', which attributes uniqueness and exclusiveness to 'our' God, or in the invocation of the Red Sea song to the King recast into a statement, 'It is true that the God of the world is our King'.

[1] In our connexion the most important reference is *De migr. Abr.* 9, in which Abraham's acceptance of the non-present as present is not accompanied by any doubt, and is derived from his 'most firm trust'; he believes because he trusts, not the other way round. Hatch, *Essays in Biblical Greek* (1889) p. 87, incorrectly attributes the same conception of faith to the Epistle to the Hebrews (see further below).

The difference between this 'It is true' and the other 'We believe and know' is not that of two expressions of faith, but of two kinds of faith. For the first, faith is a position in which one stands, for the second it is an event which has occurred to one, or an act which one has effected or effects, or rather both at once. Therefore the 'we' in this instance can only be the subject of the sentence. True, Israel also knows a 'we' as subject, but this is the 'we' of the people, which can to be sure apply to 'doing' or 'doing and hearing' (Exod. xxiv. 3, 7), but not to a 'believing' in the sense of the creed. Where it is said of the people (Exod. iv. 31, xiv. 31) that they believed, that simple trust which one has or holds is meant, as in the case of the first patriarch. When anybody trusts someone he of course also believes what the other says. The pathos of faith is missing here, as it is missing in the relationship of a child to its father, whom it knows from the very beginning as its father. In this case too a trusting-in which has faltered must sometimes be renewed.

IV

IN one version of the Epistle to the Hebrews (iv. 2) the children of Israel who were taken out of Egypt are reproached for not having united themselves 'by faith' with Moses as the hearer of God's word. The narrative from Exodus (Exod. xix. 17) is here referred to, where the people shrank from hearing the word without a medium. What is meant is that they had first refused to lay themselves open to the voice of God, and then also shunned the message of the mediator, in that they refused to him that which was decisive for his being received, 'faith'. The manifold disobedience of the wanderers in the wilderness (Heb. iii. 16 ff.) is traced back to their 'unbelief' (v. 19), and the answer of the people at Sinai, their declaration of doing and hearing, is stated to be worthless because it was openly lacking in faith. From this point it is essential that the author of the epistle should determine what is actually understood by faith. This happens (xi. 1) in a way characteristic of the Greek method of thought, which, in that hour between Paul and John, furnished Christian theology with a fundamental reinforcement and greatly influenced the following periods.

Faith is defined, not simply but in a double aspect and in such a manner that its two aspects stand unconnected beside each other, the 'assurance of what is hoped for' and the 'conviction of things unseen'. Here in a remarkable way a Jewish and a Greek concept of faith are joined together. The relation to the future, without a spark of which the natural man cannot live, hoping, becomes for the early Israelite assurance, because he trusts in the God with whom he is intimate (this is the Old Testament meaning of the word 'to know' when it is used of the relationship between God and man). In addition however there is added as a second point from Greek philosophy the familiar *elenchos*, the 'proof' or the 'demonstration', or, to do justice to the factor of the believing person, conviction; only one may not then inquire who it is who effects conviction, the man of faith himself, which would be contrary to the sequence, or as the older exegetes think, the faith, or as the later ones do, God. For neither the faith which cannot give what it is can be thought of, nor God, Who in that case must have been named, but He does not appear before the verse after the next; in addition however the objective Greek terminus does not in any way urge the question about the effecting subject, and the second part no more requires such a one than the first which is parallel to it. Nevertheless the understanding of the meaning of this *elenchos* as clearly as possible is required. The first part has as its object that which is to come, that which does not yet exist, which as such cannot yet be perceived, the second that which cannot in any way be perceived, the unseen and unseeable, that is, the eternal in distinction from the temporal, as Paul states (2 Cor. iv. 18). He who has faith in the sense of the Epistle to the Hebrews has received proof of the existence of that, the existence of which admits of no observation.

To the man of ancient Israel such a proof is quite foreign,

because the idea of the non-existence of God lies outside the realm of that which was conceivable by him. He is 'made to see' (Deut. iv. 35) that the God of Israel, 'his' God (vii. 9) is not a special God but the only God, and nevertheless also the 'faithful' God to Whom he may entrust himself; that there is 'a' God, he 'sees' apart from this. Even when it is recorded of the 'transgressors' that they deny God, it means that they presume God not to be present, not to care about the affairs of the earth.[1] Whether this man recognizes God's rule or objects to it, whether he is responsive or refractory, he lives by the fact that God is, no matter how he lives. 'Whoever cometh to God' it says in the continuation of the exposition in the Epistle to the Hebrews (xi. 6), 'must believe that He is . . .'[2] To the true Israelite this is a truism. It merely depends here—and upon this point rests the whole weight of earthly decision—upon whether an individual understands the fact of the divine existence as the fact of the actual Presence of God, and on his part realizes the relationship to God which is so indicated to him, to the human person; that is, whether he trusts in the God Who exists 'as a matter of course' as truly his God. The assurance of what is hoped for requires therefore neither a basis nor a support. On the other hand for the Epistle to the Hebrews (one of its commentators says for the New Testament as a whole[3]) the existence of God is 'not something to be taken as a matter of course, but an article of faith; man does not feel the nearness of God, but he believes in it'.

Moreover, as already shown, the category of 'things not seen' in the sense of an *absolute* imperceptibility of all eternal

---

[1] Cf. for example, Ps. x. 4 with xiv. 1; the negation does not mean 'God does not exist' but 'God is not present'.

[2] For the whole verse, cf. the next chapter.

[3] O. Michel, *Der Brief an die Hebraeer* (1936), 165.

things is also foreign to the man of the Old Testament. To be sure, God is invisible; but without prejudicing His invisibility 'He gives Himself to be seen', namely in manifestations, which He Himself transcends but nevertheless gives as His appearing, and this man experiences as such manifestations—experiences, not interprets—both historical events and natural phenomena, which stir his soul. The man who has faith in the Israelite world is not distinguished from the 'heathen' by a more spiritual view of the Godhead, but by the exclusiveness of his relationship to his God and by his reference of all things to Him. He does not need to be convinced of what he does not see: what he sees he sees in the faith of the invisible. But even the opening of the heavens at the baptism in the Jordan in the Synoptics (it too is missing in John) still belongs to the same realm of ideas as the view of the elders from the top of Sinai—whereas in John nobody but Jesus himself has a sight of God (xii. 44, xiv. 9). We must only insist on understanding such passages 'rationalistically', or rather in the highest sense realistically. Christian and late-Judaistic considering as true that God exists belongs to the other side.

In John's Gospel the faith which is expressed in 'We have obtained the faith and knowledge' is placed under the command and the judgement. It is recorded (vi. 28 ff.) how, after the feeding of the five thousand, the 'crowd', which had followed Jesus in boats over the Sea of Genesaret, asked him what they had to do 'in order to do the works of God', that is, to fulfil the will of God in their lives. He replies: 'This is the work of God, that ye believe in him whom He has sent'. 'He who believes in him', it says in another passage (iii. 18), is not judged. He who does not believe is already judged. The most profound interpretation of these words that I know[1] says that in the decision of faith there comes to

[1] Bultmann, *Das Johannesevangelium* (1939), 115.

39

light what the individual really is and always has been, but it does so in such a manner that only now it is being decided; and so the great separation between light and darkness takes place. The supposition for a decision between faith or unbelief is lacking in the world of Israel, the place for it is as it were missing, because the world of Israel grew out of covenants with God. The separation, which is announced in Israel's Scriptures, cannot be between those who have faith and those who have not, because there is here no decision of faith or unbelief. The separation which is here meant takes place between those who realize their faith, who make it effective, and those who do not. But the realization of one's faith does not take place in a decision made at one definite moment which is decisive for the existence of him who makes the decision, but in the man's whole life, that is in the actual totality of his relationships, not only towards God, but also to his appointed sphere in the world and to himself. A man does the works of God accordingly in pro- portion to the effectiveness of his faith in all things. For Israel—according to its mode of faith—everything is de- pendent upon making its faith effective as actual trust in God. One can 'believe that God is' and live at His back; the man who trusts Him lives in His face. Trusting can only exist at all in the complete actuality of the *vita humana*. Naturally there are different degrees of it, but none which requires for its actuality merely the sphere of the soul and not the whole area of human life. By its very nature trust is substantiation of trust in the fulness of life in spite of the course of the world which is experienced. The Old Testament paradigm for this is Job: he experiences and expresses without restraint the apparent godlessness of the course of the world and reproaches God with it, without however diminishing his trust in Him; indeed, whilst God Himself 'hides His face' and 'withdraws the right' from His creature, Job waits in expectation of seeing Him in the body (xix. 26 is to be understood in this way), by which sight the cruel appearance of what appears is pierced and overcome, seeing by seeing—and it happens (xlii. 5).

It must not however remain unnoticed that the setting of faith under the judgement of God—and seemingly in that same 'Christian' meaning of faith as acceptance of the truth of a proposition and of unbelief as the opposing of it—was not foreign to the Judaism of the early Talmud, as the much-discussed sentence of the Mishna (Sanhedrin X) shows, which denies a share in the 'coming world', that is in eternal life, to three categories: to those who deny the resurrection of the dead, to those who deny the heavenly origin of the Torah, and to the 'Epicureans' who, following the teaching of Epicurus, deny to God as the Perfect Being an interest in earthly affairs. But this proposition, which is indeed contemporary with the early days of the Christian Community, characteristically is not concerned at all with belief or unbelief in the existence of God or the existence of any transcendent being; the reason for the three negations being condemned obviously consists in the fact that they tend to prevent or destroy man's complete trust in the God Who is believed in. The third is the most general and fundamental: only the man who knows that the Creator-God, the God of all things, cares about him can trust Him. This caring of God manifests itself most sensibly in two acts, one in the past, yet which directly influences the present condition of the man who trusts: the revelation to Israel, through which he learns how he can fulfil God's will; and one in the future, which however acts similarly, the resurrecting of the dead, the promise of which warrants to the man who trusts that even death, apparently the end of his existence, is not able to put an end to God's concern with him and accordingly to his concern with God. The man who contests these three—

says the sentence of the Mishnah—himself destroys his relationship to God, apart from which there is no eternal life for man.

It is evident that a considerable change in relation to the Old Testament idea of faith has here taken place, and this under the influence of Iranian doctrines and Greek ways of thought. But we must not fail to recognize how strong the organic connexion with the original state of Israel's faith has remained even in this attitude. The further development, determined by the discussion with Christianity and Islam, proceeding from formula to formula and leading to the regular confession in creeds, belongs no longer in essence to living religion itself but to its intellectually constituted outposts, to the theology and the philosophy of religion.

V

T HE sentence in the Epistle to the Hebrews about the man who comes to God runs in its complete form: 'Without faith (*pistis*) it is impossible to please God; for whosoever cometh to God must believe (*pisteuein*) that He is and that He is a rewarder of those who seek Him'. Here the acknowledgment of God's existence is blended in one 'faith' with the Old Testament attitude of trust in Him, but in such a way that this second element also becomes a believing 'that' He is the rewarder. The sentence thereby seems to come near that of the Mishnah about the three categories, but this is only apparently the case. The Mishnah leaves the fundamental character of the trust intact; trust is not changed into acknowledgment, but the lack of it to denial, and that in accordance with the meaning—a person can be a confessor without really trusting, whereas the denial makes the lack of trust absolute. But it is quite foreign to the spirit of the Mishnah, as I said, that the primary certainty of God, without which man cannot be agreeable to God, as Enoch (*v.* 5) was agreeable to Him, becomes a constituent part of the

43

'believing that'. Nevertheless 'the elders' (*v.* 2) i.e. the men of faith of the Old Testament, are called as witness for this faith, naturally without it being possible to say of any one of them that, in the sense of an inner or external act of confession, he had 'believed that God is'. The strange thing is that among the evidences cited for Abraham's faith there is missing that central incident amongst the seven revelations belonging to him in the Genesis-account, where alone it is said of the patriarch (xv. 6) that, according to the usual translation, he believed in God, or rather, according to the true meaning of the word, trusted Him; it is missing here, although soon afterwards (Hebrews xi. 12) the preceding verse from the same chapter is quoted. But that gigantic figure, Paul, whom we must regard as the real originator of the Christian conception of faith, has, before the author of the Epistle to the Hebrews, based his representation of Abraham as the father and prototype of the man of faith (Rom. iv) upon this incident.

In the Genesis-narrative Abraham 'in the vision' by night is taken by God, Who in the struggles had been his 'shield' (xv. 1), out of the tent and placed in view of the starry heavens of Canaan, that he might count the stars if he were able: 'so shall thy seed be'. It is now said of Abraham that he 'continued to trust' God (the peculiar verbal form is meant to express this), and of God that He 'deemed' this 'as the proving true' of him. We must try to grasp what the narrator meant by this, in order to estimate the difference between this and what Paul derived from the text which was not only translated into Greek but virtually Hellenized, and with which he had grown up to be familiar, so that it deeply influenced his understanding of the original. What is recorded of Abraham is an immovable steadfastness: one is reminded by this use of the verb of the use of the noun in the story of the battle with Amalek (Exod. xvii. 12) where

44

Moses' right hand,[1] held up by a support and raised to the sky, is 'steadiness', that is, remains firmly steady; we might come nearest the verbal-form if we render it: 'and he let remain firm to JHVH' (no object is required here), whereby however no special action is meant but only as it were a supply of strength in relation to an existent essential relationship of trust and faithfulness together.[2] In view of a promise which he was able to believe only from this essential relationship, the patriarch enhanced this yet by strengthened surrender. This is now deemed as proving him true. As *zedek* is the pertinently-fitting verdict, the agreement of an assertion or action with reality, about which judgement is made, so *zedakah* is the manifestation of the conformity between what is done and meant in the personal conduct of life,[3] the proving true (which idea is then transferred to God as confirmation of His benevolence). Which action in the past finally attains the character of a proving true can in the nature of the case be decided neither by the individual nor his community, but by God alone, through His 'deeming', in which alone everything human becomes openly what it is. The verb, which later receives the meaning 'to think',

[1] It is to be read in the singular, corresponding with the previous verse; on the whole incident cf. the chapter 'The Battle' in my book *Moses*.

[2] According to Weiser, *Glauben im Alten Testament*, *Festschrift Georg Beer* (1933), 91, the hiphil form of the verb, where it is used of the relationship of man to God, had the meaning of a declaration in the sense of 'perceiving the relationship into which God enters with men and of recognizing it in such a manner that man places himself in this relationship'. The attitude of Abraham in Gen. xv. 6 cannot be covered by this definition; he does not place himself in a relationship, but he already stands in it, and now essentially remains in it. Even a usual verbal form like Exod. iv. 31, xiv. 31 intends to relate a consolidating of Emunah, and not a turning towards it; this is expressed so only in a late text, Jonah iii. 5, which already belongs to the beginning of the mission.

[3] Buber-Rosenzweig, *Die Schrift und ihre Verdeutschung*, 156.

originated, it seems, in the technical sphere as 'to think out, to plan'; although it slightly touches forensic language in the sense of legal attribution, it has not deeply penetrated it; its main meaning has become 'to consider', either as deliberation, plan, or as estimation, valuation. Men of course are only able to estimate and value individual phenomena as such;[1] God however can deem anything which happens in a man and which proceeds from him as the full realization of the essential relationship to the Godhead. For in this moment, in this movement of his total being, the person has raised himself to that position which is decisive for the revelation of his worth; the nature of the creature has attained the being intended by the creation, and even the most extreme 'temptation' will only be able to draw forth and realize what was then ordained.

Paul found in his Greek Bible at this point something which is immersed in a different atmosphere. Abraham does not believe 'in' God, in the sense of a perseverence in Him, but he believes Him—which to be sure does not require to mean that he believed His words (such a weakening of the sentence is not in the mind of the translator), but it does denote an act of the soul in the moment described. More important still is the fact that instead of the divine consideration, deeming, ratification, there has come into being an attributing, a category in the judicial computation of items of guilt and innocence against each other, and in connexion with this instead of the proving true, a 'righteousness', the rightness of the conduct which justifies the individual before God; both are a limitation, a deflation of that original fulness of life, a limitation common to Alexandrian and contemporary rabbinical Judaism. With its assumption by Paul however the sentence is penetrated by the principles

[1] Hence not only God (Ps. xxxii. 2) but men also (2 Sam. xix. 20) can reflect, contemplate, remember a failure of anyone.

of the Pauline faith and justification doctrine, and its import is changed: faith, as the divine activity in man, gives rise to the condition of being righteous, which the 'works', proceeding from men alone, the mere fulfilment of the 'law', are not able to bring about. The simple face-to-face relationship between God and man in the Genesis story is replaced by an interpenetration which comes about by faith and faith alone, the dialogical by the mystical situation; but this situation does not remain, as nearly always in mysticism, an end in itself; it is grasped and discussed as the situation which alone can place the individual in that state in which he can stand the judgement of God. By imparting the state of faith God Himself renders it possible as it were for Him to be gracious without detriment to His justice. When we read that sentence first in the original and then in the Septuagint we are displaced from the high-ground where God receives Abraham's attitude of faith, his persistence in Him, as proving true, to the deep valley, where the act of faith is entered in the book of judgement, as the decisive fact of the case in favour of the person judged; when we read the sentence afterwards in the context of the Pauline letters we are removed on to a rocky slope where the inner divine dialectic governs exclusively. The fundamentals of this dialectic-idea are to be found in Judaism, namely in the early Talmud, but the conception of the intercourse between the divine attributes of severity and of mercy[1] changes here to the extreme real paradox, by which for Paul (here we are obliged to anticipate for a moment the course of this investigation) even the great theme of his faith, his Christology, is supported, without it being possible to be expressed: in redeeming the world by the surrender of His son God redeems Himself from the fate of His justice, which would condemn it.

[1] Cf. below in chapter 14 further on this point.

The transformation of Israel's conception of faith by Paul becomes still clearer perhaps in another of his quotations. In the Epistle to the Galatians (iii. 6) he repeats first the reference to Abraham: all who have faith share in the blessing bestowed upon him, whereas the doers of the law 'stand under the curse'—a far-reaching verdict, which Paul bases upon the translation of the Septuagint: as the concluding sentence in the list of curses on Mount Ebal (Deut. xxvii. 26) it said, following a tradition for which we have other testimonies too, 'Cursed be the man who does not uphold the words of this instruction to do them', which is changed into 'Cursed is everyone who does not continue in all things which are written in the book of the law, to do them'. 'By law', it now runs, 'no one is justified before God'. In support of this (v. 11) the word of the prophet Habakkuk (ii. 4) about the just or rather the man proved true is referred to, who 'will live in his faith', a word which Paul quotes also in the Epistle to the Romans (i. 17) in order to characterize the 'righteousness' which is truly agreeable to God, and which 'is revealed by faith to faith'. The word from Habakkuk and the sentence about Abraham have evidently been joined with each other in his mind, as the individual fact and its general proclamation.

In the difficult and apparently mutilated verse Habakkuk speaks about an enemy of Israel. 'See', he says, as if pointing to him, 'his soul was puffed up, it did not become more upright within him'. And now he interrupts the description with the antithetical exclamation: 'But the man proved true will live in his trust' (to be understood, it seems, as an exclamation of the prophet interrupting God's speech, the like of which we know from other prophetic texts). After that it is said of that 'presumptuous man' that he has made his throat broad as hell, and insatiable as death he draws the peoples to him and snatches them up. Here is unmistakably meant the man who recognizes no other commandment than the never-resting impulse of his own force to become power. He refuses to know moderation and limitation, and that means, he refuses to know the God from Whom he holds on trust his power as a responsibility, and Whose law of moderation and limitation stands above the deployment of force by those who are endowed with it. By the action of inflated self-assurance, which has nothing in common with genuine trust and is nothing other than self-deception, genuine trust in the faithful God has become completely lost. The maddened self-assurance will bring ruin upon him. Opposed to him, and appearing only in brief exclamation, is the 'man proved true', the man who represents on earth the truth of God, and who, trusting in the faithful God, entrusts himself to Him in this confidence which embraces and determines his whole life, and through it he has life. He 'will live', for he depends upon and cleaves to the eternally living God. (One may compare the verse of the Psalm lxxiii. 26, which is probably not much later and which is to be understood in a similar way.)

The two passages in which Paul appeals to the verse from Habakkuk supplement each other. Instead of the 'man proved true' of the original text, and instead of the 'just man' of the Greek version, he understands *zaddik* and *dikaios* of the man who is pronounced righteous. The man of faith, who lives 'from faith', is pronounced righteous—so he understands the verse. Only from faith, not from the fulfilment of God's law, is a man pronounced righteous by God. The law is not 'from faith', for it does not require to be believed but to be done. Paul refers, obviously highly conscious of what is at stake, to the verse (Leviticus xviii. 5) in which God decrees that His statutes and commandments should be kept, in which and through which the man who does them lives. In these two verses Paul wants to distinguish,

49

from the point of view of God himself, two modes of life in regard to Him, according to 'wherein' they exist, on which kind of regard to God, whether the law or faith is that which in this instance or that sustains and preserves the 'life', the life that God may characterize as such. But now the law is overcome through the coming of Christ, who 'has freed us from the curse of the law'. In the place of the life derived from doing has come the life from faith; from this alone there comes and into this alone there enters now 'the righteousness of God', His declaration of man as righteous.

VI

T HE faith, which Paul indicates in his distinction between it and the law, is not one which could have been held in the pre-Christian era. 'The righteousness of God', by which he means His declaration of man as righteous, is that which is through faith in Christ (Rom. iii. 22, Gal. ii. 16), which means faith in one who has come, died on the cross and risen.

In the matter of 'faith' against 'works', which Paul pursues, he does not therefore in fact intend a thing which might have existed before the coming of Christ. He charges Israel (Rom. ix. 31) with having pursued the 'law of righteousness' and not having attained it, because it strove after it 'not by faith but by works'. Is this to mean that ancient Israel did not fulfil the law because it did not strive to fulfil it by faith? Surely not, for it is immediately explained that they had stumbled on the stone of stumbling, and that cannot apply to the former Israel and a possible insufficiency of its faith in the future coming of the Messiah, but only to the Jews of that time, those whom Paul sought for Christ and whom he had not won for him because they did not recognize in him the promised Messiah of belief. In Isaiah's word

(viii. 14), which Paul quotes here in a strange amalgamation with another (that discussed above, xxviii. 16), the 'stone of stumbling' refers to none other than God himself: the fact that His message or salvation is misunderstood and misused as a guarantee of security means that His own word brings the people to stumbling. Paul interprets the saying as referring to Christ. 'For Christ is the end of the law, so that righteousness may come to everyone that believes.' The Jews, who refuse for themselves this faith, refuse to submit to the righteousness of God. Paul prays that they may be saved, but they do not desire it, for they have a zeal for God, but they lack the knowledge.

Again Paul refers to a sentence from the Old Testament, but this time he takes it neither from the history of the time before the law nor from the prophets, but from the 'law' itself. It is the sentence (Deut. xxx. 14): 'For the word is very nigh thee, in thy mouth and in thy heart'. 'That is', Paul continues (Rom. x. 8 ff.), 'the word of faith which we preach. For if thou confess with thy mouth Jesus as Lord and believe in thy heart that God has raised him from the dead, thou shalt be saved'. Paul refers to the verse of Isaiah we have already discussed, 'he who trusts will not hasten', but in the incorrect translation of the Septuagint, which is perplexed by the difficult text and has chosen a different version; hence the sentence which Paul quotes has become: 'Whosoever believeth on Him shall not be ashamed'. This is the Pauline counterpart of the Johannine reply of the apostle to Jesus, 'We have believed and known that thou are the Holy One of God'; both statements supplement each other as only the report of a declaration by disciples who have been apprehended by the living Jesus and the authentic evidence of one apprehended by the dead can supplement each other. But with that sentence from Deuteronomy, where, as he says, (*v.* 6) 'the righteousness which is of faith' speaks, Paul deals very curiously. In the text itself the word which is not in heaven but in the mouth and heart means none other than 'this commandment, which I this day command thee' (*v*. 11), thus not a word of faith but simply the word of the 'law', of which it is declared here that it does not come from far above man, but in such a manner that it is felt to rise in his own heart and to force its way from there on to his lips. But in the sentence which Paul quotes he has omitted a word, the last word of the sentence. The text runs: 'For the word is very nigh thee, in thy mouth and in thy heart, *to do it*'. The word which God commands man speaks to him in such a way that he feels it rising in his heart and forcing its way to his lips as a word which desires to be done by him. As in the case of the 'commandment' so Paul has also left the 'doing' unnoticed. Elsewhere however (ii. 14 ff.) this 'doing' appears in him precisely in conjunction with this 'in the heart': where he speaks *of the heathen*, who 'do by nature the things of the law' because 'the work of the law is written in their hearts'. One may compare with this God's word in Jeremiah (xxxi. 33) that some day the Torah of God shall be written in *Israel's* heart. Strange are the ways of the Pauline hour and its solicitation!

'No flesh' (Rom. iii. 20, Gal. ii. 16), says Paul, becomes righteous before God by the works of the law. This thesis, of which it has been rightly said[1] that for Paul it is 'the principle which requires no proof and is exempted from every conflict of opinions', means above all (Rom. iii. 28) that 'by faith alone', faith in Jesus (*v*. 26) 'without the works of the law', the individual, heathen or Jew, is declared righteous, so that therefore—and this is the special concern of the apostle to the Gentiles—the Gentiles do not have to come through Judaism to Christ, but have their own

[1] Lohmeyer, *Probleme paulinischer Theologie*, ZNW 28 (1929) 201.

immediate approach to him. It means further, as we have seen, that the Jews who refuse to believe in Jesus, have no prop in their possession of the law, but by their refusal reject the only possibility of being declared righteous by God. But the law did not come into the world at the same time as Jesus; how is it with the generations between the two? Unlike Paul's contemporaries, they were not faced with the question as to whether they believed in Christ; but of course they have 'believed', or rather the 'believers' amongst them have trusted God and looked for the coming of His kingship. In this 'faith' of theirs they have truly fulfilled the 'law'. As men of faith, even if, which could not be, they did not believe in the Christ who had come, they have nevertheless, so we may assume, been declared righteous like their father Abraham; did the God who justified them detach their faith from their fulfilling of the law, and heed only the former and not the latter also which was done in faith? Paul expressly says (Rom. ii. 12) that the doers of the law, its true doers in faith, were, as such, declared righteous. Or are we to understand by the futile 'works of the Law' merely a performance without faith? It is however quite obviously Paul's view that the law is not capable of being fulfilled; for he bases (Gal. iii. 10) his statement about the curse under which those are 'who are of the works of the Law' upon the alleged verse of Scripture that everyone is accursed who 'does not continue in all things which are written in the Book of the Law to do them' (the decisive word 'all things' is missing in the Masoretic Text,[1] as

[1] Even in the version which contained the word and which was followed by the Septuagint and also by the Samaritan, it undoubtedly did not have the emphatic meaning, as we can see from its use in similar passages in Deuteronomy. To be sure elsewhere (Deut. xxviii. 58) the non-observance of 'all words of this Torah' is threatened with the most severe penalties, but Scripture carefully adds straightway what is meant by this total claim: 'to fear this glorious and fearful Name'.

stated), therefore the former are identical with the latter: nobody can in fact do everything which the law demands of him under the threat of the curse. The indivisible law which allows of no selection, the 'whole' law (Gal. v. 3), demands therefore according to Paul the impossible, without his differentiating between an external fulfilment which is possible and an impossible fulfilment in the complete intention of faith; evidently he already regards the outward fulfilment as impossible, without of course his indicating what makes it so.

Here not merely the Old Testament belief and the living faith of post-Biblical Judaism are opposed to Paul, but also the Jesus of the Sermon on the Mount, although from a different motif and with a different purpose.

VII

THE Jewish position may be summarized in the sentence: fulfilment of the divine commandment is valid when it takes place in conformity with the full capacity of the person and from the whole intention of faith. If we want to give a parallel formulation to Jesus' demand that is transcending it, the sentence may run like this: fulfilment of the divine commandment is valid if it takes place in conformity with the full intention of the revelation and from the whole intention of faith—in which however the conception of the intention of faith receives an eschatological character. The first of these two positions starts from the actuality of the acting individuals and the conditionality of their ability, the second on the one hand from the actuality of God at Sinai and the unconditionality of its claim, on the other hand from the eschatological situation and the readiness incumbent on it to enter into the kingdom of God which draws near. Both conflict with Paul's critical attitude to the Torah.

I say 'Torah' and not 'law' because at this point it will not do to retain the Greek mis-translation which had such far-reaching influence upon Paul's thought. In the Hebrew Bible Torah does not mean law, but direction, instruction, information. *Moreh* means not law-giver but teacher. God is repeatedly called this in Old Testament texts. 'Who is a teacher like Him?' Job is asked (Job xxxvi. 22), and the prophet promises the future people of Zion: 'Thine eyes shall see thy Teacher' (Isa. xxx. 20); man is ever expectant that the God who forgives will teach Israel 'the good way' (see especially 1 Kings viii. 36) and the Psalmist asks as a matter of inward certainty (Ps. xxv. 4, xxvii. 11): 'Teach me Thy paths'. The Torah of God is understood as God's instruction in His way, and therefore not as a separate *objectivum*. It includes laws, and laws are indeed its most vigorous objectivizations, but the Torah itself is essentially not law. A vestige of the actual speaking always adheres to the commanding word, the directing voice is always present or at least its sound is heard fading away. To render *torah* by 'law' is to take away from its idea this inner dynamic and vital character. Without the change of meaning in the Greek, objective sense the Pauline dualism of law and faith, life from works and life from grace, would miss its most important conceptual presupposition.

It must not of course be overlooked that from the very beginning in Israel itself, with the existence of the Tables, all the more with that of a 'Book of the Covenant' and more than ever of a 'Holy Scripture', the tendency towards the objectivizing of the Torah increasingly gained ground. We become acquainted with its results best in Jeremiah's great accusation (viii. 8 f.), in whose eyes the current saying, 'We are wise, the Torah of JHVH is with us' means a scorning of the divine *word*. In the period of the beginning of Christianity the Hebrew Torah conception became yet more static, a process which brought it near the conception of law, and indeed caused it to be blended with it; the narrow but deeply-felt idea that the Torah has actually been given to Israel and that Israel possesses it thereafter tends effectively to supplant the vital contact with the ever-living revelation and instruction, a contact which springs from the depths of the primitive faith. But the actuality of faith, the undying strength of hearing the Word, was strong enough to prevent torpidity and to liberate again and again the living idea. This inner dialectic of Having and Being is in fact the main moving force in the spiritual history of Israel.

For the actuality of the faith of Biblical and post-Biblical Judaism, and also for the Jesus of the Sermon on the Mount, fulfilment of the Torah means to extend the hearing of the Word to the whole dimension of human existence. This demand made it necessary to struggle against a withering or hardening, which knew of no other fulfilment than the carrying out of rules, and so made the Torah in fact into a 'law' which a person had merely to adhere to as such, rather than to comprehend its truth with every effort of the soul and then to realize it. Indeed the constant danger of the form of faith which tends to the realization of a revealed divine will, is that the keeping of it can persist apart from the intended surrender to the divine will, and can even begin as such, which surrender can alone invest the attitude with meaning and thereby with its right. The beginnings of this process of making the gesture independent go back to the early times of the Sinai-religion. The struggle against it runs through the whole history of Israelite-Jewish faith. It begins in the accusations of the prophets against a sacrificial service robbed of its decisive meaning by the omission of the intention to surrender one's self, gains a new impulse in a time of increased danger in the zeal of the Pharisees against the many kinds of 'tinged-ones', i.e. those whose inwardness is a pretence, and in their contending for the 'direction of the heart', and continues through the ages until at the threshold of our era it receives a peculiar modern form in Hasidism, in which every action gains validity only by a specific devotion of the whole man turning immediately to God. Within this great struggle of faith the teaching of Jesus, as it is expressed in particular in one section of the 'Sermon on the Mount', has a significance, to understand which one must see Jesus apart from his historical connexion with Christianity.

The teaching of Jesus is in this regard fundamentally related to that critical process within Judaism, especially to its Pharisaical phase, and yet at one decisive point stands out against it.

In the Sermon on the Mount it says (Matt. v. 48), 'Ye therefore shall be perfect,[1] as your Heavenly Father is perfect'. The Old Testament commandment, five times repeated (Lev. xi. 44 f., xix. 2, xx. 7, 26), which is likewise founded upon a divine attribute and so likewise summons to the imitation of God, runs similarly yet differently: 'Ye shall be holy, for I am holy'. In the former instance 'ye' refers to the disciples who have gone up the 'mount' to Jesus, in the latter to Israel assembled around Sinai. The address to Israel concerns the sacred principle of the lasting life of the nation, that to the disciples arises out of the eschatological situation and refers to it, as that which demands what is definitely extraordinary, but which also

[1] Torrey's opinion (*The Four Gospels*, 291, cf. *Our Translated Gospels*, 92 f., 96) that in the Aramaic original the adjective means 'all inclusive' is quite mistaken; the references from the Talmud assembled by him lack all force of proof, and Matt. xix, 21, where the word has obviously the same meaning as here, but has to be translated by Torrey by 'perfect', most clearly contradicts it. Bultmann (*Jesus* 111) understands by the adjective: faithful and straight, but proceeds from an Old Testament meaning and not that which was current in the writings at the time of Jesus.

makes it possible. In accordance with this the command to the disciples says, transcending humanity: 'as'; the command to the people says only: 'for'; in the breaking-in of the Kingdom according to the teaching of Jesus man ought to and can touch the divine in his striving after perfection, while the people in the revelation-hour of its history is only required and expected to strive, for the sake of the divine holiness, after a human holiness which is essentially different from the divine. There is in the course of history a human holiness, which only corresponds to divine holiness; there is no perfection in the course of history, and in Israel—in distinction from Greek philosophy and the mysticism of Islam—it is an essentially eschatological conception. This becomes apparent also in the only other passage in the Gospels where (probably in a secondary text stratum) the adjective occurs (Matt. xix. 21): he who would be 'perfect' must give up everything and follow Jesus on his eschatological way. It is of course possible that the Matthew-text in the Sermon on the Mount does not give the original words, which may be found in the parallel reference in Luke's Gospel (vi. 36), it too following the commandment to love one's enemy. There we find 'compassionate' instead of 'perfect', and compassion can be imitated, while perfection cannot. In this form the saying coincides almost verbally with the well-known Pharisaic one dealing with the imitation of God (Bab. Tal. Shabbat 133b, Jer. Pea 15b): 'Be thou compassionate and merciful as He is compassionate and merciful'. Nevertheless the Matthean passage remains worthy of notice as the expression of a doctrine of perfection of the Church (cf. xix. 21) in which there still dwells a strong eschatological impulse.

Some Old Testament commandments speak of perfection in quite a different way. 'And let your heart be perfect (complete) with JHVH your God', it says in the concluding sentence of Solomon's speech of consecration (1 Kings viii. 61), and certainly not unintentionally the one responsible for the redaction of the book recognizes soon afterwards in the same words (xi. 4) that Solomon's own heart did not remain perfect with JHVH his God. Obviously a general human attribute is not meant here, but a degree of devotedness to God which reaches completeness. The same is intended when, in connexion with the warning against Canaanite superstition, it says (Deut. xviii, 13): 'Thou shalt be entire (undivided) with JHVH thy God'.[1] This does not refer to a perfection which emulates the Divine perfection, but to completeness, undividedness, entirety, in the relation to God. The Torah addresses the constant nature of man and summons him to the elevation granted to him, to the highest realization of his relationship to God which is possible to him as a mortal being; Jesus on the other hand, as represented by Matthew, means to summon the elect in the catastrophe of humanity to come as near to God as is made possible to it only in the catastrophe.

The spiritual struggle within Judaism is determined by those primitive commandments, and it is concerned with their truth. In our connexion we have to deal neither with the prophets nor with the Hasidim, but with the Pharisees. The Jesus of the Synoptic tradition addresses them from the point of view of his eschatological radicalism (especially Matt. xxiii. 13 ff., Luke xi. 39 ff.) in a way which is scarcely different from that in which they themselves address those who only seem to be Pharisees;[2] it sounds like a declaration directed against unhappy confusions when the Talmud (Bab. Sota 22b) makes King Jannai, the Sadducee, tell his

---

[1] It should be noted that the Septuagint renders both adjectives, *shalem* and *tamim*, by τέλειος.

[2] Cf. Chwolson, *Das letzte Passamahl Christi* (1892), 116 ff., and *Beiträge zur Entwicklungsgeschichte des Judentums* (1910), 60 f.

wife that she shall not be afraid of the Pharisees, but 'of those tinged-ones who look like Pharisees'. Jesus misses the mark when he treats the Pharisees as people who close their eyes, and they miss their mark when they treat him as one subject to hallucinations; neither party knows the inner reality of the other. Much in the stories in which 'the Pharisees and scribes', half chorus and half spiritual police-patrols, 'test' Jesus, are snubbed by him and then begin their testings again, is certainly unhistorical, and originates from the polemical tension of early Christianity, in which the generalizing point against 'the Pharisees' may have been added in the Hellenistic diaspora[1]; yet there remains enough of real difference over against the true outlook of the Pharisees, even if never quite so great as to exceed the bounds of the dialectics within Judaism. Nevertheless, whether the sentence from the Sermon on the Mount (Matt. v. 20)—which sounds somewhat 'Pauline' and yet is not really Pauline—'For I say unto you, if your proving true is not greater than that of the scribes and Pharisees, you will not enter into the Kingdom of God' originally contained the reference to the Pharisees or not, yet undoubtedly the criticism which is expressed in it applied not to a lax observance of moral or religious commandments by some circle of the people, but to the dominant *view* about the relationship to them, a view which was essentially determined by that of the Pharisees. And in the preceding declaration of Jesus[2] (v. 17) that he has not come to dissolve the

---

[1] The *ad quosdam, non ad omnes* in the Jewish-Christian pseudo-Clementine 'Recognitions' 6, 11 is worthy of notice; cf. now Schoeps, *Theologie und Geschichte des Judenchristentums* (1949), 145 n. 2.

[2] I cannot accept Bultmann's view ('Die Bedeutung des geschichtlichen Jesus fuer die Theologie des Paulus', *Theologische Blaetter* VIII, (1921), 139, cf. *Die Geschichte der synoptischen Tradition*, 2. ed. 146 f., 157 f., *Theologie des Neuen Testaments*, 15) that Matt. v. 17–19 is not genuine and is a 'product' of the polemics of the Church'. When the 'fulfilling'

Torah but to 'fulfil' it, and this means indeed to make it manifest in its full original meaning and to bring it into life, it becomes altogether clear that here doctrine has to stand against doctrine, the true disclosure of the Torah against its current, erroneous and misleading usage. (The doing belongs of course to this, as is expressly stated in the next verse but one: as in the report of Sinai hearing succeeds doing, so here teaching succeeds doing—only on the basis of doing can a person truly teach.) The attitude of the Sermon on the Mount to the Torah accordingly appears to be the opposite of that of the Pharisees; in reality it is only the sublimation of a Pharisaic doctrine from a definite and fundamental point of view, the character of which can again be made clear by comparison. Of course there can be no question of influence, since the Pharisaic doctrine to which I refer is not attested until after the time of Jesus; here also we have only to show the homogeneous elements as such. It is to be emphasized that among the rabbis of the period other views of the subject are to be found, for the inner dialectics continues within Pharisaism itself; but the great and vital lineage of this doctrine is unmistakable.

The doctrine can best be described as that of granting direction to the human heart. The heart of man—this unformulated insight is at the basis of the doctrine—is by nature without direction, its impulses whirl it around in all directions, and no direction which the individual gathers from his world stands firm, each one finally is only able to intensify the whirl of his heart; only in Emunah is persistence: there is no true direction except to God. But the heart

is correctly understood it does not seem to me that the contrasting of the verses with 'other words of Jesus' and with the 'actual attitude of Jesus' yields any contradiction other than that which is biographically acceptable.

cannot receive this direction from the human spirit, but only from a life lived in the will of God. Hence the Torah has assigned to man actions agreeable to God, in the doing of which he learns to direct his heart to Him. According to this purpose of the Torah the decisive significance and value does not lie in the bulk of these actions in themselves but in the direction of the heart in them and through them. 'One does much, the other little', was the device of the college of Jabne (Bab. Berachot 17a) 'if one only directs the heart to heaven!' (Heaven is to be understood here, as in all related contexts, as God.) The Scripture-verse (Deut. vi. 6), 'This, which I this day command thee, shall be on thy heart' is explained (Bab. Megilla 20a) to mean that everything depends on the direction of the heart. Therefore the Temple was called after David and not Solomon because 'the Merciful One desires the heart' (Bab. Sanhedrin 106b): it is a matter, not of the one who completed it, but of him who directed his heart to God for this work and who dedicated it to Him. The doctrine applies not only to actions which are commanded, but to all: 'All thy works shall be for the sake of Heaven' it says in the Sayings of the Fathers (ii. 13). Sin is recognized by the fact that in it a man cannot direct his heart to God; he who commits it denies to God the directing of his heart to Him. Therefore the project of sin and the reflecting upon it and not its execution is the real guilt. The play of the imagination upon the sin is explained (Bab. Joma 29) as being even more serious than the sin itself, because it is this which alienates the soul from God. The most virtuous conduct in the matter of the performance of precepts can exist together with a heart which has remained or become without direction, a heart waste or devastated. On the other hand it may even happen that a person in his enthusiasm for God transgresses a commandment without being aware of it, and then not the sinful matter in his action but his intention is the decisive thing: 'The sin for God's sake is greater than the fulfilling of a commandment not for God's sake' (Bab. Nazir 23). Accordingly, he who has a waste heart cannot truly teach another the Torah; he cannot teach how to obtain the direction, and without it the individual is not able for that for which all learning by the mouth of man is but the preparation: to open his heart to the living Voice of the Divine Teacher. Therefore the Patriarch Gamaliel II ordered that it should be proclaimed (Bab. Berachot 28a) that no scholar whose inwardness did not equal his outwardness ought to enter the schoolroom. From this there was coined two hundred years later the principle (Bab. Yoma 72b): 'A scholar whose inwardness does not equal his outwardness is no scholar'.

There is much to be said for the critical view of the Sermon on the Mount which suggests that we have in it a later composition from different words of Jesus, spoken at different times, with the addition of some from the community, which probably were contained already in the source used by Matthew and Luke. It seems to me however that the blessings belong essentially together from the start, whereas the sayings which concern us here, in spite of formal elements common to them—which obviously caused them to be joined together—'Ye have heard . . . and I say unto you', are different in meaning and purpose, and are therefore probably to be assigned to different groups. Three of them (murder, adultery, oaths) derive essentially from three of the Ten Commandments and transcend them, but what they demand is to be found also in Pharisaic teachings, yet without these approaching the forcefulness of their address. The other three (divorce, formula of the talion, love to one's neighbour), which have obviously been further arranged and adapted to the form of the first three[1], refer to commandments and precepts outside the decalogue, and either contradict them (the first two) or contradict at least an accepted, apparently popular interpretation (the third); rabbinical writings present either no analogy to them or none sufficient. Only that group—in which 'the thesis' stands 'in the form of a prohibition' which 'is not rejected but surpassed'[2]—can in essence be regarded as 'fulfilment' of the Torah, and not those also which are concerned 'not with a prohibition, but with an instruction or concession', which 'is not surpassed but abolished'. That nevertheless even these sayings aim at a 'fulfilling' is shown when we place together the one in which 'Jesus directly annuls a Mosaic ordinance'[3] with the related Synoptic texts which at all events are nearer to the original version. In one of these (Luke xvi. 17 f.) a saying against divorce (which incidentally agrees with the strict view of the school of Shammai) is conjoined with one which repeats, almost verbally yet rather more sharply, a sentence from that section of the Sermon on the Mount: 'It is easier for heaven and earth to pass than for one tittle of the law to fall'. How this is to be understood becomes clear when we refer to the narrative (Mark x, Matt. xix, Luke xvi) in which Jesus actually says this against divorce, according to which the remarriage of a divorced person shall reckon as adultery. In both instances, the 'Pharisees' appeal to Moses, who

---

[1] In distinction from those they obviously do not belong originally together; *vv.* 39 and 44 derive, I presume, from the same unity (cf. Luke vi. 27 ff.); the joining of the first with the talion formula is secondary, probably also *v.* 43 and *vv.* 31 f. constitute an independent saying (see further below). In both of the first the Old Testament quotation has been, I imagine, pre-fixed subsequently: probably also in the first (cf. Luke xvi. 18); whereas in the other group the quotations are an organic part of the text.

[2] Bultmann, *Die Geschichte der synoptischen Tradition*, **144**.

[3] Wellhausen, *Das Evangelium Matthaei*, 21.

(Deut. xxiv. 1) instituted the form of divorce. Thereupon Jesus makes a significant double reply. In the first place, Moses wrote down this commandment 'because of the hardness of your hearts'; about which a modern commentator[1] truly remarks that 'lying at the basis of this hard word is the deep Jewish idea that the Torah is never a fixed law, considered apart from the persons to whom it was given, but rather "instruction" given in a dialogue between God and a partner whose heart and ear are not always open to this teaching of God'. In the second place, Jesus refers to God's word in Paradise (Gen. ii. 24) that a man shall leave his father and mother and cleave to his wife, and they shall become one flesh. Jesus understands this as a commandment: he appeals from the Mosaic revelation to that of creation. Therefore in the end it is the same with the second group as with the first: starting from the inwardness of the divine claim Jesus demands that the inwardness of men shall surrender to it. The divine claim in its outwardness has been made known in the historical situation and has reached the externality of man, the outward conduct of man; the inwardness from above presents itself in the eschatological situation and the inwardness from below can now appear before it. Fulfilment of the Torah accordingly means here disclosure of the Torah. Seen in regard to man the Pharisaic doctrine of the direction of the heart comes here to an heightened expression, and indeed to one so radical that in contrast to Pharisaism, it affects the word of the Torah itself—for the sake of the Torah. Jesus speaks throughout as the authentic interpreter: as long as he remains standing on Sinai he teaches what the Pharisees teach, but then Sinai cannot satisfy him and he must advance into the

[1] Lohmeyer, *Das Evangelium des Markus*, 200 (apparently under the influence of my hints, both verbally and in writing, to this circumstance).

67

cloud-area of the intention of the revelation, for only now his words (familiar in form also to rabbinic discussion) 'but I say unto you' or 'and I say unto you' are opposed to the tradition of the generations. Now too we hear a specifically eschatological-present command like 'Resist not the evil', which must have been unacceptable and even intolerable to the Pharisees, who supposed that they had to live and teach, not in the breaking-in of God's rule, but in continued historical preparation for it under Roman rule. They also indeed enjoined that one should not oppose with force the wrong done to one in personal life, and promised to the one who submits that all his sins would be forgiven him; but a principle which forbade action against the wrong-doer in general or which might at least be so understood, increased in their eyes the area of injustice in the world. They rejected in general the position of the Zealots; but in their heart, as is to be noticed in particular in the recorded conversations with the Romans, they obviously felt themselves to be the opponents of the evil power, which they opposed by their own spiritual methods.

From this point of view the last and highest of these pronouncements, that of love for the enemy, is also to be considered. It proceeds (v. 43) from the Old Testament commandment to 'love one's neighbour' (Lev. xix. 18) which Jesus in another place, in the reply to the scribe's question about the greatest commandment (Matt. xxii. 39; Mark xii. 31), declares to be the greatest alongside that of love to God, and appends to it the interpretation which was indeed popular but was presumably derived in part from the strong words of the Pharisees against the enemies of God, that a man is allowed to or even shall hate his enemy. He opposes this with his commandment 'love your enemies'. In its fundamental meaning it is so deeply bound up with

Jewish faith and at the same time transcends it in so particular a way that it must be especially discussed at this point.

In the quotation from the Sermon on the Mount about the command to love it is first of all noteworthy that the word usually translated by 'as yourself' is missing, whereas in the reply to the scribe the sentence is quoted in its entirety (only outwardly shortened by Luke); the reason may be that a 'love your enemies as yourself' ought not to follow it. But the 'as yourself' is only one of the three falsely rendered words which follow one another in this sentence in the Septuagint and the other current translations. The word so translated refers neither to the degree nor the kind of love, as if a man should love others as much as himself or in such a way as himself (the idea of self-love does not appear in the Old Testament at all); it means, equal to thyself, and this means: conduct thyself in such a way as if it concerned thyself. An attitude is meant and not a feeling. It does not say, one should love someone, but 'to someone'. This strange construction of the dative is found in the Old Testament only in this chapter of Leviticus. Its meaning is easy to ascertain when once the question is put in this way: the feeling of love between men does not in general allow its object—designated by the accusative—to be prescribed; whereas an attitude of loving-kindness towards a fellow creature—designated by the dative—can indeed be commanded to a man. And finally the noun re'ah translated in the Septuagint by 'the one near by, the near' means in the Old Testament first of all one to whom I stand in an immediate and reciprocal relationship, and this through any kind of situation in life, through community of place, through common nationality, through community of work, through community of effort, especially also through friendship; it transfers itself to fellow-men in general and

69

so to others as a whole.[1] '*Love thy re'ah*' therefore means in our language: be lovingly disposed towards men with whom thou hast to do at any time in the course of thy life; for this of course there was also required a soul not given to feelings of hatred, and so the commandment was premised (*v.* 17): 'Do not hate thy brother (synonym for *re'ah*) *in thy heart*'. However in order that no limitation of the idea might result in the people's consciousness to whom the first half of the sentence ('Do not take vengeance on and do not bear ill-will to the sons of thy people') could easily be misleading, later in the same chapter (*v.* 33) another commandment is added, to meet with love also the *ger*, the non-Jewish 'sojourner' who lives in Israel; 'for ye were once sojourners in the land of

[1] It is customary to base the generally accepted interpretation 'fellow-countryman' incorrectly on the fact that in the first parallel phrase of the sentence the reference is to the 'sons of thy people'. That in texts of this kind, as in general, the parallelist form of expression may not be pressed, is made clear, for example, by *v.* 15, in which 'the humble man' and 'the great man' are made parallel. Moreover, man on the threshold of history (and from such a one, I am convinced, originates the sentence transplanted into a late text) often uses 'fellow-countryman' and 'man' interchangeably, as he does the designations 'land' (own land) and earth, because he knows by living contact only that which belongs to him, and includes that which is other according to the degree in which it becomes vitally familiar to him. In Israel he says 'fellow-countryman' and means accordingly the man with whom he *lives;* when he wishes to denote him as such, he says 'companion' (*re'ah*); and because he also lives with other people as well as fellow-countrymen, that is with 'foreign-settlers' (*gerim*) [real 'foreigners', *nochrim*, he learns to know only from his or their journeyings or in war, he does not 'live' with them], he refers in particular to them. Our *idea* of 'fellow-creature' is a late one, derived from the reflection (stoicism) which strove to *overcome* the fact of foreignness, and from the great religious missionary movements in which this first became possible on a large scale (Hellenistic mystery religions, Jewish and Christian missions to the heathen).

Egypt', which means, ye have yourselves known what it means to be treated as sojourners, unloved. The first commandment ends with the declaration 'I am JHVH', the second with 'I am JHVH thy God'. Translated into our language: this is not a moral commandment but a commandment of faith; the declaration means accordingly: I command this to you not as human beings as such, but as *My* people. The connexion between the actuality of faith and the commandment to love is disclosed more deeply still to us if we turn to the passage where, in apparent contradiction to our conclusions, the commandment is construed with the accusative (Deut. x. 19): 'Ye shall love the sojourner, for ye were sojourners in the land of Egypt'. The full understanding of this sentence is first disclosed in its connexion with the three references to love in the previous verses. Israel is summoned to love God (*v.* 12); it is said of God (*v.* 15) that He loved Israel's fathers when they were foreign-settlers; and then it is said of Him (*v.* 18) that He loves the sojourner—not this or that one, but the man dependent upon a foreign nation in general, 'to give him bread and raiment', (cf. the words of Jacob on his way to become a *ger*, Gen. xxviii. 20), as He does right to the person within the nation who is dependent upon others, 'the orphan and the widow'. With God there is no difference between love and the action of love. And to love *Him* with the complete feeling of love[1] can be commanded, for it means nothing more than to actualize the existing relationship of faith to Him, as in trust so in love, for both

[1] Bultmann (*Jesus*, 105 ff.) attacks the view that a feeling is involved in the commandment to love God and one's neighbour. Certainly a 'sentimental' feeling (110) is not involved, but a great feeling is never sentimental, and the love of God is the greatest; 'to submit one's own will in obedience to God's' (105) does not describe love to God; when and so far as the loving man loves he does not need to bend his will, for he lives in the Divine Will.

are one. But if a person really loves Him, he is led on by his own feeling to love the one whom He loves; naturally not the sojourner only—it merely becomes quite clear in his case what is meant—but every man whom God loves, according as a person becomes aware that He does love him. To the loving attitude towards one's fellow love itself is added here, awakened by the love to God.

The maxim from the Sermon on the Mount stands over against this Old Testament view of the connexion between the love of God and the love of man, or, if one prefers the derived categories to original realities, between 'religion' and 'ethics'. Its kinship with the maxims of Deuteronomy and its distance from them is shown at once in the argument about the love of God for all men (v. 45). By His grace in the realm of Nature He sheds His love upon all without distinction, and we are to imitate His Love (both of these are the doctrine of the Talmud also). But 'all' does not mean in this case what it did there: not only Israel but also foreigners, but: evil and good, just and unjust. God does not select the good and the just in order to love them; so also we ought not to select them.

We have seen that the Old Testament commandment of love in its primitive meaning of re'ah does not admit of the interpretation that one ought to hate the enemy. Obviously Jesus starts from a changed meaning which had taken place in the noun. The question here is not the much-discussed problem as to whether at the time of Jesus only fellow-countrymen were included in it, because he nowhere indicates here that he has non-Jews in mind: rather it is about the fact that in his time the word referred mostly to the personal friend: over against love of a friend, love to a person who loves me, he set love towards a person who hates me. But the interpretation quoted in the text which was apparently a popular saying, that one was free to hate the enemy, misunderstood not merely the wording of the commandment to love; it stood also in contradiction to the express commandments of the Torah (Exod. xxiii. 4 f.), to bring help to one's 'enemy', 'the person who hates one'. Nevertheless amongst the people appeal may have been made, as already indicated, to certain expressions on the part of the Pharisees.

In the sayings of the Pharisees exceedingly strong expression is given to the universality of the command to love, so when (Jer. Nedarim 41c, Sifra on Leviticus xix. 18) one of two great rabbis declares, like Jesus, that the Leviticus statement about love for one's neighbour was the greatest precept in the Torah, his companion, obviously because of the possibility of the text being misinterpreted, places another verse of Scripture still higher, namely (Gen. v. 1): 'This is the deed of the generations of Adam. . . . In the image of God He created him': since everyone originates from God's image, discriminating between men or the races of men is in the end inadmissible, the question as to the worthiness of this or that person to be loved is therefore directed against God Himself. It actually says in a Midrash (Genesis rabba XXIV): 'Know whom thou despisest. He created him in the image of God', and another (Pesikta zut. on Numbers viii), emphasizing his absolute value: 'Whoever hates a man is as if he hated Him Who spake and the world was'. In sayings like these the strong basing of the morality upon the actuality of faith is not inferior to that in the saying of Jesus. What according to this doctrine God thinks in particular of national hatred becomes evident when an early school of interpretation, which attributes a share in eternal life to all men, even to evil-doers, makes God reply (Bab. Sanhedrin 105a) to the angels' question as to what He would do if David complained before His throne about the presence of Goliath, that it is incumbent upon Him to make the two friends with each other. Nevertheless a limit is often described, owing to the Biblical idea of the 'enemies of God' or 'haters of God', of whom the Psalmist (Ps. cxxxix. 21 f) avows that he hates them fundamentally as his own enemies. How shall a man, nay precisely one who is convinced of the truth of his faith easily ask himself, not hate them, and particularly those too whose 'hostility' to God manifests itself in the denial of His presence? To the question of a philosopher as to who among men is absolutely deserving of hatred, a rabbi replies (Tos. Shebuot III, 6): 'He who denies his Creator'. Especially with the increase of a formalized 'believing that', this opinion is hardened: unbelievers and heretics do not merely cause confusion in the world of man, but they disturb God's saving activity, and one must fight them and destroy them —and very rarely can hatred be absent from such a conflict. So by appealing to this Psalm, a saying comes about like that (Abot de R. Natan XVI. 32) which begins by contradicting a limitation of the commandment of love, in order then to continue: 'Love all—and hate the heretics, the apostates and the informers'. In this case it is shown crudely how dangerously unstable the boundary-line is. To one assured of his possession of the God of Israel it was but a short step to hold (Sifre 22) that one who hates Israel is 'as one who hates God'. Such opinions are easily transferred to the personal sphere, so that many among the people understand their own enemies as God's, instead of reckoning with the Psalmist God's enemies as their own. But we do not come to know the real danger on such lowlands as these, but rather upon the heights of faith. Not merely fanatics but precisely genuine prophets often cannot but attribute opposition to the message—God's message!—to malice and hardness of heart and in their zeal for it they lose the simple love. The Gospel in which the Sermon on the

74

Mount appears knows the same thing in Jesus' angry out-
bursts against the 'generation of vipers' of the Pharisees
(Matt. xii. 34, xxiii, 33), the authenticity of which, it is true,
has been justifiably contested.

All in all, the saying of Jesus about love for the enemy
derives its light from the world of Judaism in which he
stands and which he seems to contest; and he outshines it.
It is indeed always so when a person in the sign of the
kairos demands the impossible in such a way that he com-
pels men to will the possible more strongly than before.
But one should not fail to appreciate the bearers of the
plain light below from amongst whom he arose: those
who enjoined much that was possible so as not to cause
men to despair of being able to serve God in their poor
everyday affairs.

However, by our view of the difference between 'Jewish'
and 'Christian' faith and of the connexion between Jesus
and the former, we have not yet done full justice to the
saying.

'Love your enemies', it runs in the concise version of
Matthew, 'and pray for your persecutors, that you may
become the sons of your Father in heaven'. To illustrate
by paradox and with the help of a Greek conception, yet
with the greatest possible faithfulness: men become what
they are, sons of God, by becoming what they are, brothers
of their brothers.

Moses says to the people (Deut. xiv. 1): 'Ye are sons of
JHVH your God . . . for ye are a people holy unto JHVH
your God'. In the people holy unto God, because they are
that and in so far as they are that, all men are sons of God. The
prophets deny that the desecrated people belong to God,
they are no longer JHVH's people (Hos. i. 9); but they
promise (ii. 1): 'Instead of it being said to them: "ye are
not My people", it will be said to them: " sons of the living

75

God!"'' Through the new consecration of Israel its people will be newly admitted into sonship. In a late yet pre-Christian book, the Book of Jubilees, the promise is expressed in this way (i. 23 ff.): 'Your soul will follow Me, they will do My commandment. I will be Father to them and they will be sons to Me. They will all be called sons of the living God. All angels and all spirits shall know and perceive that they are My sons and I am their Father in faith and truth, and that I love them'. There has come down from the first half of the second century after Christ a conversation (Bab. Baba Batra 10) between Rabbi Akibah, imprisoned by the Romans, and a high Roman official; on the basis of a verse from Scripture the Roman asserts that the God of the Jews treats them as insubordinate slaves; Akibah refers against this to the 'Ye are sons', but the Roman sees in the difference between the two statements the difference between two stages in the relationship to God: 'If you do God's will you are called sons, if you do it not you are called slaves'. Still more precisely a Midrash text (Pesikta rabbati XXVII) holds: 'If thou doest His will, He is thy Father and thou art His son; if thou doest it not He is thine owner and thou art His slave'. The statement of Jesus about love to an enemy is to be seen in connexion with this process of a progressive dynamization of the sonship. But nowhere else is love to man precisely made the presupposition of the realized sonship to God as here, and that in the unheard-of simple form of this 'so that', in the form, that is, of open entrance for everyone who really loves. Originating from the enthusiasm of eschatological actuality, this statement, viewed from the point of view of Israel's faith, implies at the same time a supplement to it. Somewhere, apparently quite on its own accord, the most daring arc has been described, and yet a circle has thereby been completed. Seen in relation to the history of faith in Christianity, the arc must of course appear as the beginning of another figure, perhaps of an hyperbole. How this figure is continued is shown to us in the sentence in the prologue of John's Gospel (i. 12), where the Logos which appeared gives power to 'those who believe on his name' to become children of God, and in the sentence related to this (1 John v. 1), declaring everyone who believes that Jesus is the Messiah to be 'born of God', or already by Paul's direct speech to the converted Gentiles (Gal. iii. 26): 'For ye are all sons of God through faith in Christ Jesus'.

Entirely within Judaism and outside all Christian influence the question, which has concerned us here, found in its three essential points at the threshold of our age a parallel answer in Hasidism. As the clearest examples three reports from the life of the Zaddikim, from leaders of the Hasidic body, may be cited. The first concerns the 'enemy' in general. A Zaddik commands his sons: 'Pray for enemies that things go well with them. And if you think, that is no service of God: know that more than any other prayer, this is service of God'. The second story concerns the extent of the idea of the 'neighbour'. A Zaddik speaks to God: 'Lord of the world, I beseech Thee that Thou mayest redeem Israel. And if Thou willest it not, redeem the Gentiles!' The third concerns the 'enemy of God'. A Zaddik is asked by a pupil whether one can love a person who rises up against God. He replies: 'Dost thou not know that the primeval soul came from God and that every human soul is a part of it? And when thou seest how one of the holy particles has become entangled and is near to be suffocated wilt thou not show mercy to it?'

That the principle of love to the enemy in this instance has in such a way expanded in the pure form of faith, and not in a form essentially ethical, merely enjoined by God, is to be understood from the fact that even in Hasidism the

77

messianic inspiration of Judaism made one of its high flights, and that without employing in general the form of eschatological actuality: paradoxically expressed, it is a messianism of continuity. Even the Hasidim, at all events those of the first generations, experience a nearness of God's rule, yet one which demanded not the readiness to change everything, but the continuity of a life of faith which was both enthusiastic and yet strove after the cohesion of the generations.

VIII

I T has become evident that Jesus, as he speaks in the Sermon on the Mount, considers the Torah capable of fulfilment, not merely in accordance with its wording, but in the original intention of its revelation. The first he has in common with Pharisaic Judaism, in the second he meets it in certain points again and again. That there are only points which cannot be combined into a line lies in the fact that the *actual*, so to speak experimental, capability of being fulfilled in the sense of 'so far as thou, exerting thyself, art able to do here and now', is for the Pharisees more than a position, it is their vital air. For Jesus quantum satis means: that which in the heart of God is looked for from men; the Pharisees, in the higher state of their teaching, start from Scripture ('with all thy might'): God expects from thee fulfilment according to thy nature and ability, He expects in the fulfilment 'the direction of thy heart towards Him', not less, but also not more—the individual shall will to love, for daily he experiences anew whom and how he is able to love even now. Paul on the contrary—on the basis of that alleged 'in all things'—contests the fact that the Torah is capable of fulfilment at all; that he in this contradicts the teaching of Jesus also either did not enter his consciousness, or, as appears more likely to me, it is connected in a manner, the understanding for which we lack the equipment, with his resolve or his constraint not to know Christ any more 'after the flesh', and this would mean that what Jesus taught was admissible for the time during which he lived but not necessarily so for the quite different time after his crucifixion and resurrection.

What is however decisive for our undertaking is not that Paul considered the Torah to be incapable of fulfilment, but that he meant and said that it was given not in order to be fulfilled but rather through its incapability of fulfilment to call forth sin—'in order that it might abound' (Rom. v. 20), that it, through the fact of the commandment, 'might become exceeding sinful' (vii. 13)—and so prepare the way for grace. To be sure, so Paul thinks, as the will of God the Torah must be fulfilled; but its purpose is to cause man to whom it is given to be frustrated precisely by this imperative, so that he might submit to grace. Does the essence of sin consist now for Paul, as is interpreted by important instances, in that the individual who is subject to the law makes of his obedience a merit and a guarantee, that is, seeks to establish his own righteousness instead of submitting himself to God (Rom. x. 3)? Or does Paul see, as he seems to me to have meant, that this indeed is something added, but he perceives the substance of sin in the psychic–factual transgression of the law through the inevitable 'concupiscence' in the most comprehensive sense (which the Sermon on the Mount declares to be avoidable as earlier, in a stricter sense, the conclusion of the Decalogue forbids covetous envy as destroying community)?[1] At all events one

[1] Cf. my book *Moses*, 133 f.

aim of the divine Lawgiver is here set forth as being to make His own law ineffectual. The words are about tablets which must and are bound to break in pieces in the hands of those for which they are appointed.

This opinion of Paul's may claim to be regarded in conjunction with his conception (which is influenced by various sources, yet is a unity) of the theocentric history of the cosmos and of man, which, on account of a reserve commanded by the subject, he has nowhere summarized with entire clarity, and so his reader must bring it together carefully from scattered statements. Paul himself understood this conception (Col. i. 26) as the mystery pre-determined by God, kept hidden before the aeons and the generations, which has been revealed in the appearing of the risen one (cf. Rom. xvi. 25) and is now transmitted in words and therein proclaimed by him, Paul, with fear and trembling. This mystery was in particular hidden from those (1 Cor. ii. 7 f.) who were assigned the principal roles in it, namely the spirits which Paul calls the rulers of this aeon and whose leader he calls on occasion (2 Cor. iv. 4) the god of this aeon. For if they had known it 'they would not have crucified the Lord of Glory' (1 Cor. ii. 8), but this was destined for them in the mystery so that thereby they help to achieve its realization and to promote their own overthrow.

This aeon is in hands other than God's. For a period determined by Him, God has delivered up the lordship of the world to the spirits of the elements (Gal. iv. 2 f., 9), in order that they—in themselves only weakly and miserable—as guardians and trustees arouse in the creation which is 'placed under' their 'nothingness' the desire to become free children of God (Rom. viii. 19 ff.). God in the creation has put into man's 'flesh' and 'members' the 'other law' (vii, 18, 21 ff.) which is equally contrary to the divine will and to human reason and apparently identical with the Old Testament

81

'evil imagination of the heart' (Gen. viii. 21, cf. vi. 5). Man, fallen by the seduction of Satan who had disguised himself as an angel of light (2 Cor. xi. 14) and now given over by God to the 'lusts' and 'shameful passions' (Rom. i. 24, 26), has, by reason of 'the spirit of the world' (1 Cor. ii. 12) and 'the spirit of bondage' (Rom. viii. 15) which he receives from these 'powers and forces', enslaved himself to them. The gift of the law to Israel occupies a significant and indeed central position in this process, the purpose of which is the redemption of man and world; this law has not been 'ordained' immediately by God but by angels (Gal. iii. 19). They employ now the law which is in itself 'holy' (Rom. vii. 12) but incapable of overcoming the 'other' law (viii. 3), in order to make man self-righteous, that he may be forfeited completely to them, and the law, contrary to the original designation which was announced to Israel (cf. Gal. iii. 11), is no longer something which gives life and no longer effects, as was intended, the justification of man (v. 21), but sin and wrath (Rom. iv. 15); the prohibition against coveting (Exod. xx. 17 f.) provides the opportunity for sin to excite concupiscence (Rom. vii. 8), man no longer knows what he is doing (v. 15) and is 'taken captive' (v. 23). But the angels, by what they bring about, merely serve the purpose of God, Who had caused the law 'to come in besides', 'so that the transgression multiplies' and grace can hereafter 'overflow' (v. 20). So the Jews are 'kept in captivity under the law', and that which they presumed to have in their possession as 'the embodiment of knowledge and of truth' (ii. 20) castigates them as a severe task-master (Gal. iii. 23 f). It works 'death' instead of life, for the 'sting of death is the transgression, but the strength of the transgression is the law' (1 Cor. xv. 56). All this is taking place to prepare the coming of Christ (Gal. iii. 22). For with the appearing of Christ, whom God for the sake of His purpose 'delivered up' (Rom. viii. 32) to the rulers of this aeon in the concealing 'form of a slave' (Phil. ii. 7), and who now 'conquers' (1 Cor. xv. 24) and disarms (Col. ii. 15) all authorities and powers and 'delivers up' the dominion of the world to God (1 Cor. xv. 24, the same verb was used for the handing over of man to the evil and of Christ to the 'rulers'), the emancipating faith in him is offered to the Jews, whose law, the 'note of hand', has been fastened to his cross (Col. ii. 14). True he is only received by the 'remnant' known to the prophets, which grace has elected (Rom. xi. 5), but the rest have 'been made hardened' (*v.* 7), for 'God hardens whom He will' (ix. 18), but when they see the salvation of the Gentiles who have been set free from the service of the spirits of the elements, they will become envious (xi. 11) and with their grafting again into their own good olive-tree (*v.* 24) the whole fulness of the blessing will come upon the world.

The Gnostic nature of the essential features of this conception is obvious—the derivative powers, which, ruling the world, work against the primal divine power and way-lay the human soul, the enslavement of the cosmos, the problematic character of the law, the overcoming of the 'rulers' and the setting-free of man—and it has not to be discussed genetically here. None of this concerns the God-head, but the intermediate being set up or permitted by Him. Nevertheless to the God of whom Paul treats there adhere two shadows mysteriously bound together, which are both borrowed from the Old Testament, but which are deepened into something dreadful: the will to 'harden' and the double character of the purpose in the giving of the law. We must inquire into them.

In the story of the Egyptian plagues Pharaoh is wont at times after the visitation is over, to 'make' his heart 'ob-durate' or to 'harden' it or to 'brace' it. But before the seventh plague begins a new motive appears: by this time

JHVH 'hardens' or 'braces' the heart of the king who is tending to yield, as He had already proclaimed to Moses in the burning thorn-bush. For He wishes to show His signs (Exod. x. 1) and 'be glorified upon Pharaoh' (xiv. 4, 17): 'the Egyptians shall know that I am JHVH' (this means, unlike their gods, the truly Present-One). The number of repetitions worked out by the redactor[1] refers, as so often, to the theological meaning of the matter. God is ever concerned to bring the man who strives against Him to his senses—up to the turning-point where he himself begins to equip his resisting heart with inflexible strength for a renewed resistance, for now it is no longer a matter of bending the evil will but of determined destruction: now God grants the sinner, not in silence but in open declaration, the special strength to persevere in the sin. It is obvious that an extreme situation in the most exact sense is here concerned, in which it is paradigmatically given to know—that sin is not an undertaking which man can break off when the situation becomes critical, but a process started by him, the control of which is withdrawn from him at a fixed moment.

After this statement we hear of a strengthening or hardening of the human heart by God only on two other occasions, both likewise in the Hexateuch (Deut. ii. 30, Joshua xi. 20), and both in stories of wars in Canaan: to the peoples which had been condemned to destruction because of the mysterious 'iniquity of the Amorites' (Gen. xv. 16)[2] strength is granted to continue the struggle to the end. This also must obviously be noted and understood: it concerns a sinfulness of their religious tradition itself which had become inherent and indomitable in the life of these people.

[1] The text speaks of the 'bracing' of Pharaoh's heart seven times, of the Egyptians' once, and of the actual 'hardening' once.

[2] Cf. Buber and Rosenzweig, *Die Schrift und ihre Verdeutschung*, 61, where I have shown that sexual cults and rites are meant.

Yet once more Scripture speaks of a hardening, of one which indeed is not like the former caused or to be caused by God directly, but one enjoined by Him on a prophet, this time not a hardening of the heart but of the ears, yet in conjunction with a 'fattening' of the heart: in Isaiah's account of his vision in the temple (vi. 10). If we compare it with his account of a later period (chap. viii) we find that he is commanded to make large, by the proclamation of the messianic message of salvation among the people, the sense of immovable security and so to contribute to their hardening. In this case it is the people, chosen by God themselves, who shall be hardened, and this is due to the fact that they hear the true Word of God. God has already too often let Israel be warned that it should turn back to Him and to no purpose, all too often already He has stricken them in vain, now, as He once said to the young Isaiah (i. 14), He has become weary of bearing that which is intolerable: He no longer desires the turning of this generation, He will even hinder them, promising the people salvation in all the disasters which come and so hardening them into a false confidence which prevents their turning to Him. What such a design and such a request mean to the messenger is declared by his resolve, expressed in his account (viii. 16–19), to withhold from the people for the time being the message of salvation, which he dare not suppress, and to entrust it to his 'disciples' alone, to 'tie it up' and to 'seal' it as 'testimony' and 'instruction' among them, until in the hour of crisis, of 'darkness' (v. 22), when the time is come: 'To the instruction! to the testimony!' (v. 20), he may unseal and untie it, and make it known.[1]

Here, with the fearful commission of God to His prophet, Paul sets forth. But he makes God's will to harden Israel

[1] For this cf. the chap. 'The Theopolitical Hour' in my book *The Prophetic Faith* (1949).

begin to take effect on Sinai itself, at the time, that is, when it becomes Israel and His people. For the sake of His plan of salvation God hardens all the generations of Israel, from that assembled on Sinai to that around Golgotha, with the exception of His chosen 'Election' (Rom. xi. 7).

Paul quotes (ix. 17) a saying of God to the Pharaoh who was hardened by Him. He premises it (*v.* 15) with the saying to Moses (Exod. xxxiii. 19): 'I am gracious to whom I am gracious, and I show mercy to whom I show mercy'. The saying means implicitly that grace will not be dictated to as to who is worthy of it. But Paul does not wish to read this from it, but (*v.* 18): 'So He has mercy on whom He will, and whom He will He hardens'. That is to say: as the mercy is God's alone, so the hardening is His alone; as the mercy is unfathomable to human understanding, so also is the hardening; as the mercy does not need to be 'caused', so neither does the hardening. In the Old Testament meaning the hardening intervenes in an extreme situation in life, an extreme perversion in the relation of an individual or a nation to God, and makes it, dreadfully enough, into an inevitable destiny, makes the going-astray into a state of having gone-astray from which there is no returning; in Paul's usage however the process of hardening in general no longer cares about the men and the generations of men which it affects, but uses them and uses them up for higher ends. Contrary to the Old Testament Paul's God does not have regard for the people to whom He speaks out of the cloud, or rather causes His angels to speak.

Paul obviously derived also from the Old Testament the decisive stimulus for his conception of the means which his God makes use of in the hardening of Israel.

Ezekiel, the prophet of unconditional personal responsibility and therefore of the absolutely real freedom of man before God, knew of no hardening from above. The house of Israel *is* hardened (ii. 4, iii. 7), but it has not been hardened. Man and nation, endowed from the beginning and without exception with the capability for unlimited and quite real decision, are judged by God, but not for anything in the occurrence of which He had a hand either by indirect (Pharaoh) or direct (Isaiah) influence. God gave His creature freedom at the creation and He does not dispute its freedom, but makes it thereby fully responsible to Him. To bring home to the hearer of the Word that this is the actual condition of his life constitutes the content (which is modified according to changing persons and situations) of the warning which the prophet is at times summoned to proclaim (iii. 17 ff.). The restraint of God which renders human freedom possible is therefore not to be understood as though He allowed that which He introduced into the world to be without direction as to which was the right way and which the wrong. Indeed, He gives the people chosen by Him direction in the form of 'statutes and ordinances', of such a nature that the man who fulfils them gains life thereby (xx. 11, cf. Lev. xviii. 5). But the people do not follow the way shown to them, they reject the direction and with it, life (*vv.* 13 and 21), although they are admonished time and again. Then God gives them 'statutes and ordinances not-good,[1] through which they do not gain life' and makes them unclean through their gifts, 'because they bring over every first opening of the womb', every firstborn (*v.* 25 f.). Since shortly before in the book (xvi. 20 f.) and shortly after (xxiii, 37, 39[2]) the sacrifice of children is reckoned as the greatest guilt of the people, it would be a most patent

---

[1] The meaning is: which become not-good.

[2] This form of repetition, which I might describe as hermeneutic framing, the purpose of which is to prevent misinterpretation or even directly to point to the correct meaning, is not unusual; cf. e.g. the framing of Exod. iii. 14 f. by iii. 12 and iv. 12.

contradiction of Ezekiel's doctrine of responsibility if he declared that this sacrifice was commanded by God. Therefore the commandment to bring over 'every first opening of the womb' (Exod. xiii. 12)[1] which was determined for the period after the possession of the land can only be understood here as 'given' to the people in this form of words, because this does not exclude its misinterpretation and misuse: in extreme necessity any person, referring to the commandment and at the same time to the custom of neighbouring peoples (2 Kings iii. 27, xvi. 3) and perhaps even to the tradition of Abraham, may have thought himself able to soften the heart of God when he exceeded by sacrifice (cf. Mic. vi. 7) the conceded equivalent, namely the bare dedication and ransom by the alleged fulfilment of the surrender demanded by sacrifice. By the 'not good' character of such statutes is therefore meant their latent ambivalence, that is the occasion which they afford for false interpretation: God makes a claim which He at once modifies symbolically, but the claim is cast in the form of a word and it remains to the individual freely to imagine that satisfying it literally is superior to the conceded equivalent. So the disobedient are punished by the possibility of perverse obedience.

Paul fitted into his conception of the world-process what he found in Ezekiel, in that he transferred that which applied to the individual commandment to the whole range of the law, that which applied to a few generations to every one up to his own, and that which was a possibility to a necessity, for the law according to him is incapable of fulfilment because in his opinion it is intended to be fulfilled *only* as a whole ('in all things'), and its non-fulfilment, which is unavoidable in this sense, stands under the curse. And this

[1] The whole expression (with the verb 'to bring over') only appears in these two references in Scripture.

motif, which was thus changed about, was combined by him with the changed motif of the hardening. In order to harden Israel and for the benefit of the plan of salvation, 'until the fulness of the Gentiles is brought in' (Rom. xi. 25), God, whom Paul speaks of as the God of Israel, gave them the law in order to cause them to be frustrated by the fact of it being incapable of fulfilment. He has actually 'shut them all in unbelief', the Gentiles without the law and the Jews who possess it, 'so that He might have mercy upon all'. (v. 32).

When I contemplate this God I no longer recognize the God of Jesus, nor his world in this world of Paul's.[1] For Jesus, who was concerned with the individual human soul and with every single human soul, Israel was not a universal entity with such and such an appointed function in the plan of the world, nor was it for him the mere totality of Jews living in his day and who stood in a certain relationship to his message: every soul which had lived from Moses to himself belonged in concreto to it. In his view for everyone of them, when they had gone astray, turning was allowed,

---

[1] Bultmann's view (*Theologie des Neuen Testaments*, 3) that the preaching of Jesus is in line with the apocalyptic hope, the presupposition of which is 'the pessimistic-dualistic perception of the satanic corruption of the whole course of the world', seems to me to be insufficiently founded. The only word of Jesus cited for this, 'I saw Satan fall as lightning from heaven' (Luke x. 18) belongs to Isaiah xiv. 12, not to Rev. xii. 8 f. The image of the world shown here is the prophetic, not the apocalyptic. The principle, which causes contradiction and corruption and which is hurled down from the circle of the powers, never governed the structure of the world in this image. Like the prophets, Jesus sees this aeon as that in which powers struggle, not as that of a rule of evil. In the world there is a kingdom of Satan (Luke xi. 18), which opposes the coming of the kingdom of God, but the world only contains it, it is not it. Therefore the one called to overcome it (v. 22, cf. 2 Sam. xxiii. 7, the saying about the man who shall strike the worthless, *beliya'al*, and is 'invested with spearhead and shaft') can be chosen from mankind itself.

and everyone of them when they did turn back, was the lost son returned home. His God was the same Who, though He might at times also 'harden' and perhaps even at times give a statute which was 'not good', yet answered in every generation to the person interposing for Israel: 'I have pardoned according to thy words' (Num. xiv. 20). In Paul's conception of God, where the generations of souls in Israel from Moses to Jesus are concerned, this characteristic is supplanted by another, which alters everything. I do not venture to give it a name.

In our era a philosopher, Hegel, has torn the Pauline conception away from its root in the actuality of faith and transplanted it into the system in which now the god of the philosophers, 'Reason', forces by its 'ruse' the historical process unwittingly to urge on its perfection.

IX

W<small>E</small> have found a critical attitude towards 'the works of the law' not only in Paul but also in Jesus, as well as among the Pharisees. The works which are criticized in this and that place are nevertheless of a different kind, in part of a fundamental difference. For the Pharisees they are those done without the doer directing his heart to God. Jesus means the works a person finds prescribed and which are done as prescribed, without recognizing the purpose of God enshrined in the precept and without rising to it in doing them. Paul meant by 'the works of the law' chiefly those in the performance of which the individual is deceived into thinking that he obtains merit before God and becomes righteous; but behind this there exists for him the whole problem of the law as a 'law of sin and death', to which is opposed henceforth and now for the first time the 'Spirit-law of life in Christ Jesus' (Rom. viii. 2) which sets one free, and is now and only now revealed, so that in the end all works done for the fulfilling of the law apart from faith in Jesus as the Christ are rejected for ever. That 'he who loves his neighbour has fulfilled the law' and therefore 'love is the fulfilling of the law' (Rom. xiii. 8, 10, cf. Gal. v. 14) is to be sure spoken in the spirit of Jesus, and Jesus in this consideration has not deviated from the teaching of the Pharisees; but even love, the fulfilling of the law, is not valid for Paul as fulfilment of the law, but only when it is through faith in Jesus as the Christ.

The life-problem of the man who comes from the world of the 'law' is therefore for the Pharisees and Jesus: how do I get from an apparent life in the revealed will of God to a true life in it, which leads to eternal life? The difference is that 'revealed' means for the Pharisees: through the historical revelation in the Word brought into the tradition of Israel and manifest in it; for Jesus however the tradition of Israel has not adequately preserved the historical revelation in the Word, but now it is adequately disclosed in its meaning and purpose. For Paul however man's problem, derived from the 'law', is: how do I get from a life from the revelation in the Word, a life which of necessity becomes false owing to its ambivalence and its counter-law implanted in me, to true life into which the will of God for me enters undistorted?

The specific answer which was developed among the Pharisees is the *lishmah* doctrine, which is narrowly connected with that of the 'direction of the heart', and yet goes beyond it. The meaning of this doctrine has already been repeatedly referred to,[1] but it cannot too often be done. *Lishmah* means: for the sake of the thing itself. By this word there is expressed first of all the fact that man should learn the Torah for its own sake and not because of what it yields; he is to fulfil the commandment for its own sake

[1] The most important texts are assembled in their proper sequence according to meaning (which I retain) by Schechter, *Some Aspects of Rabbinic Theory* (1909), 160 f.

and not for its advantageous consequences; constantly the note is clearly sounded; for the sake of the teaching, for the sake of what is commanded, and thus it is as mentioned comprehensively expressed: 'All thy works should be for the sake of God'. The only thing which matters is that everything should be done truly for God's sake, from love to Him and in love to Him. The decisive force of the 'for His sake' penetrates into a depth in the relation of man to the Torah, in which this makes known an ambivalence whose tension is not less than that maintained by Paul, but without, as in his case, the faithfulness of the Revealer to the human person as such becoming questionable—on the contrary, the effect of the Torah is placed directly in the hands of this person. The Torah is not an objectivum independent of the actual relationship of man to God, which would bestow of itself life upon the one who receives it: it does that only to one who receives it for its sake in its living actuality, that is, in its association with its Giver, and for His sake. To the man who engages in it for some other reason the Torah 'breaks his neck' (Bab. Taanit 7a). Not that there are different parts of the Torah, which effect good and bad: the same words 'enliven' the one who does it 'for its sake' and 'slay' the one who does not do it 'for its sake' (Sifra on Dt. 32. 2). If accordingly, as is emphasized (Midrash Tehillim on Ps. xxxi. 9), the real difference 'between a righteous man and a wicked one' (Mal. iii. 18) is to be recognized just at this point, it must nevertheless be borne in mind at the same time that the possibility is given to every wicked man in 'turning' to attain to the stage 'upon which those who are completely righteous are not able to stand' (Bab. Berachot 34b). The dynamic character of the *lishmah* doctrine is only here fully disclosed: it is not concerned with two types of men who are opposed to each other, but with two human attitudes to the divine manifestation, which are to be sure fundamentally different and yet so related to each other that a way can lead from the negative attitude to the positive. Since it does not lie within the will of man to do what he does for God's sake and yet it does lie within his will both to learn the Torah and to keep its commandments, he must therefore begin to do both so far as he is able, in such a way that the 'for the sake of the thing' is given to him merely as a direction and not yet as motive. If he seriously does what he can he will 'advance from the "not for its sake" to the "for its sake"' (Bab. Berachot 17a).

In the place where this doctrine is found amongst the Pharisees, that is as the answer to man's life-problem, there is found in Jesus the summons to follow himself. Since, over against the current tradition of Israel, he referred to the undefaced purpose of the Revealer as that which had been made known to him ('But I say unto you') his answer could be only a personal one. By the proclamation of the rule of God which is come near, as it were has come within range, he had aimed at calling the people in Israel to it, especially the 'sinners' (Mark i. 17 par.), so that they, healed by him, may 'take it by force' (Matt. xi. 12) through the storming power of their turning. Contrary to the Pharisaic teaching—known to us to be sure only through later utterances—that one ought 'not to force the end', this maxim declares that the kingly grace, which even now inclines to the world of men, expects in return the greatest effort to meet it, to enter into it and to make it by this into an earthly reality; the sinners who are turning must stand in the centre of this effort, since no power on earth is equivalent to that of turning.[1] What he says to the crowd is directed

[1] Schweitzer, *Das Abendmahl* II (1901), 27, goes however too far when he says of this that 'a pressure as it were' is intended which is exercised to 'force' the kingdom of God 'to become apparent'. R. Otto's words

to those still concealed in it who ought to follow him. When he meets one or other of them alone or in pairs apart from his preaching, perhaps at work, and recognizes them as ones who belong to him, he calls to them: 'Come after me' or 'Follow me'. They follow him. What this following means however becomes clear when (Mark x. 17. ff. par.) one, who is no sinner but who knows that he has kept the commandments and yet does not find the way to eternal life, steps out from the crowd to him and questions him; Jesus replies that he must sell everything and give to the poor, and then 'Come, follow me'. That is, he is to be concerned now, in the perihelium of grace, to hold on to nothing, to allow nothing else to prevent him from meeting it, but to become free for storming the rule of God as he does who goes before and whom one ought to follow. Jesus says this more radically still to the crowd, after he has called them together 'with his disciples also' (Mark viii. 34), obviously so as to make entirely clear to those amongst them who belong to him that they ought to come over to him, as well as to the disciples themselves, what is required of those who follow: it is a question of 'abandoning themselves', getting free of themselves, 'self' meant as the epitome of everything to which a man is attached; this is the proper expression for the surrender, to make one's self free. No general verbal definition of the way leads beyond this preliminary condition of following, but only the way itself. The highest effort is not to be paraphrased; a man comes to know it in the actual following. In following a man attains to true life in the revealed will of God. Jesus speaks from the being and consciousness of the man who has 'abandoned

seem to me correct (*Reich Gottes und Menschensohn*, 87): 'only by summoning all one's power, and with the most strenuous determination, does one penetrate into it'.

himself'; therefore he can give this personal answer instead of an objective one.

The fiery centre in the history of Christianity is the endeavour to keep this following alive after the death of Jesus. In order to bridge the interval Paul summons to an indirect following (1 Cor. xi. 1)[1]: 'Be my imitators, as I am of Christ'. The Johannine circle, because it is 'the last time' (1 John ii. 18), believes that it can preserve the direct following (ii. 6): 'to abide in him' means to walk as he walked; for John's Gospel (xiii. 15), emphatically going beyond the Synoptics, had made Jesus say: 'I have given you an example, that you should do even as I have done to you'. The example is passed on from generation to generation chiefly through living recollection; but also after the recollection is broken generation after generation produces for itself the picture as something to be imitated, and in later times as often as the presentiment of the end of time becomes strong the stimulus to follow becomes strong too.

Of course neither Paul nor anyone other than Jesus himself could offer this following as the answer to man's life-problem. Whoever asked about the how, from him Jesus demanded that he should join him, and when the challenge touched the man's very heart, 'he went after him' and shared his life. This simple going-before could not be replaced by any command to follow the Master. The answer which Paul gave to the life-question of the man who came from the world of 'law' and wanted to attain to true life in the revealed will of God and the answer with which he anticipated this question was the summons to have faith in Christ. In this way he did precisely what Jesus, in so far as we know him from the Synoptic tradition, did not do, and whatever was the case with his 'messianic consciousness',

[1] The usual theological distinction between following and imitating does not affect the course of our argument.

obviously did not wish to do. He might indeed cry to the disciples in the ship when they were alarmed at the storm (Mark iv. 40) 'Why are ye fearful? have ye still no faith?' But what he missed in that case—if one disregards the miracle-story[1] with which the saying has been conjoined— was merely that unconditional trust in the grace which makes a person no longer afraid even of death because death is also of grace. Afterwards Jesus does indeed ask whom he is considered to be, but he does not desire that a man should hold him to be anyone in particular. The situation for Paul is that a man shall recognize Jesus with all the strength of faith to be the one whom he proclaims as the door to salvation. This is indeed 'the word of faith which we preach' and that to which 'the word is nigh to thee' from the Torah is referred (Rom. x. 9): 'If thou shalt confess with thy mouth that Jesus is Lord and believe in thy heart that God has raised him from the dead, thou shalt be saved'. To be sure, much more than this is necessary, but everything, even that which is most extreme, the 'dying with Christ' in the midst of life, is necessary from this starting-point: for it means the Risen-one (Rom. v. 8 f.), it is based upon faith in his resurrection. And this faith is a 'belief that' in the pregnant sense of the word,[2] which is essentially different

---

[1] I use the concept in the meaning of the critical section of Bultmann's important essay 'Zur Frage des Wunders', according to which the idea of miracle has become impossible and must be given up, because of the 'impossibility of conceiving as real an event contra naturam' (Bultmann, *Glauben und Verstehen*, 1933, 216: cf. also his 'Neues Testament und Mythologie' in the symposium *Kerygma und Mythos*, 1948, 18).

[2] Wissmann, *Das Verhaeltnis von πίστις und Christusfroemmigheit bei Paulus* (1926), 39, says rightly: 'The faith which for Paul and his congregations constitutes the essence of a Christian is above all entirely believing (*fuerwahrhaltender*) faith'. (Wissmann however considers quite wrongly that this is the essence of late-Judaistic religion, as can be proved from most of the references cited by him for this from Hellenistic Judaism.)

from the faith of the Jews that on Sinai a divine revelation took place, as it signifies the acceptance of the reality of an event, which is not destined, like the former, to confirm and strengthen the hereditary actuality of faith of the Jewish person who hears about it, but fundamentally to change it.

If one would understand the nature of the faith which Paul demands, it is indeed quite correct to proceed from faith in the resurrection of Jesus. The conception of the divine world-plan is entirely dependent upon the resurrection (or the ascension from the cross): if it had not succeeded the death of the one crucified by the angel-powers, who are the rulers of this aeon, they would have overcome God and frustrated His work of salvation. It is therefore quite consistent when the apostle (1 Cor. xv. 1 ff., 11) first brings home to the Corinthians that the resurrection of Christ is the chief article of his preaching and their faith, and then (v. 14), his language becoming ever more daring, declares: 'But if Christ has not been raised then our preaching is vain and your faith also is vain'. The resurrection of Jesus, as the one preceding the resurrection of the dead in the form of its first-fruits (v. 20, cf. Col. i. 18), is the beginning of the victory of God—already promised in the Old Testament prophecy (Is. xxv. 8)—over 'the last enemy' (1 Cor. xv. 26), over death as the principle of those powers in whose hands the world is; through the resurrection Christ is appointed 'as the Son of God in power' (Rom. i. 4). The central character of belief in it is obvious. It has been pointed out[1]

Bultmann in *Theologie des Neuen Testaments*, 310 ff., has not been able to convince me that Paul understood *pistis primarily* as an act of obedience; it is however undoubtedly to the point that *pistis* in a decisive way here means 'acceptance of the message'.

[1] Goguel, *Trois études sur la pensée religieuse du Christianisme primitif* (1931), 37.

that without it, if the disciples had merely kept the expectation that the Master would rise at some future time with all the dead, then perhaps a reformation of Judaism might have taken place, but certainly not a new religion; in point of fact every true *reformatio* intends precisely that which found its strongest expression in the sayings of Jesus which begin with 'But I say unto you': to return to the original purity of the revelation.

There is much to be said for the view[1] that in the period after the death of Jesus the idea of his ascension from the cross existed alongside that of his resurrection, and indeed preceded it—the idea of a removal, analogous to that told in the Old Testament of Enoch and Eliah, later also of Moses and others. The rise of this idea—which might more immediately result in the explanation of the visions of the Exalted One rather than the other—has been facilitated by the fact that from the legendary tradition according to which the chosen servants were removed by a personal intervention of God, a divine 'taking' (Gen. v. 24, 2 Kings ii. 3, 5. 9 f.) of the living body, has been spiritualized in the hope of the Psalmists: when they say (Ps. xlix. 17, lxxiii. 24) that God will 'take' them instead of letting them sink into the underworld, they mean that He will raise up their souls in death. 'If this idea', writes Johannes Weiss, as it appears to me correctly, 'had become generally dominant, we should have heard nothing at all about a resurrection'. A pre-Pauline mission which was based on this conception may have won Jews by means of it, as it would not be difficult

[1] Cf. Johannes Weiss, *Das Urchristentum* (1917), 19, and *Das Problem der Entstehung des Christentums*, Archiv fuer Religionswissenschaft XVI (1913), 474 ff.; Bertram, *Die Himmelfahrt Jesu vom Kreuz aus*, Festgabe fuer Deissmann (1927), 187 ff., cf. also Schrade, *Zur Ikonographie der Himmelfahrt Christi*, Vortraege der Bibliothek Warburg, 1928–1929 (1930), 75 ff., as well as Rudolf Otto, *Aufsaetze das Numinose betreffend* (1923), 160 f.

for them to place a third alongside the two who had been removed to heaven. However the idea of the resurrection was already in the centre of Paul's mission, although that motif still operated in him, and of course resurrection alone could be used for a coherent statement of the events. The Jew of the time, the majority of whom were Pharisaic in matters of faith, believed to be sure in the final resurrection of the dead as a great community; but the resurrection of an individual in the course of history was unknown to him from Scripture (the legends of the miracles of coming to life again do not apply here, because in them the decisive point, the rising again from being lost in the underworld, is missing) and he could not in general make himself believe in it: the peculiarly austere realism of the Jew in things of the body and physical death could be conquered by an eschato-logical view of the whole, but only rarely[1] by contradictory reports of an individual instance. On the contrary the Hellenistic 'heathen's' belief in the dying and rising gods of the Mysteries opened the way; the message, that now in his own life-time such a one had lived, died and risen in the little land with the curious traditions, transferred this belief from the mythical remoteness of symbols and mystic dis-appearance of experiences into the ordinary world, and in this way provided his need for a concrete relationship with the sphere of the gods with a unique impulse, which in-creasingly overcame the opposition of the rational instances. The Corinthians who opposed refused to believe, not that Christ was risen, but that the dead as a whole will rise, and Paul met them with an argument, which apparently did not seem conclusive to them (I Cor. xv. 16), that if the former is not true then the latter is neither. The resurrection of the individual is incredible to Jews, that of the mass ('the

[1] So Acts ii. 27, 31 might be understood, if we could consider the Pentecost narrative *in extenso* to be historical.

resurrection of the dead' Acts xvii. 32) to Greeks; for them resurrection is an affair of the gods of the Mysteries and their kind—one only needs to make the Christ the God-man to make him credible to them. Hellenistic Judaism on the other hand, which knew how to comprehend ingeniously Greek speculation and that dimension of life which was determined by tradition alongside each other, appears to have remained as a whole unresponsive to the message of the resurrection of Christ. The apostolate, which of necessity suppressed the idea of removal by that of the resurrection, and so demanded from the Jews an act of faith hardly capable of being effected, decided, without desiring it, for the Gentiles. As the risen-one who gave himself to be seen by the vanquished angel-powers and to whom they are henceforth subordinate (Eph. i. 21, 1 Pet. iii. 22), Christ has now been 'preached among the Gentiles' (1 Tim. iii. 16).

X

UT the motif of removal leads to something even more important, the consideration of which will be useful to our concern of comparing two kinds of faith. We must touch at the same time upon the enigma, which in the end may well be reckoned insoluble, and which has been called the 'self-consciousness' of Jesus. What this glance at his personal connexion with the Jewish world of faith will bring us to is necessarily hypothetical, yet is capable of helping towards the clarification of the problem.

Critical research tends to refer all that the gospels make Jesus say about the suffering and death which await him before the journey to Jerusalem to the category of *vaticinia ex eventu*. That certainly applies to the sacral formula which is repeated three times in all the Synoptics (Mark viii. 31, ix. 31, x. 33 par.), ascending to an even more urgent tone—first 'suffer much', then 'be given over into the hands of men', finally introduced by 'Behold, we go up to Jerusalem'. But such, in my opinion, is not the case with a variant of the first of these statements,[1] which Luke (xvii. 25) has preserved as belonging to the journey to Jerusalem, and he alone (that he alone has not simply replaced the sentence, like Mark and Matthew, with the dogmatic formula, but allowed it to stand alongside it, is no evidence against its genuineness). Referring to the prediction known also to Matthew (xxiv. 27) about the flashing lightning (*v.* 30 understands it as a 'revealing') of the 'Son of Man' who was previously hidden—the wording of which in Matthew sounds more Greek, but in Luke more Semitic— it runs: 'First however he must suffer much and be rejected by this generation'. Both 'suffer much' and 'be rejected' we know also from the formula, but how much smoother and more historical it sounds here without all 'the elders and high-priests and scribes'! And, read with the saying about the lightning, how much more natural and sensible the allusion to the—elsewhere variously quoted—verse of the Psalm (cxviii. 22) about the 'rejected' stone which has become the corner-stone! The connexion between the present hidden and the future revealed condition of the 'Son of Man' 'in His day'[2] is here, in opposition to the precision of the resurrection-formula, left in doubt, obviously because the mind of the speaker was uncertain. He knew himself as

---

[1] Also I cannot think that Luke xii. 50 is not genuine, if only we detach it from a context foreign to it (cf. Wellhausen on the passage)— in distinction from Matt. xx. 22 f., where the same tradition appears in a later modification—although I do not know any satisfactory interpretation of the statement. I cannot conceive how it could have originated in the primitive community (or even in the Hellenistic church).

[2] This of course does not mean that 'his' day is put in the place of the Old Testament 'Day of JHVH' (Bousset, *Kyrios Christos*, 12): it is the day of his becoming revealed. Also it does not follow that Jesus by the figure of the lightning 'made his own person a myth': the author of Is. xlii. 7 f. would have been able to say the same about the day of his future becoming revealed, the 'day of salvation'.

the prophet of the coming Basileia and at the same time as its appointed human centre (Matt. xi. 5, Luke vii. 22, cf. Is. xlii. 7 and lxi. 2); the crowd who were eager to hear recognized him as the former, but only the devotion of the disciples confirmed him as the latter, and he now knew from experience that the power granted him to-day was not that sufficient for the work of mediator of the kingdom. He knew himself as existing in the state of concealment. Is the transformation imminent in the course of life, so that he may flash as unexpectedly as the lightning—be made to flash? Will the voice which once summoned him (that the baptism in Jordan was accompanied by a personal experience of faith for him of such a kind need not be doubted, in spite of the legendary character of the narrative) testify to him before the flock of men which he shall unite into the core of the kingdom? Or must the transition be of a different kind? The statement—which is surely in the wrong place chronologically—about the wedding-guests from whom the bridegroom is 'taken'[1] away (Mark ii. 19 f. par.) appears to me to go back to a genuine tradition, even if it can no longer be reconstructed.[2] Will he be 'taken' like Enoch and Eliah, whom God removed to a special office and bestowed

[1] In the Aramaic original the verb which appeared in the Old Testament texts about the removal was obviously used here (Franz Delitzsch uses it in his translation into the Hebrew).

[2] One must not see in the statement 'a Christological utterance' (Dibelius, *Gospel Criticism and Christology*, 48). It has been rightly compared with IV Ezra x. 1 f. where the spouse, which is Zion, says: 'But as my son entered his bridal-chamber, he fell down and was dead. Then we overturned the lights'. (For this cf. Joachim Jeremias, 'Erloeser und Erloesung im Spaetjudentum und Urchristentum', *Deutsche Theologie*, II, 1929, 111 f.). The strange reference of this 'casus' (thus the Latin version) to the fall of Jerusalem is obviously secondary. Jesus seems to me to make use of a figure previously found in the tradition of the removal of the 'servant', against which the Ezra passage represents a varying form of the same motif.

the power for it, the one to a heavenly office as the 'Prince of the Presence', the angel of the immediate proximity, the other to an earthly office as the 'Angel of the Covenant', the helper in need and herald of the kingship, who had just appeared as John the Baptist and had performed his office? Or must it happen otherwise? It was written of yet another, of the 'servant of JHVH' (Is. liii) that he was 'taken' and 'cut off from the land of the living', and then 'his grave' and curiously enough 'his deaths' (*v.* 9) were spoken of, but then it was proclaimed that he would prolong his days and the will of God would prosper through him, after he 'had interposed for the rebels' and 'poured forth his soul unto death'. This too is a removal, a removal also to a particular, especially elevated office: he shall become a light to the nations (xlii. 6, xlix. 6) and a 'covenant for the people', the embodied covenant of the people united from amongst them, and he 'shall restore the earth' (xlix. 8) by setting free those held in prison and darkness (xlii. 7, lxi. 2) and establishing justice upon earth (xlii. 4); through his mediation the salvation of God shall rule unto the borders of the earth (xlix. 6).

That which has been proclaimed in this way is only to be adequately understood as the modification of the image of the Messiah.[1] In order to make this quite clear the nameless prophet, who, taking up again the concept of 'apprentice' introduced by Isaiah (Is. viii. 16, l. 4), conceived himself as a

[1] The opinion expressed by Bultmann in his discussion of Otto's 'Reich Gottes und Menschensohn' (*Theologische Rundschau* IX, 1937), 28 that the Messianic interpretation of Is. 53 is only found in Judaism since the second Christian century, is answered by the artificial and biased character of the interpretation referred to, directed against the meaning of the prophecy, which contradicts the familiar hope of the nation. This meaning was not officially accepted, but later on, when it threatened to become popular, it was opposed by that vulgar-messianic interpretation.

posthumous disciple of Isaiah, renewed the main motifs of his Messianic prophecies with an altered meaning,[1] in which everything which refers to David is expunged from the person of the Messiah; the Messiah now is not a royal but a prophetic man, one who no longer needs to raise his voice in the streets (xlii. 2) and the 'sure mercies of David' pass over to the community of Israel 'gathered' by God's compassion to an 'eternal covenant' (lv. 3 f., liv. 7), which community he represents. Added to this however is the fact that several lives come into existence from the one earthly life of the Isaianic Messiah, that—according to the Masoretic Text, the authenticity of which need not be questioned—he must die several 'deaths', that his soul is removed in the moment of dying (the spiritualized understanding of the 'being taken' already governs in this case, as we know it from the Psalms) and returns, until he is raised out of concealment into openness and may complete his work of salvation: now for the first time the world of men understands what he suffered of old for them, for the 'many' (Is. liii. 11 f., cf. lii. 14 f.), and what they failed to appreciate. In the concealment, when he lay hid like an unused arrow in God's quiver (xlix. 2), he did not even understand himself in his sufferings and his toil, all this seemed to him vain and fruitless, until it was made known to him what the office was which God kept for him; but even now he does not yet know when, at which stage of his way the fulfilment will come. The anonymous prophet, who speaks in the first person in his songs of the 'servant' knows himself as part of this way, without knowing which part.

If, as it has been repeatedly supposed,[2] the Messianic

[1] Cf. for this and the subject in general the chapter 'The Mystery' in my book The Prophetic Faith.

[2] Cf. especially Schweitzer loc. cit. 89 ff. (English edition, The Mystery of the Kingdom of God (1925), 236 ff.) and Joachim Jeremias, loc. cit., 118.

mystery of Deutero-Isaiah exercised a far-reaching influence upon Jesus, this powerful motif of the removals and of the way from the hidden office of suffering to the public office of fulfilment belongs essentially to it. We can scarcely surmise at what hour the germ of this motif came into the mind of Jesus—it may have been at the time of Peter's confession, perhaps shortly before it; but it must certainly have been a time of very painful fruitfulness, the effect of which we can feel in many a genuine saying. It is to be described as painful because already in Galilee Jesus had certainly learned to suffer through man being as he is, especially if the notable report in John's Gospel (vi. 66) about the disciples who left him may be traced back to a genuine tradition.

If we view the connexion rightly Jesus understood himself, under the influence of the conception of Deutero-Isaiah, to be a bearer of the Messianic hiddenness. From this follows straightway the meaning of the 'Messianic secret'. The arrow in the quiver is not its own master; the moment at which it shall be drawn out is not for it to determine. The secret is imposed. It is put by Jesus into the heart of the disciples[1]—whose confession indeed confirms him in it—

Against the argument, important in itself, which Bultmann (loc. cit., 27) has advanced, that in none of the words of Jesus is there a certain reference to the suffering servant of God, is to be considered the fact that Jesus' silence about his relation to a tradition which appeared not as prophecy but as mystery and spoke its language, is quite understandable. To be sure the idea of a suffering Messiah was 'strange and alarming' to the disciples, as to most of the Jews of that time (this was changed apparently from the breakdown of the Barcochba rising); but this is not to say how it appeared to Jesus. The decisive point is that in the servant of God mystery it is not the Messiah who must suffer but his previous stages; hence the particular *lability* which originates from its influence.

[1] This genuine tradition of an objective Messianic secret in Jesus' understanding of himself appears to me to have been worked over and intensified later on especially by Mark in his demon-stories.

like Isaiah once 'sealed up' the message of salvation in the heart of his own. Only when in sight of the end does the attitude of Jesus appear to change. But the story of his last days is so thickly overlaid by dogmatic certainty that one cannot venture any attempt at the reconstruction of his genuine utterances from this period. Nevertheless one single reference seems to be admissible.

In the account of the trial,[1] which is not to be considered as fundamentally historical, a noteworthy saying of Jesus is quoted (Mark xiv. 62), which as it stands can no more have come from his lips than the question which it answers could have come from the high priest, but which may be derived from the content of a genuine statement. Neither the connexion of the 'I am' with that which follows is to be retained, nor that of 'sitting' with 'coming', nor the 'power' which sounds rather like a Gnostic concept; but the reference to the 'son of man' or man, who would be 'seen' coming with the clouds of heaven, given in the answer to a question about himself, Jesus, has a peculiarly authentic character. 'Who art thou?' he has just been asked himself, as he earlier had asked the disciples who he was, but he, looking into realms beyond, replies in effect: 'Thou

[1] Cf. especially Lietzmann, *Der Prozess Jesu, Sitzungsberichte der Preussischen Akadamie der Wissenschaften, Phil-hist.* Klasse 1931 (cf. also his discussion with Buechsel ZNW 1931-2); of the earlier works: Goguel, *Juifs et Romains dans l'histoire de la passion* (1910); cf. also the same, *À propos du procès de Jesus* ZNW XXXI (1932) 294 ff. The historicity of the report has not been proved in my opinion even by the thorough essay of K. L. Schmidt, *Der Todesprozess des Messias Jesus, Judaica* I (1945), 1 ff. (Incidentally Schmidt's remark about Klausner's statement that the verdict is 'not consistent with the spirit of the Pharisees': 'Klausner, who as a Jew cannot avoid speaking in a certain sense *pro domo*' is regrettable. When Christian and Jewish scholars cannot concede to one another, even about this subject, that throughout they speak *pro veritate*, then we are seriously going back.)

shalt see the one whom I shall become'. *He* sees him now: I am he. He does not say it, but there are those who hear him who mean to hear it, because they see him, the one who sees. That he imagines himself in his own person as the one who will be removed and afterwards sent again to an office of fulfilment, in the figure of the vision of Daniel, is suggested strongly enough. The one who is now removed from the state of concealment and thereupon entering not a further concealment, but a Messianic revelation, must come from above, since now he is equipped with the other realizing power which was not granted him in the former state: he who experienced the lack of this power cannot think of it any more as confined within earthly conditions. If we may presuppose such a change of view, then the biographical fact is given, around which after the death of Jesus and the visions of the disciples the crystallizing of the mythical element lying ready in the hearts of those influenced by Hellenism took place, until the new binitarian God-image was present. Not merely new symbols but actually new images of God grow up from human biography, and precisely from its most unpremeditated moments.

The figure of the Messiah of Israel had changed twice in the pre-Christian period—both times in connexion with great national wars and periods of suffering—without however the new configuration supplanting the old; rather they continue to exist side by side, the old, pre-exilic remaining dominant, with characteristics from the others being taken into it. This first form may be called that of the king who fulfils.[1] It has its origin not in mythical imagination but in the view of historical reality in the prophetic perspective. Messiah, Christ, JHVH's Anointed, means in Israel the king as the receiver of sacramental anointing with oil in the

[1] Cf. the chapters 'The rule of God and the rule of Man' and 'The Theopolitical Hour' in my book *The Prophetic Faith*.

house of God. He was placed according to its intention, as understood by the prophets, under a special command from heaven, under a commission which allowed the prophets to set him time and again before the actual will of God; they confront him with the specific demand, which has been issued and is being issued to him, the demand to realize justice in Israel. As the kings fail to fulfil their task, the prophets reply with the prediction about the coming one who will fulfil the anointing. With the break-up of the Judaean Kingdom the old Messianic hope becomes problematic. It is not destroyed by it, indeed it springs up afresh with the first movement for return, but in the meantime a new, quite unheard-of form has appeared on the scene, the proclaimer of which treated the former as historically settled. The Messianic commission in its actual form was divided by him into two during the period of suffering in the Exile: the task of beginning, the leading back of Israel to its land is now transferred to a foreign prince, Cyrus, as JHVH's anointed (Is. xlv. 1), but the actual commission—and with it the fulfilment of the 'new' prophecy against the 'first' one—the establishment of the righteous community of Israel as the centre of the freed nations of the world devolves upon the new man from Israel, upon the 'servant of JHVH'. The commission to him embraces two functions, two phases, which are divided among different persons, who however represent only two manifestations of the same figure; this becomes ever more clear to us as we proceed from one to the other of the four songs (xlii. 1–9, xlix. 1–9a, l. 4–9, lii. 13–liii, 12), and so apparently the prophet himself gained increasing clarity through his experiences and disappointments. The first function, which is preparatory, is a suffering: the 'servant' of the period of suffering takes upon himself in his own present condition of prophetic concealment the burden of the sins of the 'many' from the nations of the world, he who is guiltless exculpates them and thereby makes possible the speedy breaking-through of salvation (if the reading in the Masoretic text 'in his deaths' may be accepted, as I think, then earlier suffering prophets may be regarded as manifestations of the servant). The second function, the Messianic fulfilment, is reserved for another, public appearance of the 'servant'; then for the first time will the nations of the world with Israel recognize how and through whom the preparation took place. (Essential to the understanding is that the one appointed for public recognition remains in the 'quiver' until he is drawn out, i.e. this his special Messianic vocation can be surmised indeed beforehand, but not actually known.)

Both forms of which we are speaking however—the pre-exilic form of the king and the exilic form of the prophetic 'servant'— have this in common, that the Messianic man is here an ascending and not a descending one. He steps forth from the crowd of men and is 'chosen' by God (Deut. xvii. 15, Is. xlii. 1)—which of course can mean different things: with the king the beginning of a testing, with the 'servant' the ratification. The commission which he receives is conferred upon him on earth, he is not sent down from heaven to earth with it. For the prophetic man too it is the specific tradition that he comes to know his mission in the call, and although he is aware of having been 'known' by God before his birth and sanctified by Him (Jer. i. 5) he is not affected by any thought of a heavenly pre-existence; and Deutero-Isaiah certainly does not think of the final, fulfilling appearance of the servant of God as one which has been sent down from heaven to earth. This changes with the second crisis and period of suffering for the people, the Syrian. People tend then not merely to despair of the saving achievement of the king, but of that of earthly man in general. The world can no longer be redeemed by the world. As the first change had been expressed in the book of the anonymous prophet, which originated from pamphlets amongst the exiles, so the second change was in the Book of Daniel. The 'one like to a man', the eschatological representative of Israel, is conveyed 'with the clouds of heaven' before the throne of God. This still indefinite image is developed in the Book of Enoch to a heavenly pre-existence of the Messianic man, although at first only in outline: his election had taken place before the creation of the world (xlviii. 6) and his dwelling is for ever 'under the wings of the Lord of the spirits' (xxxix. 7). But now the 'servant' of Deutero-Isaiah in his form as the one who fulfils is also incorporated into him: the 'from the outset hidden' (lxii. 7) heavenly 'Son of Man' is he who, having come down, will be 'the light of the nations' (xlviii. 4).[1] Accordingly the one who had been seen by the anonymous prophet as his own future, the one who is removed and who returns, proceeds from an earthly to a heavenly nature: nevertheless he remains in essence the one removed from earthly life, for instance that of Enoch, into the heavenly: the pre-existent one appears, as it were, like a vessel, which contains the man. Not the person, but the form is pre-existent.[2] Here, in a continuation of Deutero-Isaiah's conception, the ascending man is interwoven with the descending into an earthly-heavenly dual life. Jesus finds this in the popular

[1] The separation made again recently by Sjoeberg, *Der Menschensohn im aethiopischen Henochbuch* (1946) between the songs of the servant is unfounded, as I have shown in the chapter 'The Mystery' of my book *The Prophetic Faith*.

[2] I do not refer to chapters 70 and 71 of the *Ethiopian Book of Enoch* in which Enoch himself becomes the 'Son of Man', because I must associate myself with the doubt as to their authenticity. Otto's view, loc. cit., 164 ff., which is constructed from them, seems to me, as to Bultmann, untenable.

conception;[1] and so he appears to conceive his own present and future in a personal crisis, the office of suffering for the preparation and that of glory for the fulfilment.

If this is so then the idea of the 'servant'[2], modified by the Apocalypses, has stepped once again into the actual life-story of a man and in virtue of the biographical character so obtained has operated from this point as it has operated. It seems to me that here, especially through Paul, and later especially through John, the process of deification began, which it is true either dropped the name 'Son of Man', as Paul did, or retained it, as John, following the Synoptics, did, only on the lips of Jesus himself. The first presupposition of this work or process was that the removal, as associated with a purely human life (without pre-existence), was completely replaced by the resurrection, for which there was no analogy; its only trace remains in the ascension of the risen-one. As the second presupposition there was joined to it pre-existence, and differently from Jewish Apocalypses as a distinct essence and person, so that the fundamental and persistent character of the Messiah, as of one rising from humanity and clothed with power, was displaced by one substantially different: a heavenly being, who came down to the world, sojourned in it, left it, ascended to heaven and now enters upon the dominion of the world which originally belonged to him. Now it is declared (John iii. 13): 'No man ascended to heaven except him who came down from heaven, the Son of Man'. Only one step had to be taken from this to deification.

[1] I mean precisely this and not that Jesus 'had lived among the ideas of the Enoch tradition' (Otto, loc. cit., 176).

[2] So is the figure called in the Ezra Apocalypse xiii. 32, 37, 52 and in the Baruch Apocalypse lxx, 9 ('of my servant, the Messiah').

XI

THE colloquy with the rich man, whom Jesus advises to give up everything and to follow him, is opened by the question (Mark x. 17 par.): 'Good Master, what shall I do that I might inherit eternal life?' and the reply begins with the words: 'Why callest thou me good? There is none good but God alone'. Then follows: 'Thou knowest the commandments . . .' If one wants to preserve the continuity, 'good' must not be understood either by moral perfection or goodness; had that been the case Jesus would have uttered before the reply a reproof which was quite unconnected with it. It is different if the speaker uses 'good' in the sense of 'excellent', that is, intends to say that by his big question he is referring to one who, by the eminence of his mastership, is qualified to answer it adequately. Precisely this Jesus rejects. As in all things, so also in this, God alone is 'good', He alone is the good Master, He alone gives the true answer to the question about eternal life. And He has given it, in the commandments of His 'teaching', the Torah, from which Jesus now quotes several. Only when the questioner asserts that he has kept them all from his youth upwards, Jesus regards him lovingly and adds: 'Thou lackest one thing', by which he merely confirms the feeling which led the man there and the implicit expression of which inspired love in Jesus. And now he adds the entirely personal advice: therefore give up everything to which thou holdest fast (the 'treasure in heaven' is an unaccented parenthesis in the sense of the current doctrine of rewards, which Jesus does not wish to question but yet which in his view does not say the decisive thing) and follow me.[1] This is not intended to complete the divine instruction; there is no such thing, man only needs to grasp the original intention of the commandments of God, and what that means thou wilt come to know sufficiently if thou goest with me. God teaches His doctrine for all, but He also reveals His way directly to chosen people; he to whom it is revealed and who goes in it transfers accordingly the doctrine into personal actuality and teaches therefore 'the way of God' (Mark xii. 14) in the right manner of man. So Jesus knows himself to be a qualified means to teach the good Master's will, but he himself does not will to be called good: there is none good, but God alone.

No theological interpretation can weaken the directness of this statement. Not only does it continue the great line of the Old Testament proclamation of the non-humanity of God and the non-divinity of man in a special way, which is distinguished by the personal starting-point and the point of reference: against the tendencies towards deification of the post-Augustan ecumeny, its thirst after becoming a god and making gods, it also opposes the fact of remaining man. The historical depth of the moment, in which the word was spoken, is to be understood from the point of view of the

[1] Matthew obscures the meaning with his 'If thou wouldest be perfect', which transfers the idea of v. 48 to this place, with which it does not fit: the man is not concerned with perfection but eternal life.

deification which the one who spoke it attained after death. It is as if he warded this off: as if, for the sake of the faith-immediacy to God in which he stands and to which he wants to help man, he warded off this belief in himself. It is truly an instance here of Emunah.

What was the way which could lead from this declaration of Jesus—which was preserved in spite of the Christology opposed to it and accordingly the genuineness of which can hardly be doubted—to his apotheosis? 'The sonship of God', writes Usener in his book *Das Weihnachtstest* (1888) which is still not out of date, 'was given, and faith must have been irresistibly driven to develop the idea of divinity'. By the 'givenness' of the sonship we are to understand here that in the oldest tradition of the baptism of Jesus the heavenly voice chose and raised him to be the son of God. Recently it has been taken for granted that originally the resurrection was regarded as the moment of this appointment, and only later on the baptism.[1] If that is so, then the report of the baptism, which Mark places at the beginning of his account of the Messiah as the 'divine birth'[2] of Jesus, cannot well go back to any personal communication of Jesus about his own experience at the baptism, and there is no pathway from his understanding of himself to the process of deification. It is a different matter if—as appears to me correct now as before—the baptism tradition is in essence genuine[3] and a saying of Jesus lies at the basis of this

[1] Cf. the comprehensive account by M. Dibelius in *Die Religion in Geschichte und Gegenwart* (2nd ed.), I. 1559.

[2] Usener, *Das Weihnachtsfest* (2nd ed., 1911), 49.

[3] Cf. Windisch, 'Jesus und der Geist nach synoptischer Uberlieferung' (in *Studies in Early Christianity*, 1928), 223: 'The style of the narrative is mythical and the interpretation is determined by the Old Testament figure of the Spirit-anointed servant of God. But an historical kernel is very probable'.

essential part.[1] In the Synoptic Gospels such a saying has not been preserved, perhaps because of the disparity between it and the accepted report. But it seems to me that a trace of such a declaration is preserved in one place in which one hardly looks for it. It is also of importance for our concern.

The beginning of the Nicodemus-pericope (John iii. 1-8) seems to me to belong, in a shorter setting which is to be inferred approximately from the one given us, to the enclaves of genuine tradition in St. John's Gospel, which have not yet been adequately investigated, and which only yield their character when translated back into Aramaic or Hebrew.

A Pharisee town-councillor, Nicodemus, whom some exegetes[2] want to identify with the rich man who seeks the way to eternal life, comes by night to Jesus—probably not secretly, but in the atmosphere of secrecy. He addresses him 'from the sure basis of the scribes ('we know', v. 2) and recognizes him as having an equal right (he calls him 'Rabbi'), as authorized by God to be a teacher'.[3] The signs, he says, which Jesus does prove that he has 'come from God' and that 'God is with him'. These words are 'as to the form a simple address, as to the matter a question',[4] to which Jesus indeed 'replies' (v. 3). What is Nicodemus asking about? Bultmann means that the question ought not to be 'particularized'; it seems to me that one is driven by the text to do this, but one must guard against reading

[1] Cf., amongst others, Burkitt, 'The Baptism of Jesus', *Expository Times*, 38 (1926), 201.

[2] Bacon, *The Fourth Gospel in Research and Debate* (1910), 382; cf. *The Gospel of the Hellenists* (1933), 413.

[3] Bultmann in a correspondence with me (long before the publication of his commentary on John).

[4] Bultmann, *Das Johannesevangelium*, 94.

anything into it. The speaker asserts Jesus' empowerment from above in his word (*v.* 2a) and his work (*v.* 2b) and is then silent. His silence expresses his question: he does not understand this empowerment. Silently he asks: how does this come about in your case? whence have you this? with what have you acquired it? Jesus, questioned about himself, gives information about himself, but in such a way that precisely by it the questioner learns that no information can be given about such a question concerning the nature of its subject. Yet at the same time the questioner has acquired information concerning something about which he had not intended to ask or at any rate not then, and something he needed to know.

How does it come about that one, as Nicodemus expresses it, 'comes from God', without having been at pains about it? Jesus answers (*v.* 3): the particular thing about which you ask, the teaching and acting empowered by God, is derived from the fact that a man sees the kingship of God which has drawn near; but he can only see it if first—here the text becomes ambiguous[1]—he has been 'begotten from above' or 'born anew'.

'The kingship of God', for the Synoptics the beginning of the preaching of Jesus, appears in John only in this section, which was received by him. Whoever, says Jesus, sees and proclaims the kingship of God now, at the time of its greatest proximity to the world—and to announce it is my teaching, of which you speak—he it is who comes from God. For this however he must first be 'begotten from above'.

---

[1] Cf. Goguel, *Trois études*, 105; Cullmann, *Der johanneische Gebrauch doppeldeutiger Ausdruecke*, *Theologische Zeitschrift* IV (1948), 365 f. The ambiguity of ἄνωθεν in my opinion originated in this case in the translation and henceforth has been utilized for the addition of *v.* 4b (I consider 4a is original). In the original it ran 'from above'.

Jesus now gives to an incidental question, which sounds more dialectic than naïve (originally only *v.* 4a), an answer that leads more deeply and precisely into his meaning: only the man who has been begotten by water and spirit can see God's rule and enter into it—two phases of the same event. 'Water and spirit' refer in the Jewish circle of ideas (as already Clement of Alexandria perceived) to the creation of the world: the breath of power from above, which blows down on the awakened potentiality of all living creatures and which brings them to life.[1] But in the language of Hellenistic Judaism—as we know from several characteristic references in Philo—the creating of God was called a procreation, apparently in connexion with early Israelitish use of words, related to North-Syrian;[2] Adam too was considered to have been 'begotten' by God, as in addition to Philo the conclusion of the Lukan Joseph-genealogy (Luke iii. 38) shows. So it may be assumed that in the earliest tradition of the colloquy[3] Jesus spoke of people being created

[1] The attempt of Odeberg, *The Fourth Gospel* I (1929 ff.), 51 ff., to use for the explanation of the reference the idea, already known from the Book of Enoch, of a coupling of the waters above with those below, leaves unnoticed the fact that the Spirit at the beginning of the creation-story broods *over the waters above* (which are still undivided from those below). The Haggadic conception of the Spirit as hovering between the waters above and those below cannot be justified by the Scripture-text; moreover it belongs to another group of ideas to that of the coupling of the waters.

[2] The verb *qanah*, which in Hebrew appears to have originally meant parental procreation, is used in the Ras Shamra texts for the mother of the gods as 'procreatoress'.

[3] Justin's logion, *Apol.* I, 61. 4: 'If thou are not born again, thou wilt not enter into the kingdom of God', which seems to me to be derived from the earlier version of the Nicodemus conversation (cf. Merx, *Die vier kanonischen Evangelien* II, 2, 1911, 54), does not contradict this. References like 1 John iii. 9; 1 Peter i. 23 belong to a later development, which sensualizes more strongly the 'begetting'.

anew by water and spirit (the idea of water, which disappears in the sequel, is taken from the remembered experience, but does not adhere to it, but refers to the creation
exposed to the operation of the creating spirit) and in the
translation the begetting-anew took its place; this was explained as being born anew it seems, only as the second half
of the intervening question and verse 7[1] which destroys the
connexion and alters the meaning were added. It is to be
borne in mind that on the one hand neither the Synoptics
nor Paul knew of a second birth, and on the other that Paul
knows of a creating-again,[1] which he expresses (2 Cor.
v. 17, Gal. vi. 15), speaking it is true only of Christians and
not of Christ, by the word 'new creation', which was
already current in early Rabbinic thought for the activity
of God which regenerated a person in the midst of life; so,
for example, Abraham (Midrash Tanchuma on the reference) at the time of his being brought forth from his native
country (according to another conception (Midrash Genesis
rabba xxxix, 11), at the time of the promise of his 'seed', as
the endowment with new power of procreation), is 'made'
into a 'new creature'. The first stimulus towards this idea
may originate in the narrative of the first king to be anointed, who, after the anointing, as the Spirit of JHVH
falls upon him, 'is turned into another man', because God
'turned into him another heart' (1 Sam. x. 6, 9). The servant
of God in Deutero-Isaiah[2] (Is. lxi. 1) also traces back to an
anointing the presence of God's Spirit 'with him', which
portion Jesus in Luke (iv. 18) reads in the synagogue as fulfilled in him by the experience of baptism. The fact that in
the translation of the Nicodemus colloquy into Greek

---

[1] Cf. Loisy, *Le quatrième évangile*, 2nd. ed. (1921), 160.
[2] I ascribe Is. lxi, 1 f. to Deutero-Isaiah himself; that which follows
is a later elaboration which reduces the universalist conception (cf. xlii
6 f. and xlix. 6) into a particularist one.

begetting-again enters in the place of the new creation is explained also by the powerful influence which the divine saying at the baptism in the original Lukan setting, which addresses the son with the adoption-formula from Psalm ii. 7, 'To-day have I begotten thee', exercised upon early Christian thought.[1] According to that late Messianic doctrine the Messianic man, raised in the course of life by God to be His son, ascends from humanity to a heavenly existence and mission.

That Jesus now says, in correspondence with the preceding sentence, that what issues from flesh is flesh but that which issues from spirit is spirit, has originally a meaning quite different from instructing an inquisitive questioner that one cannot understand spiritual birth from the idea of physical birth. Immediately before it had been stated that on him who has personally entered into the renewal there takes place anew the never-ending event of creation, again the spirit of God hovers above the waters of becoming, but in a new, as it were, spiritual work: the human nature in which the formative breath from above and the chaotic flood from below meet one another is remodelled by the working of the spirit. But it is now said of this person that he, this 'other man', as originated from the spirit, is spirit; obviously it does not mean that henceforth he is 'only' spirit and not flesh, but that the spirit has blown down into him in such a manner that a kind of being which belongs to the spirit has become his own. Once again this requires elucidation, which must follow.

What follows is that Spirit-Wind simile, over which the Western translators have so laboured until in the end the same word *pneuma* in the same sentence is rendered once by wind and once by spirit[2]; from the point of view of

[1] Cf. Usener, *Das Weihnachtsfest*, 40 ff.

[2] Cf. Buber and Rosenzweig, *Die Schrift und ihre Verdeutschung*, 160 ff., 280 f.

readers of the Greek text this is an absurdity. 'Simile,' I said, but actually it is no simile.[1] It is not about two things, in which one was compared with the other, but only about one thing, the *ruach*, the *pneuma*, the *spiritus*, the divine breath, which, experienced from the beginning in religious sensuality, blows towards the cosmos the stirring and enlivening 'wind' and inspires the mind of man with the stirring and enlivening 'Spirit'.[2] This One-from-above, which must not be misunderstood as two, appears at the beginning of the story of creation above the upper waters and now, in the new creation of the man who is called, above the baptismal water of Jordan.[3] This, the *ruach* of God, sent down by Him, is that which ever again creates men and renews the face of the earth (Ps. civ. 30). In Luther's translation it is said of it: the wind blows (earlier he wrote as Meister Eckhart did: der Geist geistet), but in the Greek text: *to pneuma . . . pnei*, in which the oneness of the root of the noun and verb is obviously not fortuitous. But is this common root original? The intention is to point at the situation of the creation; but in the story of the creation it is not said of the *ruach* of God that it blows but that it hovers; the symbol is (cf. Deut. xxxii. 11) that of a bird which, with outspread wings, hovers above its nestlings, the tips of its wings vibrating powerfully, rather than that accepted by some old versions and commentaries of the brooding hen-bird. Here too the translation or adaptation upset the meaning. If it may be assumed (as I consider likely) that Jesus conducted the conversation with scribes in Hebrew, then the Greek translator has exceeded—like the majority of

[1] In contradistinction to Eccles. xi. 5, as the remodelling of which the statement may be seen.

[2] Cf. loc. cit, 33 ff., 60 ff.; K. L. Schmidt, *Das Pneuma Hagion, Eranos Jahrbuch*, 1945, 194 ff., and Kerenyi, *Die Geburt der Helena* (1945), 32 ff.

[3] Cf. Loisy, *Études évangéliques* (1902), 199 ff.

alliterations and assonances in the Old Testament—the intentional sound-pattern *ruach-merachefet*, which he could not reproduce. The *pneuma*, according to the account of the baptism, flew down 'like a dove' (Mark i. 10 par.), as the Babylonian Talmud (Chagiga 15a) made it hover at the beginning of the creation of the world 'like a dove' above the waters; one hears the rustle of its wings,[1] but does not know whence it has come or whither it will go. So, we may understand, it happened to Jesus himself. But we know too already from the story of Eliah (1 Kings xviii. 12) the motif, that the *ruach* carries the prophet 'I know not whither', and he cannot be found; which again is to be taken along with the fact that Jesus after the baptism is driven into the wilderness by the spirit. The sentence 'You know not . . .' provides the connecting link with the direct answer which follows to Nicodemus' silent question: 'Even so is everyone who is begotten by the spirit'. What applies to the spirit applies also to the one renewed by it: one cannot know whence he comes and whither he goes.[2] Nicodemus had asked, how is it that you come from God without having gone our way? Concerning the way of one re-created by the *ruach*, replies Jesus, you cannot know the nature of it; for it is the way of the *ruach* itself.

In this way the writer of St. John's Gospel understood the statements as an expression by Jesus of his pneumatical

---

[1] Cf. Ezek. i. 24a LXX; Rev. ix. 9a: φωνή is not used in Biblical Greek for the rushing of the wind (Ps. xxix. 5 LXX is no evidence against this: this is about JHVH's voice, which manifests itself in the storm). The Vulgate understands voice (et vocem ejus audis), and this appears to refer to what Jesus heard at the baptism; but—unlike the apocryphal Nazarean Gospel—in the Synoptic Gospels the voice of God and not that of the Spirit is heard in the account of the baptism.

[2] Cf. Overbeck, *Das Johannesevangelium* (1911) 397.

inscrutability, when the Nicodemus colloquy had not yet undergone its final revision. In his account of the Feast of Tabernacles pilgrimage (viii. 14) he makes clear reference to it and in the same language, directly after (vii. 50 f.) Nicodemus 'who came to him before' has spoken on his behalf, and he makes Jesus say to the Pharisees: 'I know whence I am come and whither I go: but you do not know whence I am come or whither I go'. Nicodemus had said: 'We know . . .' Jesus replies in this instance: 'You know not'. It is implied: you cannot know.[1]

Schlatter rightly understands the saying about flesh and spirit when he says:[2] 'What is begotten has what he who begets is. He transfers his nature to that which is made by him'. But it is incorrect when from the fact that there are two factors which beget, flesh and spirit, he infers: 'There are therefore two kinds of life, two classes of people'. The original statement does not lead to Paul's doctrine (1 Cor. ii. 14 f.) of the two classes of men, the psychic and the pneumatic. By what he says Jesus does not intend to bar the way to heaven to his nocturnal visitor, but to open it. Nicodemus hoped nevertheless, when he asked Jesus about his way, that he would so find his own, as in Mark x. 17 the question is openly asked: 'Good Master, what shall I do to inherit eternal life?' And in the end Jesus answers in this case too: 'Follow me'.

Here also the great faith is taught by the personal experience of great faith: submit to the Spirit of God and you will have to give yourself up to it. So Jesus speaks in this instance also only as a man of faith and not as a possible object of faith; he declines in both instances, in the former explicitly and here implicitly, to be made the object of faith. Here he

[1] Cf. Bernard, *A Critical and Exegetical Commentary on the Gospel according to St. John* (1928), I, 107.

[2] *Der Evangelist Johannes* (1930), 89.

says, from his experience of faith, what it means to become a son of God: to be created anew by Him, to be 'begotten' by Him, as he has experienced it. But this personal experience he expresses as one open to men in general: 'Except a man . . .' (*v.* 3) and again 'Except a man . . .' (*v.* 5) and then most clearly and forcibly (*v.* 8): 'Even so is *everyone* who is begotten by the spirit'. This doctrine, which continues the line of the Old Testament doctrine of the divine sonship promised to the true sons of Israel (Hos. ii. 1), the writer of the prologue, who (John i. 13) sets the generation by God Himself in the place of the generation by the spirit, has transferred into his theological language and world in this way (*v.* 12): 'But as many as received him to them has he given the power to become children of God'. And this declaration passes over immediately (*v.* 14) into the dogmatic proclamation of the glory of the incarnate *logos* 'as the only-begotten from the Father'.

Finally the assertion of being the only-begotten one is put also on to the lips of the Synoptic Jesus in that curious 'ancient interpolation'[1] (Matt. xi. 27), standing between a prayer and an invitation, which are by all means both of his spirit, while it is unconnected with both and foreign to both in style and content. In the word 'And no one recognizes the Father except the Son and he to whom the Son may reveal it' the sonship is particularized in the most extreme fashion. Once it ran 'Love your enemies so that you may become sons of your Father in heaven'. The way in was open to all: only love was demanded. Now Jesus is made to say: 'I am the door (John x. 9) and 'I am the way' (xiv. 6); the only door, the only way: 'nobody comes to the Father but by me'.

The sentence 'And nobody knows the Father save the

---

[1] Wellhausen, *Das Evangelium Matthaei* 57; cf. also Arvedson, *Das Mysterium Christi* (1937), 110 f.

Son' which, as is well known, is to be found almost word for word in the hymn to the Sun of Amenophis IV, has been called a 'majestic self-testimony'.[1] Certainly it is that. But when we hear Jesus himself speaking of the sonship something greater than this majesty is present.

[2] Bousset, *Kyrios Christos*, 62.

XII

Mark's story of Jesus begins with the account of the baptism in the Jordan; in John it ended originally with the account of the overcoming of Thomas' doubt in the physical reality of the risen-one, as with the 'goal and full-stop'.[1] If I do not place my finger in the marks of his wounds, he says (John xx. 25), 'I will not believe'. He wishes also to see the marks of the nails, but that may not be sufficient, for one can also see ghosts; in order that he may believe that this is Jesus himself and not a ghost he must be able actually to touch the wounds with his hand: indeed, he must establish with this hand the authenticity of the wounds and so of the person. But when Jesus appears and calls him to place his fingers in the marks of his wounds, sight is enough for Thomas. He invokes the risen-one: 'My Lord and my God!' In John's time the Caesars ordered that they should be called this;[2] but Thomas does not utter his cry because commanded. Also it is not the sight but the speech which forces it from him: no ghost speaks

[1] Deissmann, *Licht vom Osten*, 4th ed. (1923), 309. cf. Eng. trans. *Light from the Ancient East*, (1911), p. 366.

[2] Deissmann, loc. cit., 310.

like this to a man. Now the doubter believes. But he does not only believe that Jesus is risen; he believes also that he is 'his God'. Did the other apostles also believe that? Till then they have not said anything which might be so understood. Thomas believes and expresses his faith: Jesus, whom he recognizes as risen, is his God. We are not told what caused him to believe this, and we get no suggestion about it. We can only realize anew that the resurrection of an individual person does not belong to the realm of ideas of the Jewish world. If an individual as individual is risen then here is a fact which finds no place in this circle of ideas. Thomas does not intend broadening this circle of ideas. That he, as we have come to know him in the mood of his doubt, has not the power to do this is understandable. What he thinks in this moment is apparent: since no man can rise as an individual, then this is no man, but a god; and since he had been for him *the* man, his man, now he is his God. But with this the Jewish world of belief, which knows no god but God, suddenly collapses for the Thomas of the narrative. Amongst all the disciples of Jesus he is the first Christian in the sense of the Christian dogma. The first Christian must have appeared like this to the evangelist, for whom everything, his whole heaven-reaching theological building, rose up upon the foundation of the 'faith' that this *is* and that it is so: a man who avoids for as long as possible the belief that there is 'this sort of thing' and when it is no longer possible, then casts his world from him and worships the dead and living one, who has spoken to him. Therewith the presence of the One Who cannot be represented, the paradox of Emunah, is replaced by the binitarian image of God, one aspect of which, turned towards the man, shows him a human face. Thus and not otherwise from the starting-point of the Johannine presuppositions must the binitarian image of God have been established.

The objective expression of this faith in an article of faith was still required. This arises in the same circle of men from which the fourth gospel came, and apparently originates from its author. At the end of the first Epistle of John we read of Jesus Christ: 'This is the true God and eternal life'. The definite article before 'true God' has obviously to express the fact that here no new image of God is set up, but the old, until now partly hidden one, has been revealed in its completeness: until now, that is, eternal life has been 'with the Father', but now it has 'appeared to us' (1 John i. 1), yet not as something added to the true God, but as He Himself. It is this which, in other words, the beginning of the prologue of the Gospel says, which intends to tell the beginning of the creation-story again, as only now revealed in its meaning: here it is the *logos* which was 'with God', already 'at the beginning', and yet 'the *logos* was God'. The word of creation, which God, revealing Himself in it, speaks, is itself He. One might describe this as a compound of Jewish and extra-Jewish hypostases-speculation and stand by that, if the 'Word', the 'eternal life', did not show us just that human countenance, the face of the risen one, who invited Thomas to place his hand in his wounded side. For the 'Christian' who exists henceforth, God has this countenance; apart from this countenance He is, what He was and is for the Jew, without a face. There were plenty of anthropomorphic ideas in the faith of Judaism too, but they were an affair of men. Men saw appearances of God and depicted them, the men were different and the visions were different, the men passed away and the visions passed away with them, but God remained unseen in all His appearances. But now, in Christian existence, that countenance adhered, unchangeably, in spite of all the imagination which tried its hand at it, to the divine being. The Christian could not help seeing it when he turned to God. When he prayed he for the most part spoke to it, implicitly or explicitly. Already Stephen when dying (Acts vii. 59) yields his spirit not to God, as Jesus did when dying (Luke xxiii. 46, cf. Ps. xxxi. 5), but to the 'Lord Jesus'.

The work of deification was a process, a compulsion, not arbitrariness. Only in this way indeed do new images of God ever originate. But in this case there was something which had not been. 'Israel', from the point of view of the history of faith, implies in its very heart immediacy towards the imperceptible Being. God ever gives Himself to be seen in the phenomena of nature and history, and remains invisible. That He reveals Himself and that He 'hides Himself' (Is. xlv. 15) belong indivisibly together; but for His concealment His revelation would not be real and temporal. Therefore He is imageless; an image means fixing to one manifestation, its aim is to prevent God from hiding Himself, He may not be allowed any longer to be present as the One Who is there as He is there (Exod. iii. 14), no longer appear as He will; because an image is this and intends this, 'thou shalt not make to thyself any image'. And to Him, the ever only personally Present One, the One Who never becomes a figure, even to Him the man in Israel has an exclusively immediate relationship. He 'sets Him ever before him' (Ps. xvi. 8), he is 'always with Him' (lxxiii. 23). That is something quite different from what man tends to understand by monotheism. This usually means a part of a general view of the world, its highest part; exclusive immediacy however is not a worldview, but the primal reality of a life-relationship. To be sure, this man of Israel recognizes his God in all the powers and mysteries, but not as an object among objects, but as the exclusive Thou of prayer and devotion. Again when Israel confesses (Deut. vi. 4) that JHVH is its Lord, JHVH the One, it does not mean that there is not more than *one* God—

this does not need to be confessed at all—but that 'its' God is the One to Whom it is related by such an exclusive immediate Emunah, by such love of the whole heart, the whole soul and the whole might of the being (*v.* 5), as one can only be related to One who cannot be represented, which means One who cannot be confined to any outward form. In scripture this is called 'to be wholly with God'. This reality of faith and life is that which the Christian—not professedly but actually—opposes, when in the reality of his own faith and life he assigns to God a definite human countenance, the countenance of the 'great God-Saviour' (Titus ii. 13), of the 'other God' (Justin), of the 'suffering God' (Tatian), of the God who has acquired His Community with His own blood' (Acts xx. 28). The God of the Christian is both imageless and imaged, but imageless rather in the religious idea and imaged rather in actual experience. The image conceals the imageless One.

A new and different kind of immediacy is to be sure obtained by this. It is that which can be compared with the immediacy to a beloved person, who has just this and no other form and whom one has chosen precisely as this form. It is a Thou, which, determined as it is, as it were appertains to one. From this a concreteness of relationship arises, which craves sacramental incorporation of the Thou, but personally can go further, to the merging of self, to the self-bearing of this suffering, to the self-receiving of these wounds and wound-marks—and to a love for man which 'proceeds from Him'. Thomas the doubter, who renounces touching, the last figure in the story of Jesus, stands at the entrance to the way of Christ, in the later stages of which we find persons like Francis of Assisi. What a great living paradox this altogether is! Indeed that first paradox, immediacy to the Imageless One, the One Who hides Himself and appears again, Who bestows that which is revealed and withholds that which is concealed (Deut. xxix. 29), is given up.

Nathan Soederblom quotes at one point[1] the statement made in conversation by a French admiral: 'There have been times in my life when I was an atheist. But I would have called myself a Christian had I dared'. 'In our time', Soederblom continues, 'the same thing has certainly happened to more than one. Christ is to them the rock of their religion and of their heart. No other name is given to them. He is the sun of the world of the soul, Leader, Saviour, Lord—God in the same measure as that is God, upon which the heart entirely relies . . . One may at times feel a doubt about the Godhead of God, but not about the Godhead of Christ'. One of my late Christian friends, Christian Rang, who had prefixed the name Florens before his own in order to hint at Angelus Silesius' 'frozen Christ' who had come into bloom, once said to me about the most difficult time in his life: 'I should not have survived if I had not had Christ'. Christ, not God! I have since often mentioned this testimony to genuine Christians of my acquaintance from whom I knew that I should hear the candid truth of their soul. Several of them have confirmed it as the expression of their own experience. We find its great literary expression in some works of Dostoevski: a clinging to the Son when turning aside from the Father is the main attitude of Ivan Karamazov, and in the novel about the possessed, the Christian, when forced to the wall, falteringly has to confess that he indeed believes in Christ, but in God—he will believe. I see in all this an important testimony to the salvation which has come to the Gentiles through faith in Christ: they have found a God Who did not fail in times when their world collapsed, and further, One Who in times when they found themselves sunk under guilt granted

[1] *Vater, Sohn und Geist* (1909), 60.

atonement. This is something much greater than what an ancestral god or son of the gods would have been able to do for this late age. And something akin to that testimony resounds to us from the cries and groans of earlier generations to Christ. Only one must not miss hearing the other thing when listening to their fervour and piety.

At the close of the first Epistle of John there follows on the confession that this Jesus Christ is the true God and eternal life the somewhat abrupt admonition: 'Children, guard yourselves from idols!' One commentator[1] sees in this a proof 'that this confession has nothing to do with a weakening of monotheism'. That to be sure agrees perfectly with the aim of the confession, but not in the same measure with its effect. I presume of course that by 'monotheism' in this case something different has been understood from the world-view so widely current in the ecumeny which was satisfied to replace the concrete claims of the Pantheons by a claim which was general and free from all reality, and in which there was nothing to be weakened.

I may give expression here to a personal impression which always returns whenever I think of three Pauline passages taken together, and of which I can only think of as taken together. Paul, who in his genuine letters apparently never[2] claims for the pre-existent Christ the character of God, nevertheless speaks of him as made in the form of God (Phil. ii. 6) and directly assigned a share in the work of God (1 Cor. viii. 6) and this, in spite of its partly formulatory character, in a confession of elemental intensity: the world knows many gods and many lords, 'but for us there is one God, the Father, of Whom are all things and we to Him,

[1] Buechsel, *Die Johannesbriefe* (1933), 90.
[2] If one detaches in Rom. ix. 5, the benediction of the 'God over all' from that which precedes it and refers it to the Father, which corresponds to the same use of words i. 25 and 2 Cor. xi. 31.

133

and one Lord, Jesus Christ, through whom are all things and we through him'. In the Father is the origin and end of all being, in the Son its permanence and salvation. But in the Epistle to the Romans (xi. 36) we find a changed confession. There it is said of God: 'For of Him and through Him and unto Him are all things'. The difference leads me to assume that in the meantime Paul had noticed that the danger of a ditheism threatened and that he wished to obviate this. But now it still seems to work in the mind of this man who strove for the truth of his vision:[1] in the confession of unity he had not let Christ have his right, and so he must do it now. So originates the most mature expression of his intention (Col. i. 15 ff.), in which he seeks to preserve the unity and at the same time to extol the heavenly Christ: 'he is the image of the invisible God, the first-born of all creation, for in him all things have been created', 'all things were made through him and unto him'. Here the Christ is included both in the creation and in the creating of God, and in him the revelation centres, for he is the true image, in which He Who remains invisible becomes visible. So Paul contended for both things at once, for loyalty to the highest possible conception of his Master and for the 'unweakened' maintenance of monotheism.

[1] With regard to the chronology of the Pauline writings I follow the view of Dodd, 'The Mind of Paul: Change and Development,' *Bulletin of the John Rylands Library* 18 (1934), 3 ff.

XIII

AUGUSTINE, was, I think, the first to refer to the fact that Paul, who says such great things about the love of men between themselves—that is to say as members of the Church of Christ—says very little about the love of men to God. This is all the more strange, since from childhood he had heard everyday in the summons 'Hear, O Israel' the commandment to love God with his whole soul, and indeed he knew also the saying of Jesus in which this was called the first commandment of all. The rare use which Paul makes of the word *agape*, love in the religious and ethical sense, in the sphere of the relation of men to God, has been explained[1] by the fact that for him 'love' is characterized as 'made known through the cross of Christ', and that accordingly human devotedness to God, unspontaneous and uncreative as it is, at best has to be accounted as the reflexion of it.

In point of fact there is scarcely one sentence in Paul which speaks of a human love to God which is to be understood as

---

[1] Nygren, *Agape and Eros* I (1932), 92.

spontaneous; when for him man loves God we can be quite sure that God Himself in that case works in man, and we are tempted to think of Spinoza, for whom the love of man for God is in truth nothing but God's love for Himself. The depreciation of man is foreign to genuine Judaism. That man exists at all is for it the original mystery of the act of creation—which is expressed in the twofold simile, incorporation of the divine 'form' and inbreathing of the divine 'spirit'; only in the spontaneity of man does it become evident what an unfathomable mystery the fact of creation implies. The Old Testament command to love, in its threefold repetition of the claim on the whole man, appeals to his unbroken spontaneity: thou shalt, thou canst love God with all thine heart; and it is given to us to feel that the heart will not become whole except by such a love for Him. Pharisaic Judaism went a step further in that it wished to symbolize this task imposed upon man also in the dimension of time. 'Love Him', it is said (Sifre on Deut. vi. 5) 'unto the squeezing-out of the soul'. One must understand this by realizing the last moment of the agony, even the agony of the martyr, and in this way it was testified to by action. God does not attest Himself, but He desires to have man whom He has endowed with spontaneity for His 'witness' (Is. xliii. 10, xliv. 8), and the 'servant' Israel, whom He chose for suffering, belongs to such (xliii. 9) when he bears his suffering by his own will as one who loves. The suffering which was understood as springing from the love of God and borne in the innermost spontaneity of love to Him was called by Pharisaic Judaism 'suffering of love'. When this Judaism wishes to point to the mystery of the creation of man in the form of a theologoumenon of human existence, it says indeed (Bab. Berachot 33b): 'Everything is in the hands of Heaven except the fear of Heaven', but it straightway prevents this from being misunderstood by illustrating the sentence by a verse from Scripture which explains the command to love (Deut. x. 12): God demands from Israel that it should fear Him and love Him[1]—fear belongs to love as the door belongs to the house—like fear that does not flow into love, so love that does not comprehend fear is only one of the ways of serving God as an idol. We see that the God Who speaks here speaks of a partner, in whom He Himself does not arouse or effect, by the power of His own love, this love towards Himself, but rather even if He dreadfully hides himself and His love from him desires to be loved as He is feared. 'Even if He takes thy soul from thee': so Pharisaic Judaism (Bab. Berachot 61b) interprets the command to love. It is none other than God who 'squeezes out' the soul, but it is not He, precisely not He, but the soul itself, in the original mystery of its spontaneity, that loves Him, even then, and shall do it and can do it.[2]

It is evident that Jesus, in so far as we are able to unravel his historical reality, occupied a position within this circle of belief. Equally obvious is the fact that Paul had turned from it when he devoted himself to the mysterium of Christ. We cannot but ask how he came to this estrangement. He tells us nothing about it. But it seems to me that at one point a slight clue is given to us. In Romans v. 8 ff. he says first: 'God proves His love towards us in that, while we were yet sinners, Christ died for us', and then: 'If we have been reconciled to God as enemies through the death of His

[1] In this passage, where the fear of God appears united with the love of God, it is at all events to be understood in its concreteness and not polished into a synonym of piety.

[2] In view of this reality of faith the opinion—recently repeated even by Bultmann (*Theologie des Neuen Testaments*, 23)—that in the piety of Judaism God is 'removed to far away', while for Jesus He became again a God Who was near at hand, is not to be upheld.

son . . .' Paul is speaking here not in the first place about the atonement for his sins (as in 2 Cor. v. 19), but of the reconciliation of the enmity which he, the sinner, had. He, who was in enmity against God, is now reconciled to Him, since God has now proved His love. In calling himself a former enemy of God, Paul does not refer to his previous attacking the Community of Christ. He has been 'reconciled' not through the appearance of the Exalted One but through the death of Jesus, even if it was only when the meaning of this death came to him, to wit that God proved His love to man in it. When the love of God had not been proved to him, he was God's enemy. He was the enemy of a loveless God—One Who seemed to him loveless. From hence I understand his path; its traces show themselves sufficiently now.

To Pharisaic Judaism the creation of man and the revelation are works of the divine love. That man is created in His image and all the more that he comes to know this, that Israel is chosen for sonship and all the more that this is made known to it, proceeds from God's love (Abot III. 14). But Israel alone learns that this love is imperishable. From Scripture words like the statement which reaches sinful Israel 'from afar' in its wilderness (Jer. xxxi. 2), 'With everlasting love have I loved thee' and even more the exhortation to Hosea (iii. 1), to continue to love the debauched woman 'like JHVH's love to the children of Israel', the living doctrine steadies the existence of the people even under the rule of the Romans. Paul tells us almost nothing about this primeval, historic and everlasting love of God for His creation. The love of God, of which he speaks, has scarcely anything other than an eschatological meaning, it is—with the exception perhaps of an isolated mention of Israel beloved for the fathers' sake (Rom. xi. 28 ff.), which also however is intended eschatologically—

always connected with Christ as Lord of the Community of the final age, rather, it 'is' in Christ (viii. 39), it subsists and makes its appearance in him alone. 'The twofold subject experienced as a unity'[1] which we know from an early epistle (2 Thess. ii. 16), 'But He, our Lord Jesus Christ and God our Father, Who loved us', most exactly expresses Paul's view. Similarly he knows in fact no other grace of God than that which has now appeared in Christ; only once (in the passage noted above, Rom. xi. 29) he speaks of Israel's 'gifts of grace' that they are 'irregrettable', irrevocable. There are great gifts of grace (ix. 4); but if the 'conclusion of the Covenant' and the 'giving of the law' are reckoned as such we cannot banish from our memory how questionable these blessings appear in the Pauline conception of history. Not even here, from the abyss of time between election and salvation, does any loving countenance of God look forth.

This abyss is full of 'wrath'. In the Old Testament God's wrath is told, predicted and proclaimed in song, but it is always a fatherly anger towards the disobedient child, from whom even the wrathful does not want to withdraw his love, and the sheer anthropomorphisms serve here as elsewhere to preserve the personal relationship. The wrath of Paul's God, Who 'to manifest His wrath and to make known His power has endured in much long-suffering the vessels of wrath destined for destruction' (ix. 22) has nothing fatherly about it, neither the primitive wrath of the creator, who (v. 21) possesses the potter's power to make vessels for degraded use from the neutral mass, nor wrath of reprisal, which smashes them after they have been tolerated for long enough.[2] Indeed, this latter is not really God's own

[1] Dibelius on 1 Thess. iii. 11.
[2] It is instructive to compare the Pauline text with the parables of the potter in the prophets (Is. xxix. 16; Jer. xviii. 3 ff.).

wrath at all.[1] He does not grow angry, He makes 'the wrath', 'almost a form of demonic power',[2] rule in His stead. It does not sound un-Pauline when a letter, probably not genuine, speaks (1 Tim. iii. 6) about a 'judgement of the devil'. The wrath, which recalls the Old Testament 'destroyer' (Exod. xii. 23), is granted power over mankind, like the spirits of the elements, which power lasts until the end, for Jesus is called (1 Thess. i. 10) 'our deliverer from the wrath to come'. In all this there is no longer any place for the direct relationship of God to His creation, as was retained in the Old Testament even in the most extreme wrath: God is not wrathful, He gives men into the hand of the mighty power of wrath and lets it torment him—until Christ appears to deliver him.

At all times in Israel people spoke much about evil powers, but not about one which, for longer than the purpose of temptation, was allowed to rule in God's stead; never, not even in the most deadly act of requital by God, is the bond of immediacy broken. Paul, had the theological question been raised in one of his Churches, would certainly not have contested the direct participation of God in the fate of the human race, but he does not himself acknowledge it. The divine plan of salvation does not square with the fact that all the souls crying in their need to heaven were met by a deaf and blind, inevitably functioning fate, instead of by a God of grace. For Paul's 'wrath' is obviously of the same nature as that fate called by the Greeks *heimarmene*, the fate determined by the spirits of the elements or stars. Paul does not name the Greek idea. But the apostle certainly derived his conception from it already during his pre-Christian period, and in this instance the influence on him of Hellenistic Judaism of a popular variety, which

[1] Cf. Wetter, *Der Vergeltungsgedanke bei Paulus* (1912).
[2] Loc. cit, 51.

knew how to combine ingeniously God and fate more or less with one another[1], becomes clearer than at almost any other point of his contemplation of existence. It is the movement of a huge interlocked cog-wheel, which as objective 'wrath' crushes the individual, until God causes His Son to draw forth the elect from the machine.

As we have said Paul sets no divine compassion in the dimension of pre-Christian history over against the demonic power of the 'wrath', which rages with a kind of full power. Apart from the mercy shown to Paul himself and perhaps to a Christian community he talks about none other than a mercy which is at the end of time or related to the end. This mercy is to be sure the goal of the divine world-plan: the treatment of the vessels of wrath occurs for the sake of that of the vessels of mercy. Indeed, in a passage already mentioned (Rom. xi. 32), Paul goes beyond this distinction, although again only in an eschatological sense: God has shut up 'all' in disobedience in order to have mercy upon 'all'. The 'shutting up' in this case is effected neither by the 'wrath' nor by other 'powers', but by God Himself. He Himself, apparently entirely apart from Christ, makes those once chosen by Him unfree in order to be able to set them free by Christ, He makes them deserving of wrath in order to deliver them from wrath. God alone is to be perceived in the work of 'shutting up'; in the work of deliverance He almost disappears behind Christ, who only at the end of the ages will hand over the rule to his Father (1 Cor. xv. 24). The Highest Beings stand out from one another as dark omnipotence and shining goodness, not as later with Marcion in dogma and creed, but in the actual experience of the poor soul of man; the one cast it into bonds and the other frees it from them. That Christ is the one who will sit

[1] Josephus assimilates the Pharisees to himself when he makes them ascribe everything to the fate and God.

141

on the judgement-throne is as little opposed to this elemental sentiment of the man who as a Christian reckons himself amongst the saved (1 Cor. i. 18, 2 Cor. ii. 15 f., iv. 3) as the fact that it is God Who, appearing out of His darkness at the end of all things, makes everyone who has worked for Christ share in His praise (1 Cor. iv. 5).

XIV

THE experience of suffering as innocently borne works at times in the history of faith both as a destructive factor and as an element of renewal. One can endure pain, but not the God Who sent it: one rejects either Him or the image one has made of Him. The first case, indeterminate as it is, will not be discussed here; in the second the experience can be rectified by a greater proximity, i.e. a being drawn up, to the divine mystery, as the reality of the cloud is rectified by that of the lightning. The resulting change in the history of faith is then both stirring and constructive for succeeding generations if the experience of personal suffering was embedded in that of the suffering of a personally united community. Such was the situation with the Jewish nation from that historic moment in which its naïve trust in God was shaken. It was the time of Megiddo. At last the king, expected and proclaimed by the prophets, he who undertook to fulfil the divine commission conferred in the sacrament of anointing, sat upon the throne. In the certainty of empowerment from above, Josiah marched forth to fight against the

Pharaoh for the reign of God which was about to begin, and was killed. How could this come about?[1] In this way the new questioning of the justice of God arises, of the meaning of suffering, of the value of human effort on behalf of the right way, which surged up in the two centuries before the catastrophe, then in this itself, and then in the miseries of the Babylonian exile. Its effect has been preserved in the outcries of Jeremiah, the dialectical theologoumena of Ezekiel, the accusing speeches of 'Job', the Psalms of tormented souls and the songs of the suffering servant of God. All these records of a great spiritual process point beyond personal suffering to that of Israel. They concern the monstrous thing which has come to pass between God and Israel. So man penetrates step by step into the dark which hangs over the meaning of events, until the mystery is disclosed in the flash of light: the *zaddik*, the man justified by God, suffers for the sake of God and of His work of salvation, and God is with him in his suffering. This re-birth of trust in God has already lost its real vitality in the second kingdom, which attempted to restore it in an as it were institutional way. Centuries afterwards, during the period of suffering under the Syrians, the discovery had to be made anew. The legends of the readiness for martyrdom in the Book of Daniel, those of actual martyrdom in the Second Book of the Maccabees, above all the figure of the 'righteous one' (cf. Is. liii. 11) in the 'Wisdom of Solomon', which corresponds to that depicted by Deutero-Isaiah, the man who is called a son of God and is condemned to a disgraceful death, bear witness to this, of course in a later, derivative diction. Under the Hasmoneans the problem of

---

[1] Cf. Hempel, *Die Mehrdeutigkeit der Geschichte als Problem der prophetischen Theologie* (1933), 13: 'The problem concerning the possible interpretation of history becomes that of the existence of the Jahveh religion in general'.

suffering again recedes for a time. In the third, the Roman distress, it re-appears, but on a characteristically larger scale.

Three principal types of answer must be distinguished here.

The Hellenistic Judaism of common coinage, as we know it for instance from the statements of Josephus on his mode of thinking, an eclecticism from an attenuated Biblical tradition and a not less attenuated Stoic philosophy, is satisfied to associate God with a power of fate, which causes the suffering of the righteous. Josephus knows nothing more about the daring undertaking of Josiah and its result than to observe: 'Fate, I take for granted, drove him to it'. The philosophic Hellenism of Judaism, which strove to take seriously the contribution both of Israel and Greece and which could not take such an illusionary way, does not occupy itself with the problem; Philo does not go beyond the conception that God in the creation of the world made use of the 'powers' and that these hypostases also henceforth occupied a position between Him and men. Apocalyptics, which is influenced by Iranian dualism, and yet opposes it, approaches the problem differently. In its greatest product, the Ezra–Apocalypse, which was written at the time of the destruction of Jerusalem, but which was obviously constructed out of older ideas, there speaks the man who despairs of history, the son of an 'aged' world, who 'tries to understand the ways of the Most High'. He is acquainted with the doubtfulness of all human righteousness; Israel too is sinful and deserving of punishment. But why does God not show mercy to His chosen people, why must they suffer more than all others, why does He crush them and spare those who have trespassed more gravely? The answer is eschatological, but when all is said it is no answer, because at the End grace passes away and only judgement remains, at which nobody can any longer be a substitute for another, and 'the many who have come' must go into destruction, although God, Who loves His creation, has not desired it; from Israel too only a few (amongst them 'Ezra' himself) are saved. But the answer does not touch the fundamental question with which the questioning began. The speaker had reproached God (vii. 20 ff.) with not having influenced Israel in the hour of revelation to it, so they might receive it truly: 'But Thou didst not take the evil heart away from them, in order that Thine instruction might bring forth fruit in them. . . . A lasting sickness began: in the heart of the people both the instruction and the root of evil. The good disappeared and the evil remained'. But the root of evil, common to all men, grew out of 'the grain of evil seed' which 'at the beginning was sown in Adam's heart'. This question or rather complaint means that God (in that He did not take away the evil heart) preferred the freedom of man to the salvation of man, but behind it there stands the thought that He (in that He allowed the sowing to take place) put this freedom to too difficult a test. At this point 'Ezra' unmistakably goes beyond 'Job'. He too obtains no explanation. But while for the latter the sound of the divine Voice, the actual fact of the presence and the interest of God gives a most real answer, one that is more than words, for the former, in spite of the weight and melancholy of the request, everything which happens to him from above by way of answer remains vain and without comfort.

It seems to me that Paul before his conversion had got into the circle of ideas which found its most mature expression in the Ezra-Apocalypse; in the intellectual elaboration of what happened to him on the road to Damascus, he obtained an answer to those questions, which he expressed in his epistles, particularly in the Epistle to the Romans,

146

probably a decade or a little more[1] before the composition of the Ezra-Apocalypse. That the influence of that circle of ideas upon him could become so strong and so fruitful is to be understood apparently by the way it worked together with the extremely personal and violent self-reflection of his last pre-Christian period, in a great tumult of soul, the memory of which has been preserved and worked up in the seventh chapter of the Epistle to the Romans (vv. 7-25). The view that the 'I' of these texts is a rhetorically constructed description of 'the situation of the Jew under the law'[2] seems to me (from v. 24) to be unacceptable;[3] and about his present condition as a Christian Paul could not speak in this way; yet there is this direct present tense! I can only account for it in that he uses the memory of his pre-Damascus personality in its deepest experience of itself as a pattern for an inner description of the natural man (vv. 7, 8b, 9a) and man under the law (vv. 8a, 9b. 10), so that 'I' means at the same time 'I Paul' and 'I Adam', and then 'I, a Jew of the law'.[4] The path of the Jewish

[1] This follows whether we accept Eduard Meyer's dating of the Epistle to the Romans or the argument of Lake (*The Beginnings of Christianity* V, 464 ff.). I agree with Torrey, *The Apocryphal Literature* (1945), 121, in putting the publication of the chief genuine part of the Ezra-Apocalypse at the beginning of the year 69.

[2] Bultmann, *Neueste Paulusforschung* (*Theologische Rundschau* VI 1935) 233.

[3] This is not an 'emotional judgement' as Kuemmel, *Roemer 7 und die Bekehrung des Paulus* (1929) supposes, but one based on style-criticism: in a non-poetic text the I of such an exclamation must be understood precisely as I—in the rhetoric of the world's literature, so far as I know it, *this* tone is not to be found. (The texts cited by Kuemmel, loc. cit, 128 ff., from the Talmud and Alexandrian literature are of quite a different kind.)

[4] I cannot so generally admit, as Lietzmann thinks, that Paul had never been, even in childhood innocence, 'without the law' (v. 9). It is the sacramental expression of a deep reality of life that the Jewish boy only

person from the natural man, as the Jew is understood to be up to the moment of the conscious taking upon himself of the 'yoke of the rule of God and the yoke of the commandments', to the man of the law is apprehended from the point of view of that former self-reflection which is moved into the powerfully illuminating light of the present existence of the Christian. As it directly comes home to his mind, the apostle cries: 'Wretched man that I am! Who will set me free from the body of this death!' and confesses at once from his present condition that he has been freed—the I which is involved in this 'Thanks be to God', which I cannot look upon as rhetorical, entirely proves to me the autobiographical background of that which precedes it. The most significant thing in the account from our point of view is the sentence: 'But I see another law in my members, which strives against the law of my reason, and takes me captive', in connexion with which it must be held fast that immediately before it Paul is speaking about the law of God, to which he, precisely with his reason, joyfully consented. The law revealed to man by God and the 'law' set in his members by God in creation are recognized as opposed to one another. Here, unexpressed, but vibrating powerfully behind the words, to that question concerning the compatibility of evil in the sense of suffering with God's existence, is conjoined that about the compatibility of evil in the moral sense with it; it has obviously become the real stimulus to Paul's Gnostic view of the world. From this point that conception of the primitive wrath of God as the 'potter' who makes and destroys vessels of wrath becomes clear to us. Paul is not content, like the apocalyptic writers, to complain that God has allowed it to happen, that a grain of evil

becomes a 'son of the commandment' at the age of 13. To be sure he lives before this also in the atmosphere of that which is commanded, but not yet as one from whom it is—as a whole—demanded.

seed was implanted in man, from which guilt and punishment spring up; he says that God, in creating man, inflicted him with a 'flesh', in which 'nothing good dwells' (*v.* 18) and the consequence of which is that each man does the evil which he does not will (*v.* 19). But also in view of the revealed law of God, he, Paul, cannot tolerate Ezra's complaint that God has not taken away the evil heart from those who receive His revelation. For the law, which in itself is 'holy, just and good', is, he says, nevertheless so constituted that in the unredeemed man, the non-Christian, through the commandment not to covet, arouses the desire (*v.* 7 f.), calls sin into existence and drives the soul to death (*v.* 9). Since God has given the law precisely for such a purpose (*v.* 13) it could not be His will to remove the evil heart from those who received it. The man who has both, flesh and law, the still unsaved man in Israel, is 'sold under sin' (*v.* 14). But both the creating of the flesh and the giving of the law serve God's purpose of saving the world, like the enslavement of man under the forces of fate does. Creation and revelation have taken place as they are for the sake of salvation; for God's way to salvation leads through the 'abounding' (v. 20) of human sin and through its propitiation. Paul does not pray, as Ezra does again and again, for the mitigation of the judgement on humanity; God's sense of justice inexorably demands the appropriate, i.e. measureless, punishment for the 'sin which is sinful beyond measure' (vii. 13). Only God Himself can effect the propitiation of an infinite guilt, by making His Son, the Christ, take the atoning suffering upon himself, so that all who believe on Christ are saved through him. In this way Paul laid the foundation for the doctrine, which to be sure first arises after him and beyond his struggle, the doctrine in which Christ is declared a Person of the Godhead: God suffers as the Son in order to save the world, which He as the Father created and prepared as one which needs salvation. The prophetic idea of man who suffers for God's sake has here given way to that of God Who suffers for the sake of man. By this the new image of God is erected, destined to give power and consolation to Christian people during a thousand years of development and a thousand years of their struggles. The problem of the meaning of unmerited suffering however is thrown back to the position of Job's friends: there is no unmerited suffering; the only difference is that now it is taught that every man is absolutely guilty and absolutely deserving of suffering, and yet everyone can, by accepting the belief in the suffering of God, be redeemed through this suffering.

Over against this sublime religious conception, which in the fascination of its content has scarcely an equal, there stands in Pharisaic Judaism the plain effort to preserve the immediacy of the Israelite relationship to God in a changed world. For this it must guard against two ideas which had penetrated into Jewish Hellenism—the one into its popular form, the other into its philosophy as well as into its apocalyptics: the idea of a fate, which is not identical with the rule of God, and that of a mediator, different in nature from the occasional intervention of earthly and heavenly powers.[1]

In order to erect the first safeguard, every semblance of a fate had to be kept away from the idea of Providence. The latter means God's presence in and His participation in everything that happens, therefore the continuation of the creation in every moment. From a transcendent reality of this kind, which more exactly expressed is a reality which remains transcendent in immanence, nothing can be inferred, least of all anything apt to limit the self-dependence

[1] Neither the *logos* of Philo nor the pre-existent heavenly being of the Book of Enoch is a mediator in the christological sense, but each of them indicates a tendency towards it.

of man as a source of events. That is the fundamental meaning of the oft-cited sentence of Akibah, (Abot III. 15) that everything is foreseen and the licence is given. The doctrine which first received this form in the first third of the second century is actually much older, indeed early-Pharisaic, for it is evident that Josephus misunderstands it when he attributes (Ant. XVIII. 1) to the Pharisees the opinion that all things are determined by fate, but the freedom of impulse is not denied to man, indeed God lets the two work together. A 'working together' is out of the question in this case. On the one hand the thought has gone definitely further than in the sentence, that all things are in the hands of God except the fear of God: there is nothing now which does not stand in the eternal sight of God. On the other hand that which has been set free there and which possesses the character of a point, of a starting-point, freedom and potentiality to fear God, has become now a freedom in all things, an inmost potentiality in all, which is granted to man. 'Our works are in the choice and power of our souls', it says (ix. 7) in the Psalms of Solomon, the so-called Psalms of the Pharisees, a century before Paul. Transcendence and actuality do not stand in each other's way, but neither do they supplement each other, just as little as God and man supplement each other, but the one is wholly the reality of God and the other wholly the reality of man. They constitute jointly the irreducible mystery of the relationship between God and man, and we must give credit to the great men of faith amongst the Pharisees for having a presentiment of this in its depth. If however we would understand it theologically, i.e. with reference to that side of existence which is removed from us, we must speak of a relationship in God Himself, that is, as one tends to say, between attributes of God, but more correctly, between God as One Who foresees and God as One Who grants freedom. God does not hand over His creation to any kind of fate, but He sets it free and holds it at the same time.

From this point the way to the other safeguard—the guarding against the mediatorship—is already to be perceived.

The problem with which we began, that of the meaning of the suffering of the righteous, is now answered by an idea which takes up again the great theme of the servant of God who suffers 'for the many' and at the same time interprets the contemporary event which was the most important for those who gave the answer, namely, martyrdom. Already in the so-called Fourth Book of the Maccabees, presumably originating from the same period as the Psalms of Solomon, and which expresses Pharisaic piety in a form borrowed from late Greek rhetoric, it says (vi. 29, xvii. 22) of the martyrs, that the country is purged by their blood and their soul is 'taken' as a ransom for the sinful souls of the people. This basic view is now transferred to the lingering illness of great teachers, which atones for their generation. Although at times in conjunction with this there are allusions to Messianism, the conception is not essentially eschatological. But by it reference is already made to the non-eschatological relationship, the relationship manifesting itself in the course of the human generations, between the rigour and the grace of God, between judgement and mercy. The difference in Pharisaic Judaism goes beyond that in Philo of the creative and the gracious, the royal and the law-giving powers of God; it leads to the conception of a dramaticism within the Godhead. The two are understood as *middot* of God, this according to the original meaning of the word as His measures or His modes of measuring.[1] In the Pharisaic view the *middot* are neither forces nor attributes, but according to the meaning of the word,

[1] So also in Philo, Sacr. xv, 59.

modes, modes of behaviour, fundamental attitudes, consequently they are understood as essentially dynamic; but the peculiar disposition of the Haggadah towards anthropomorphic metaphorism, a further development of the Old Testament anthropomorphism, results at times in a more static imagery. God 'proceeds from the *middah* of judgement and comes to the *middah* of mercy' (Jer. Taanit 65), consequently from position to position, or (Tanchuma Buber III, 55a) He exchanges the one 'measure' for the other. It always remains a movement, a walk, a passage from mode to mode. Yet the *middot* are always united; now and then one predominates, but it never works alone, the other is never excluded from its operation. The living God always embraces the whole polarity of that which happens to the world, good and evil. The creation of the world too took place not through grace alone, but through its working together with rigour; but also no act of chastizing justice is accomplished without the participation of mercy. 'When God created man, He created him by the *middah* of judgement and the *middah* of compassion, and when He expelled him, He did so by the *middah* of judgement and the *middah* of compassion' (Midrash Genesis rabba XXI. 6). The 'walk' means consequently nothing more than that at one time the one, at other times the other exercises the direction, always in accordance with the nature of what God intends to accomplish. Yet—and this is the most important—they are not equal to one another in power: the *middah* of grace is the stronger. It, and not rigour, is the right hand, the strong hand (Sifre 50). Because this is so, the world is preserved; were it otherwise, it could not continue. And what applies to the existence of the world, applies to that of man. It is the right hand which God, Who judges with the left, stretches out towards the sinner who turns back to Him and with which He raises him to Himself. In the whole course of human history, and not only in salvation, grace prevails; 'the measure of the good is greater than the measure of reprisal' it runs in an early text of the Talmud (Tos. Sota IV. 1). In that saying about the providence of God and the 'licence' given to man Akibah continues: 'The world is judged by goodness'—a sentence which has for its subject not only the last judgement but also the constant rule of God. The dynamic unity of justice and grace stands opposed in this instance to the Pauline division of the justice of God in this aeon and His saving grace at the End. Accordingly the full immediacy to the just and gracious God in one is established anew. One is not allowed to turn towards only one of the *middot* and to turn away from the other: one must submit without reservation to the movement between both in the unity of God, praying for mercy but not resisting the judgement, with fear and love in one, as God is both fearful and loving, but with a love which is above fear, as in God grace is above judgement. This immediacy of the whole man is directed towards the whole God, that which is revealed in Him and that which is hidden. It is the form in which Pharisaic Judaism by its doctrine of the *middot* renewed the Old Testament Emunah, the great trust in God as He is, in God be He as He may. It excludes the two great *imagines* which the Pauline world-view set over against the immediate Emunah; the demonocracy, to which this aeon is given over, and the mediatorship of a Christ at the threshold of that which is to come.

XV

I N Luke's Gospel (xi. 1) it is related that one of the
disciples, evidently on behalf of all, asks Jesus to teach
them to pray, 'as John also taught his disciples'. Jesus
then teaches them the 'Our Father'. From the critical
side it has been said, certainly rightly,[1] that it cannot indeed
be determined how far this prayer, in essence composed
from Jewish prayer-sentences but distinguished by the
simplicity of the whole form, really goes back to Jesus, but
that it is 'at least characteristic of him'.

The first petitions are really nothing but introductory invocation and glorification in accordance with Jewish
custom.[2] The three last, the truly personal petitions of the

---

[1] Bultmann, *Jesus*, 166.

[2] Cf. amongst others, Klein, *Der aelteste christliche Katechismus* (1909),
257 f. Isaak Heinemann refers me to the fact that the words in the
Kaddish prayer which follow 'Hallowed be His great Name'—'in the
world which He created according to His pleasure'—are missing here.
In my opinion one ought not to conclude that in Jesus a tendency towards the Pauline 'cosmic pessimism' is to be observed, but a difference
in the point of view from the world-acceptance of the Kaddish is nevertheless recognizable.

community of those who pray, constitute a unity, which gives the impression of a particular authenticity related to a specific situation. The little band, which wanders through the Galilean country with their master, is without all economic security and is thrown completely upon God, Who will let them be sustained by those amongst the people well-disposed towards them: they pray first of all that He may further help them to get the necessary daily ration in order to be able to travel on and to do service. But now, after this indispensable petition, they express the most essential personal petition, which reminds us at once of the preaching of the Baptist. He proclaimed 'the baptism of turning for the forgiveness of the sins' (Mark i. 4 par.);[1] they pray for the forgiveness of the sins. That is to be sure also universally understandable, but it receives its significance from the nature and life of those who pray. 'I have not come'[2], says Jesus (Luke v. 32 par.) at the beginning of his course, after he had called the first disciples and while he sits at table with them and other 'tax-gatherers and sinners', 'to call the righteous to turning but sinners'. The verse may or may not be genuine (I fancy that it is genuine precisely as it stands in Luke); the one which precedes it, which is not being questioned, says the same: 'the healthy do not need a doctor, but the sick'. Sinners who by following Jesus have accomplished their turning, the sick in soul who by the fact that he has drawn them unto himself have become well, represent the praying band. They know themselves liable to fall back, they experience time and again how easy it is even for the man who has turned to the

[1] 'Forgiveness' belongs, in my opinion, like Luke xxiv, 47, to turning, not, like Acts ii. 38, to baptism.

[2] Originally rather: 'I have not been sent', as Luke iv. 43; it seems to me that here and in other related references a 'Johannine' revision is present.

way of God to fall again into sin, therefore they pray to God to forgive them their sins—and not to lead them into temptation, for they fear lest they will not be able to withstand it.

If it is a fact that Jesus taught his disciples to pray in this way, then he speaks from their situation and from their minds, but at the same time from the depths of the Jewish tradition of prayer. 'True prayer', it has been said,[1] 'is the creation of the Jews'. What can this mean if we consider Jewish prayer against the background of the great Indian, Babylonian, Egyptian and early Persian prayers? Hardly anything else but that here the turning to God is accomplished in a peculiar direct way. To teach how to pray means above all forms of words: to teach how to turn one's self thence. In an imageless religion that is a very particular thing, but even more in one which perceives ever more clearly that 'heaven and the heavens of heavens (i.e. that seen from heaven would appear to one as heaven and so forth) do not contain Him' (1 Kings viii. 27); the All no longer offers to a person a support for the act of turning. This can only take place, not towards the remoteness, but towards a nearness and intimacy, which can no longer be co-ordinated with the space-world: the first word, that which results from the act itself, is directed to God as Father, and only after it God as the Lord of the *Basileia* is addressed; this is the sequence in Jewish prayer also. But the immediacy is deepened again in the personal petitions, in which the 'Thou' ('Thine') no longer is the leading word as in the first, but, included in the imperative, is bound up with this strong imploring 'to us'. These requests can be completely understood only from the Jewish doctrine of sin and forgiveness.

According to Jewish doctrine sin is the disturbing by

[1] Wellhausen on Matt. vi. 9.

157

man of the fundamental relationship between God and man, so that as a result man is no longer identical with the creature of God. Forgiveness is the restoration of the fundamental relationship by God after man through turning to Him is set again in the condition of his creatureliness. Turning, provided the individual exerts his whole soul to accomplish it, is not prevented by anything, not even by the sin of the first men. The latter changed the situation at the beginning without being able to impair the freedom and power to overcome it, for the will of God in creation is not to be injured by any act of that which is created. Man always begins again and again as God's creature, although henceforth under the burden of a humanity cast out from Paradise into the world and history, wandering through world and history, yet, because the expulsion and the impulse to wander happened with both 'judgement and grace', ever now and always capable, as bearer of the historically increasing burden, of proving true before God. That he sins belongs to his condition, that he turns back belongs to his holding his own in it. He sins as Adam sinned and not because Adam sinned. Historically he is no longer in the original condition nor does he have the original power of decision, but fundamentally everyone is, since according to the doctrine of the Talmud (Bab. Nidda 31a) there are three who create in every child—father, mother and God; so God is always present and His participation is strong enough to enable the sinner to turn back. But no one goes out in order to turn without grace coming to meet him, and 'whoever comes to purify himself is helped' (Bab. Shabbat 104a). Because the way of humanity ever begins again, no matter how far it has gone astray, the man who prays speaks the truth when, on waking every morning, he says to God: 'The soul which Thou hast given me is pure'. True, everyone sins, but everyone may turn back. 'The

158

gates are never closed' (Midrash Tehillim on Ps. lxv), or, as Jesus expressed it, 'Knock, and it shall be opened to you'. God withholds nothing from him who turns back 'unto God'. It says (Is. lvii. 19): 'Peace, peace, to him that is far off and to him that is near'—first to him that is far off, then to him that is near. For God says, 'I do not reject any creature, no one who in turning has given me his heart'. (Midrash Tehillim on Ps. cxx). Forgiveness is not eschatological, but eternally present. Immediacy to God is the covenant established in the creation of man, and it has not been and is not annulled.

He who prays 'Forgive us our sins' delivers himself to the God Who here and now wills to forgive; as it is described in the Talmud, employing a Biblical expression for the venture, he places his soul in his hand and delivers it to Him. Prayer takes place in the immediacy and for the sake of the increase of the immediacy. Those who turn back pray that God, Who has received them, may hold them.

Once again we must glance back at the parting of the ways.

I have just described Israel's doctrine of sin, which is that of the Pharisees and of Jesus. Apocalyptics means an intrusion into it, yet not a complete one. True, the most woebegone of all, 'Ezra', cries (4 Ezra vii. 118): 'O Adam, what hast thou done!' and complains about those of Adam's sons to whom was promised an immortal world but who did mortal deeds: the garden of bliss was shown to them, but they would not enter; he has nothing to say about forgiveness. But even he knows (loc. cit 127) the 'meaning of the struggle which the earth-born struggles' and in which he can conquer. And from the Apocalypse of Baruch (xlviii. 42) there resounds still more urgently: 'O Adam, what hast thou done to all of those who are descended from thee!', but then (liv. 15) it says as if in answer to this that each of his descendants procures for himself torment or honour. It is different with Paul (Rom. v. 18 f.): through the disobedience of the one the many have been made to sin, through the one trespass has come the condemnation of all men; there is no deliverance except through Christ. Paul is almost completely silent in his letters about the turning to which Jesus, like the prophets and the Pharisees, had summoned men; he is only acquainted with that joining with Christ through which alone the fundamental relationship may be restored. In opposition to the apocalyptists, he knows of an eschatological forgiveness, but only for those amongst sinful men who profess Christ. There is for him in the course of history no immediacy between God and man, but only at the beginning and the end; there extends in between over the whole area between God and man that fate which is only broken through for the Christian by Christ. 'Ask and it will be given you', Jesus had said, and he did not mean only those who followed him, for 'the Father gives good things to those who ask Him' (Matt. vii. 11): nobody is excepted. Now this is no longer the case: there is a power of God unto salvation, but only for those who believe in the message of Christ (Rom. i. 16); for all others even now, as before, the wrath of God is revealed from heaven (v. 18), which condemns them to destruction (ii. 12), but those who believe, they alone, are 'freely justified' (iii. 24), to them alone are their sins forgiven (v. 26). Immediacy is abolished. 'I am the door' it now runs (John x. 9); it avails nothing, as Jesus thought, to knock where one stands (before the 'narrow door'); it avails nothing, as the Pharisees thought, to step into the open door; entrance is only for those who believe in 'the door'.

In Matthew's Gospel the 'Our Father' is inserted in the Sermon on the Mount, consequently the request of the disciples is missing, and in its place we hear sayings about prayer, the last of which (vi. 8) surprises one again and again by its genuine, entirely 'personal' sound: 'For your Father knows what ye need before ye ask Him'. This is one of the most important of man's words about prayer as the very essence of immediacy towards God. God does not require to hear in order to grant, that is, in order to give to the individual what he really needs; but He desires that the individual should apply to Him in such an immediacy.

In Paul we do not find again this teaching of Jesus about immediacy in prayer. His statements about prayer arise from a different basic situation. The most significant of them (Rom. viii. 26, and 2 Cor. xii. 7 f.) speak of a man who sometimes does not know how to pray 'as was fitting' and to whom in this his need it happens that the Spirit comes over him, 'intercedes for him' and speaks no longer in an ordered sequence of words, but 'in wordless groans', a thing divine speaking to God; then of one who, in the extreme misery of soul, beaten with fists by the messenger of Satan, prays to the 'Lord', to the exalted Christ; what is called in the answer which he receives 'my strength', which is perfected in weakness, is 'the strength of Christ' which dwells within him. These statements of the Christian man of the Spirit, which are of incomparable significance as witnesses for a faith-intercourse with mediating powers, are outside immediacy. It is as if, since Jesus gave his disciples that instruction, a wall had been erected around the Deity, and it is pierced by only one door; he to whom it is opened beholds the God of grace Who has redeemed the world, but he who remains far from it is abandoned to the messengers of Satan, to whom the God of wrath has given over man.

XVI

THE periods of Christian history can be classified according to the degree in which they are dominated by Paulinism, by which we mean of course not just a system of thought, but a mode of seeing and being which dwells in the life itself. In this sense our era is a Pauline one to a particular degree. In the human life of our day, compared with earlier epochs, Christianity is receding, but the Pauline view and attitude is gaining the mastery in many circles outside that of Christianity. There is a Paulinism of the unredeemed, one, that is, from which the abode of grace is eliminated: like Paul man experiences the world as one given into the hands of inevitable forces, and only the manifest will to redemption from above, only Christ is missing. The Christian Paulinism of our time is a result of the same fundamental view, although it softens down or removes that aspect of the demonocracy of the world: it sees nevertheless existence divided into an unrestricted rule of wrath and a sphere of reconciliation, from which point indeed the claim for the establishment of a Christian order of life is raised clearly and energetically enough, but *de facto* the redeemed Christian soul stands over against an unredeemed world of men in lofty impotence. Neither this picture of the abyss spanned only by the halo of the saviour nor that of the same abyss covered now by nothing but impenetrable darkness is to be understood as brought about by changes in subjectivity: in order to paint them the retina of those now living must have been affected by an actual fact, by the situation now existing.

I will illustrate my position from two books, which are very different from each other; I choose them because the view of which I am speaking comes to light clearly in them. For this reason I have chosen one from the literature of modern Christian theology, because I do not know of any other in which the Pauline view of God is expressed so directly; it is *The Mediator* by Emil Brunner. The other, one of the few authentic similes which our age has produced, is the work of a non-Christian poet, a Jew, Franz Kafka's novel *The Castle*.

I am only concerned in Brunner's book with what he has to say about God, and not about Christ; that is, with the dark foil and not the image of glory which stands out against it. We read: 'God cannot allow His honour to be impugned'; 'the law itself demands from God the reaction'; 'God would cease to be God if He allowed His honour to be impugned'. This is said of the Father of Christ; therefore it does not refer to one of the gods and rulers, but to Him of Whom the 'Old Testament' witnesses. But neither in this itself nor in any Jewish interpretation is God spoken of in this way; and such a word is unimaginable from the lips of Jesus as I believe I know him. For here in fact 'with God all things are possible'; there is nothing which he 'could not'. Of course the rulers of this world cannot allow their honour to be impugned; what would remain to them if they did! But God—to be sure prophets and psalmists

show how He 'glorifies His Name' to the world, and
Scripture is full of His 'zeal', but He Himself does not
assume any of these attitudes otherwise than remaining
superior to them; in the language of the interpretation:
He proceeds from one *middah* to the other, and none is
adequate to Him. If the whole world should tear the
garment of His honour into rags nothing would be done
to Him. Which law could presume to demand anything
from Him?—surely the highest conceivable law is that
which is given by Him to the world, not to Himself:[1] He
does not bind Himself and therefore nothing binds Him.
And that He would cease to be God—'God' is a stammering
of the world, the world of men, He himself is immeasurably
more than 'God' only, and if the world should cease to
stammer or cease to exist, He would remain. In the immediacy we experience His anger and His tenderness in
one; no assertion can detach one from the other and make
Him into a God of wrath Who requires a mediator.

In the Book of Wisdom, scarcely later than a hundred
years before Christ, God is addressed in this fashion: 'But
Thou hast compassion upon all, since Thou canst do all
things'—He is able to have compassion even upon us, as
we are!—'and Thou dost overlook the sins of men up to
their turning'—He overlooks them, not that we should
perish, but turn to Him; He does not wait until we have
turned (this is significantly the opposite of the Synoptic
characterization of the Baptist's preaching: not repentance

---

[1] Brunner explains: 'The law of His being God, on which all the
lawfulness of the world is based, the fundamental order of the world,
the consistent and reliable character of all that happens, the validity of
all standards . . .' Precisely this seems to me to be an inadmissible deriva-
tion of the nature of the world from the nature of God, or rather the
reverse. Order and standards are derived from the act of God, which
sets the world in being and gives it the law, and not from a law which
would determine His being. Cf. E. Brunner, *The Mediator* (1934), 444.

for the remission of sins, but the remission of sins for repentance)—'. . . for Thou lovest all creatures and abhorrest
nothing that Thou hast made'—here the creation is obviously
taken more seriously than the Fall—'. . . Thou sparest all
things because they are Thine, O Lord, Who willest good
to the living. For Thine incorruptible Spirit is in all'. It is
as if the author wished to oppose a doctrine current in
Alexandria about the Jewish God of wrath.

Kafka's contribution to the metaphysics of the 'door' is
known: the parable of the man who squanders his life
before a certain open gateway which leads to the world of
meaning, and who vainly begs admission until just before
his death it is communicated to him that it had been intended
for him, but is now being shut. So 'the door' is still open;
indeed, every person has his own door and it is open to
him; but he does not know this and apparently is not in a
condition to know it. Kafka's two main works are elaborations of the theme of the parable, the one, *The Trial*, in the
dimension of time, the other, *The Castle*, in that of space;
accordingly the first is concerned with the hopelessness of
man in his dealings with his soul, the second with the same
in his dealings with the world. The parable itself is not
Pauline but its elaborations are, only as we have said with
salvation removed. The one is concerned with the judgement under which the soul stands and under which it
places itself willingly; but the guilt, on account of which it
has to be judged, is unformulated, the proceedings are
labyrinthian and the courts of judicature themselves
questionable—without all this seeming to prejudice the
legality of the administration of justice. The other book,
which especially concerns us here, describes a district
delivered over to the authority of a slovenly bureaucracy
without the possibility of appeal, and it describes this
district as being our world. What is at the top of the

government, or rather above it, remains hidden in a darkness, of the nature of which one never once gets a presentiment; the administrative hierarchy, who exercise power, received it from above, but apparently without any commission or instruction. A broad meaninglessness governs without restraint, every notice, every transaction is shot through with meaninglessness, and yet the legality of the government is unquestioned. Man is called into this world, he is appointed in it, but wherever he turns to fulfil his calling he comes up against the thick vapours of a mist of absurdity. This world is handed over to a maze of intermediate beings—it is a Pauline world, except that God is removed into the impenetrable darkness and that there is no place for a mediator. We are reminded of the Haggadic account (Aggadat Bereshit IX) of the sinful David, who prays God that He Himself may judge him and not give him into the hands of the seraphim and cherubim, for 'they are all cruel'. Cruel also are the intermediate beings of Kafka, but in addition they are disorderly and stupid. They are extremely powerful bunglers, which drive the human creature through the nonsense of life—and they do it with the full authority of their master. Certain features remind us of the licentious demons into which the archons of Paul's conception of the world have been changed in some Gnostic schools.

The strength of Pauline tendencies in present-day Christian theology is to be explained by the characteristic stamp of the time, just as that of earlier periods can explain that at one time the purely spiritual, the Johannine tendency was emphasized, and at another the so-called Petrine one, in which the somewhat undefined conception 'Peter' represents the unforgettable recollection of the conversations of Jesus with the disciples in Galilee. Those periods are Pauline in which the contradictions of human life, especially of man's social life, so mount up that they increasingly assume in man's consciousness of existence the character of a fate. Then the light of God appears to be darkened, and the redeemed Christian soul becomes aware, as the unredeemed soul of the Jew has continually done, of the still unredeemed concreteness of the world of men in all its horror. Then to be sure, as we know indeed from Paul too, the genuine Christian struggles for a juster order of his community, but he understands the impenetrable root of the contradiction in the view of the threatening clouds of wrath, and clings with Pauline tenacity to the abundant grace of the mediator. He indeed opposes the ever-approaching Marcionite danger, the severing not only of the Old and New Testaments, but that of creation and salvation, of Creator and Saviour, for he sees how near men are, as Kierkegaard says of the Gnosis, 'to identifying creation with the Fall', and he knows that a victory for Marcion can lead to the destruction of Christianity; but—this seems to me to be more strongly recognized again in Christendom to-day—Marcion is not to be overcome by Paul.

Even Kierkegaard, a century ago, gave expression to the fact that there is a non-Pauline outlook, that is, one superior to the stamp of the age, when he wrote in his Journal a prayer, in which he says: 'Father in heaven, it is indeed only the moment of silence in the inwardness of speaking with one another'. That to be sure is said from the point of view of personal existence ('When a man languishes in the desert, not hearing Thy voice there'), but in this respect we are not to distinguish between the situation of the person and that of man or mankind. Kierkegaard's prayer, in spite of his great belief in Christ, is not from Paul or from John, but from Jesus.

A superficial Christian, considering Kafka's problem, can easily get rid of him by treating him simply as the unredeemed Jew who does not reach after salvation. But only he who proceeds thus has now got rid of him; Kafka has remained untouched by this treatment. For the Jew, in so far as he is not detached from the origin, even the most exposed Jew like Kafka, is safe. All things happen to him, but they cannot affect him. He is not to be sure able any longer to conceal himself 'in the covert of Thy wings' (Ps. lxi. 4), for God is hiding Himself from the time in which he lives, and so from him, its most exposed son; but in the fact of God's being only hidden, which he knows, he is safe. 'Better the living dove on the roof than the half-dead, convulsively resisting sparrow in the hand.' He describes, from innermost awareness, the actual course of the world, he describes most exactly the rule of the foul devilry which fills the foreground; and on the edge of the description he scratches the sentence: 'Test yourself on humanity. It makes the doubter doubt, the man of belief believe'. His unexpressed, ever-present theme is the remoteness of the judge, the remoteness of the lord of the castle, the hiddenness, the eclipse, the darkness; and therefore he observes: 'He who believes can experience no miracle. During the day one does not see any stars'. This is the nature of the Jew's security in the dark, one which is essentially different from that of the Christian. It allows no rest, for as long as you live, you must live with the sparrow and not with the dove, who avoids your hand; but, being without illusion, it is consistent with the foreground course of the world, and so nothing can harm you. For from beyond, from the darkness of heaven the dark ray comes actively into the heart, without any appearance of immediacy. 'We were created to live in Paradise, Paradise was appointed to serve us. Our destiny has been changed; that this also happened with the appointment of Paradise is not said.' So gently and shyly anti-Paulinism speaks from the heart of this Pauline painter of the foreground-hell: Paradise is still there and it benefits us. It is there, and that means it is also here where the dark ray meets the tormented heart. Are the unredeemed in need of salvation? They suffer from the unredeemed state of the world. 'Every misery around us we too must suffer'— there it is again, the word from the shoot of Israel. The unredeemed soul refuses to give up the evidence of the unredeemed world from which it suffers, to exchange it for the soul's own salvation. It is able to refuse, for it is safe.

This is the appearance of Paulinism without Christ which at this time when God is most hidden has penetrated into Judaism, a Paulinism therefore opposed to Paul. The course of the world is depicted in more gloomy colours than ever before, and yet Emunah is proclaimed anew, with a still deepened 'in spite of all this', quite soft and shy, but unambiguous. Here, in the midst of the Pauline domain, it has taken the place of Pistis. In all its reserve, the late-born, wandering around in the darkened world, confesses in face of the suffering peoples of the world with those messengers of Deutero-Isaiah (Is. xlv. 15): 'Truly Thou art a God Who hides Himself, O God of Israel, Saviour!' So must Emunah change in a time of God's eclipse in order to persevere steadfast to God, without disowning reality. That He hides Himself does not diminish the immediacy; in the immediacy He remains the Saviour and the contradiction of existence becomes for us a theophany.

XVII

THE crisis of our time is also the crisis of the two types of faith, Emunah and Pistis.

They are as fundamentally different in nature as in their origin, and accordingly their crisis is different.

The origin of the Jewish Emunah is in the history of a nation, that of Christian Pistis in that of individuals.

Emunah originated in the actual experiences of Israel, which were to it experiences of faith. Small, then great numbers of people, first in search of open pasture-land, then of land for a free settlement, make their journey as being led by God. This fact, that Israel experienced its way to Canaan, which was its way into history, already in the days of the 'Fathers' as guidance, sensually as guidance through wilderness and dangers—this fact which took place historically once only is the birth of Emunah. Emunah is the state of 'persevering'—also to be called trust in the existential sense—of man in an invisible guidance which yet gives itself to be seen, in a hidden but self-revealing guidance; but the personal Emunah of every individual remains embodied in that of the nation and draws its strength from the living memory of generations in the great leadings of early times. In the historical process of becoming individual the form of this embodiment changes, but not its essence. Even when a rabbi of the late Hasid Sect sees the 'Shekinah', the 'indwelling' of God, approach him at a crossing of the road, something of the former guidance is present. In our day for the first time the connexion is increasingly becoming loose. In the generations of the period of emancipation the People of Faith is being broken up increasingly into a religious community and a nation which are no longer organically bound together, but only structurally. In the secular nation Emunah has no longer a psychical foundation nor in the isolated religion a vital one. Therefore the danger which threatens personal faith is to become impoverished in its essential spontaneity in the time of eclipse and in its place to be succeeded by elements of Pistis, in part of a logical and in part of a mystical character. But the crisis of the People of Faith extends further. For the purpose of the guidance, which was expressed at the beginning of the revelation, was actually (Exod. xix. 6) that Israel might become 'a royal sphere of direct attendants (this is the original meaning of the word *kohanim*, usually: priests, preserved in this and a few other places) and a holy nation' (that is, consecrated to God as its Lord). When the breaking-up is completed this purpose is repudiated. Then only a great renewal of national faith would be able to provide the remedy. In this the ever-existent inner dialectic of Israel between those giving up themselves to guidance and those 'letting themselves go' must come to a decision in the souls themselves, so that the task of becoming a holy nation may set itself in a new situation and a new form suitable to it. The individuals, regenerated in the crisis, who maintain themselves in Emunah, would have fulfilled the function, when it comes about, of sustaining the living substance of faith through the darkness.

Christian Pistis was born outside the historical experiences of nations, so to say in retirement from history, in the souls of individuals, to whom the challenge came to believe that a man crucified in Jerusalem was their saviour. Although this faith, in its very essence, was able to raise itself to a piety of utter devotedness and to a mysticism of union with him in whom they believed, and although it did so, yet it rests upon a foundation which, in spite of its 'irrationality', must be described as logical or noetic: the accepting and recognizing as true of a proposition pronounced about the object of faith. All the fervour or ecstasy of feeling, all the devotion of life, grew out of the acceptance of the claim and of the confession made both in the soul and to the world: 'I believe that it is so'. This position, in its origins arising from a Greek attitude, a thorough acknowledgment of a fact which is beyond the current circle of conceptions, yet an acknowledgment accomplished in a noetic form, came into being (in distinction from the major part of the later history of conversion) as the action of the person who was sharply separated thereby from the community of his nation, and the demand was directed just to such an attitude. To be sure Jesus also addresses himself to the individual, or, when he speaks to a number of people, to the individuals amongst them; but one has only to listen how (Matt. xv. 24) he speaks about the 'lost sheep[1] of the house of Israel'; he sees even them still in the frame of the 'house'. The like is not heard after him. Paul often speaks about Jews and Greeks, but never in connexion with the reality of their nationalities: he is only concerned with the newly-established community, which

[1] The expression (see Jer. l. 6; Ezek. xxxiv. 4, 16; Ps. cxix, 176) is to be understood of animals which have strayed from the herd.

172

by its nature is not a nation. The conception of the 'holy nation' in its strict sense has faded altogether, it does not enter into the consciousness of Christendom, and soon that of the Church takes its place. The consequence of all this is that even in the mass-baptisms of the West—occurrences which were far removed, both phenomenologically and psychologically, from the individual act of Hellenistic Pistis—the individuals as individuals, not the nations, became Christian, that is, subject to Christ: the 'People of God' was Christendom, which in its nature differed from the nations, and these remain in their own nature and their own law as they were. Therefore those who believed in Christ possessed at every period a twofold being: as individuals in the realm of the person and as participants in the public life of their nations. This state of existence remained, preserved from the crisis so long as the sphere of the person was able to assert itself against the determining power of public affairs. The crisis grows according to the degree in which the sphere of the person has been penetrated, in our era, by this. The blessing of Christian salvation, the true consistency of the redeemed soul, is imperilled. A hundred years ago Kierkegaard recognized this severely and clearly, but without estimating adequately the causes or showing the seat of the malady. It is a question of the disparity between the sanctification of the individual and the accepted unholiness of his community as such, and the disparity is necessarily transferred to the inner dialectic of the human soul. The problem which rises here points to the task inherited by Israel—and to its problematic nature.

But in connexion with this we are allowed to anticipate in our thought that here also there is a way which leads from rigid Paulinism to another form of Pistis nearer to Emunah. The faith of Judaism and the faith of Christendom are by nature different in kind, each in conformity with its human basis, and they will indeed remain different, until mankind is gathered in from the exiles of the 'religions' into the Kingship of God. But an Israel striving after the renewal of its faith through the rebirth of the person and a Christianity striving for the renewal of its faith through the rebirth of nations would have something as yet unsaid to say to each other and a help to give to one another—hardly to be conceived at the present time.

AFTERWORD
David Flusser

I N one of my last conversations with Buber, I talked with him about the meaning of the commandment to love one's fellow man.* I reminded him that his interpretation of the Biblical verse Lev. 19:18[1] is contained for the first time in Jesus Sirach (28:2–5). Whereupon Buber replied: 'Yes, I have put it down, somewhere, on a piece of paper.—Surely, one can rely much better on you, the philologists, than on us, the philosophers'. 'But, don't forget, there are dumb philologists'. 'I am talking about the good ones'—and then, after drawing a brief breath, he suddenly went on in Yiddish: 'And, I am a *Stückele Schraber,* a bit of a writer!' Well, a writer, a poet, according to this pious sigh of the great Buber, is even less reliable than a philosopher is!

I admit that, until now, I still have not fully recovered from this remarkable conversation with Buber. I bring it up mainly to prevent Buber's words from getting lost and also

*See M. Buber in the present edition, *Two Types of Faith,* trans. Norman P. Goldhawk, pp. 68ff.

in order to show that Buber's sublime poetic talents, in my opinion, have veiled the truly deep merits of his *Zwei Glaubensweisen*[2] [*Two Types of Faith*[3]] under a marvelous gown. I am writing this afterword so that Buber's significant findings with regard to the comparison of a Jew's and a Christian's faith can appear overtly and bear good fruit.

In comparison with the lasting value of this work by Buber, unfortunately little known, any objections that might be brought up against some issues of his theses are of little weight. The faith of Jews is called *Emuna* in Hebrew, and the Christian faith is called *pistis* in Greek, which is the original language of the New Testament. The essay ends: 'The faith of Judaism and the faith of Christendom are by (their) nature different in kind, each in conformity with its human basis, and they will indeed remain different' [pp. 173–74]. Any opposing separation evokes from its core dangers that lie in wait. And the first step in this matter is, almost inevitably, to identify oneself with one of the two ideological antagonists—and then, with every inclination to objectivity, the opponent's part will be debased—and Buber acknowledges that he professes the Jewish faith. Hence, it is easy to understand that, at one time, Buber's friend, the philosopher Hugo Bergmann, called the book 'an apologetic book, with all the merits and faults of an apologetic statement. . . . It is my impression, without being able to prove it, that you are doing wrong to Christianity and to Paul'.* Perhaps the reproach has some foundation, and this is true not because Buber does not keep silent about the dark sides of the opposing ideology. It may rather be, and this is the principal point, because Buber pictures Jewish faith as flawless—though, to my understanding, ruptures and shades can be perceived on both

*See M. Buber, *Briefwechsel aus sieben Jahrzehnten,* vol. 3 (Heidelberg, 1975), pp. 197, 160 Brief.

sides—and, moreover, even objections to the common root of the two types of faith may appear to be legitimate. How should we know then whether the one and only God of the Jews, the Christians, and the Moslems is truly as good, just, and merciful as the revealed monotheistic religions preach that He is? But Buber once told me: 'Faith is a risk'. Maybe, somewhere, he has written down this sentence as well.

But: if in our case a polarity in fact does exist, a fundamental inconsistency in reality, then indeed no man of thought may close his eyes to it! And that, as it seems to me, sore duality of the two types of faith is, to my regret, a fact independent of the one who is looking at it. It is a fact that one should approach with loving care, as would a physician, trying to heal the ancient fracture. Buber was right in saying that the faith of Jesus is a part of the tradition of Jewish faith. The Christian faith, in contrast, was amended decisively, namely with the faith in Jesus Christ and with which the faith of Jesus finds itself, let us say, in a psychological discrepancy. And in the hearts of most Christians lies, as we shall see, the acute danger that the faith in Jesus might threaten or supplant the good tidings of faith, the Gospel of Jesus. It is correct, indeed, that the Gospel of Jesus is wholly Jewish and that the faith in Jesus was incorporated neither into Judaism nor into Islam. But this, by itself, does not mean that the amendment, the novelty of the Christian type of faith, must subjugate, from the Christian side, Jesus' type of faith. Thus, it seems to me that the two types of faith are an internal problem of Christianity; beforehand, however, we must return to the dichotomies as Buber recognized them.

Highly problematic in Buber's essay is his statement that the Christian type of faith, the Pistis,[4] a thorough acknowledgment of a situation,[5] is, from its sources, an eminently Greek attitude (p. 172). Nevertheless, from the point of linguistics, this statement cannot be maintained. The Greek

Pistis actually means the same as the Hebrew *Emuna,* and much the same is true for the Greek and Hebrew verbs that go with them. To clarify things as they stand: in Athens, I once saw an inscription: *Trapeza emporikes pisteos,* which in German, i.e., in translation, reads literally, 'die Bank des kaufmännischen Glaubens'. In English, one would say, 'Commercial Credit Bank'. And, at the times of Jesus and Paul, *Pistis,* among other meanings, holds also this one: 'credit'! Apparently, it is linguistically correct that in antiquity one could hardly speak in Hebrew about *Glauben, dass* [believing, that]—for this purpose other verbs were available. This limitation then, most probably, was true also for profane Greek. In the New Testament, in the Christian usage of language, however, it is possible to write: 'Thou believest that there is one God' (James 2:19).[6] One should investigate this fact more closely. It might be that from the point of linguistics Buber is, to some extent, right about the Greek *Glauben, dass* [believing, that]; to speak about faith as such, however, it is a common human need that comes up, time and again, out of necessities beyond religiosity. The question then is, at what time and how did faith obtain a religious meaning?

Certainly, in paganism there existed no urgent religious necessity to speak about the faith in one or the other god. No more than two examples are known to me where I found Greek faith within the realms of religion, and they occur, as one could have expected beforehand, when a need for self-defense arose against the threat of atheism. In one of his writings, Lukianos, the highly talented and witty author (c. 120-c. 180 C.E.), attacks the problematic and fashionable guru Alexandros of Abunoteichos.* Among

---

Alexandros, or the false prophet, chap. 38. It is important to know as well that, as Seneca states in the letters to Lucilius 95:50, that the prime condition

other things, he relates that Alexandros invented a mystery play of three days' length. However, ahead of the plays' performances, he proclaimed habitually the following warning: 'In case an Atheist or a Christian or an Epicurean man has come to this place in order to partake in this mystery play, then he should flee from here. But those who believe in God I hail with best wishes for their initiation! The famous Plutarchos (c. 46–120 C.E.) lived and wrote prior to Lukianos. In his study on the goddess Isis (chap. 23), significant for the history of religion, he takes a polemic stand against the Greek founders of religion, who, to his understanding, are atheists. He reproaches them in that they 'exterminate and root out the pious faith that is the common internal heritage of almost all men from birth on'. Thus, in both cases, during the days of pagan Greek antiquity the religious faith is played off against the threats of atheism. It is difficult, then, to speak of any specific content of faith in Greek paganism.

From this derives the difficulty to presuppose any pagan Greek definition of religious faith. But perhaps this is not what Buber intended to say. Apparently he just wanted to say that the Christian type of faith stems from the Greek world of thought.

'That the faith-principle of acknowledgment and acceptance, in the sense of a holding henceforth that so-and-so is true, is of Greek origin requires no discussion. It was made possible only through the comprehension reached by Greek thought of an act which acknowledges the truth' (p. 11). But apart from this, the conception of Christian faith as *Glauben, dass* [believing, that]—in contrast to Jewish faith

---

of religion is to believe in the (existence of the) gods: 'primus est deorum cultum deos credere'. Here too, then, the subject is a repudiation of atheism.

in God (see pp. 30ff.): this conception stands less unequivocal than Buber's study might lead us to understand.

How much is the Christian type or faith indeed a faith in a certain fact? Lessing perceived such a faith already as an aporia [problem, question beyond answer] as such.* 'All of us believe that Alexander lived, he who conquered all of Asia within a short time. But who would want to risk on this faith anything of long-lasting value, which, if lost, can find no replacement?' Lessing, following Leibnitz on this, speaks about 'accidental true facts in history' and calls the aporia a 'wretched wide trench'. Lessing thus perceives *Glauben, dass* [believing, that] as a *contradictio in adiecto*. But I—not Buber—allow myself to claim that the faith in historical facts, i.e., in any event of salvation, constitutes the paradoxical strength of the Jewish-Christian type of faith. Hence, in a specific way, there is yet *Glauben, dass* [believing, that]—this, however, being only one part of the complex picture.

In paying little respect to the *Glauben, dass* [believing, that], Buber found himself allies not only in Lessing, but also—in Martin Luther. Martin Luther, for his part, writes about the two types of faith:† 'Here it must be noted that there are two types of faith. First of God, that is, when I believe it to be true, what is said about God, just like when I believe what is said about the Turk, the devil, and hell. This faith is more of a science or knowledge than it is faith. On

---

*G. E. Lessing: 'Über den Beweis des Geistes und der Kraft', in *Werke* (München, 1979), vol. 8, pp. 9–14. As one knows, Kierkegaard highly esteemed this work by Lessing.

†See *D. Martin Luthers Werke,* vol. 10 (Weimar, 1907), p. 389. The small prayer book came out in the year 1522, and Luther took this passage word by word from his 'kurzen Form der zehn Gebote' [short form of the Ten Commandments] in 1520. That text, too, is in vol. 7 (1897), p. 215. Here we adjusted the spelling to modern usage.

the other hand, there is the faith in God, that is, when I do not believe what is said about God, but set my trust in him, move and weigh to act with him, and believe without doubting at all that he will be and act thence with me as it is said about him, things of the kind that I would not believe of the Turk or any man regardless of the greatness of his public appraisal, for I believe easily that a man may be good, but I do not dare to count on him. Such [is the] faith that trusts in God, as is said about Him, in life and in death, that makes the Christian man, and [he] receives everything from God that he wishes; this faith will have no evil [i.e., intentionally] wrong heart, for it is a living faith, and it is commanded in the First Commandment; hence [it] says there: I am your God, thou shallst have no other gods. Therefore, the small word *in* is placed very well and should be observed with care, that we may not say: I believe God the Father, or of God, but *in* God, the Father, *in* Jesum Christum, *in* the Holy Spirit'.[7] The passage we just read is an introduction to the Christian profession of creed [*Glaubensbekenntnis*]. The decisive word *in* is taken from the Latin Credo. Later, Luther will speak about the *Glauben* an *Gott* [giving credence *to* God or trusting *in* God].

This implies that Luther would have firmly opposed the claim that, in principle, a Christian's faith should be understood as a *Glaube, dass* [belief, that]. Although Buber's understanding of the Christian type of faith is not refuted with Luther's words, its strength, however, is basically weakened. With regard to the essence of the Jewish-Christian concept of faith, it is important to see that Luther, at this point, calls attention to the religious concept of *Glauben an* . . . [confession of 'certitude']. By the way, Buber himself acknowledged the gravity of this term (p. 46). This significant type of speech is unknown to the Greeks and uncommon with the Hellenistic Jews. Then, one would not speak of having faith *an Gott* [in God], but of trusting *dem Gott* [to trust God—in His words, deeds, etc.].* The phrase [*Wendung*] *Glauben an* [to believe—i.e., trust] is, at the least, a Hebraic term. But to me it appears that it can also carry a semantic weight within the Jewish type of faith.† For us, it is decisive that already in the New Testament—and this in contrast to the original Greek usage of speech—one speaks, in many cases, not only of *Glauben* an *Gott* [having faith in God] but also in many cases of *Glauben an Jesus* [having faith in Jesus].

Faith in the Hebrew Bible is a complicated matter‡ on positive grounds for this reason. It is also a complicated matter because linguistic theology can never be purely objective. The difficulties are to some extent owing to the fact that the respective Hebrew root itself has several linguistic meanings. During the times of Jesus and Paul, the situation, as far as the Hebrew language is concerned, calmed down more or less. In those days, a religious concept of faith, also with regard to its linguistic use in Hebrew, established itself, a concept that then became of decisive relevance for the Christian concept of faith. I believe that one could cut the Gordian knot with the help of this simple insight: instead of beginning with the religious concept of faith, one should begin with the profane one. And from there one should recollect furthermore that man simply[8] needs a word for faith and therefore must take a word from his language in order to express what he considers worthy of belief and what he finds unbelievable. In Biblical Hebrew, the choice was cast onto the root *amn* and here, in particular, on the

*By the way, it is this way in the Greek original version of the text also. See footnote on p. 178.

†But see Prov. 26:25!

‡For the Hebrew root *amn*, see Alfred Japsen, *Theologisches Wörterbuch zum Alten Testament* (Stuttgart, 1973), pp. 313–48.

form of the verb *ha'amin*. It is possible to paraphrase the meaning of this verb in scientific terms with 'Beständigkeit gewinnen' [to gain stability], 'sich verlassenauf jemanden' [to rely on someone], 'einer Botschaft Glauben schenken' [to have faith, to believe in a message], 'sie für wahr halten' [to consider it to be true], or 'jemandem vertrauen' [to trust someone].* But aren't these definitions more or less valid for the German word *glauben* [to have faith, to believe], the English word *to believe,* and so forth? Hence, we read in Proverbs 14:15, 'The simple believeth every word',[9] or in Proverbs 26:25, 'When he (man) speaketh fair, believe him not'. This is a warning against credulous trusting. And what does the poet Horatius say in Latin? 'This may believe the Jew Apella, but not I'.[10]†

Buber calls the Jewish type of faith in Hebrew *Emuna*. But the word *Emuna* holds various meanings in Biblical Hebrew, for example 'Verhalten aus Zuverlässigkeit'

*Ibid., p. 331.

†Horatius, *Satirae* 1: 5, 100. See G. Büchmann, *Geflügelte Worte* (Berlin, 1986), p. 280. This saying by Horatius is reminiscent of the later Greek criticism of the Christian conception of faith. 'If one would have asked an educated heathen of the second century [C.E.] to summarize briefly and poignantly the distinction of his profession from the Christian one, he would have said that it was the difference between "logismos" and "pistis," between an established conviction and a blind faith' (R. E. Dodds, *Pagan and Christian in an Age of Anxiety* [Cambridge, 1965], pp. 120–23). Among other proofs, Dodds points to two passages in the anti-Christian text of Kelsos (178 C.E., in Origines c. Cels 1:4 and 6:11). According to this pagan philosopher's view, Christians follow the principle 'Don't examine, have faith'! and 'Your faith will save you'. In other words: 'Have faith, if you want to be saved; otherwise clear off'! Kelsos thus understood correctly the soteriological peculiarity of faith in Christianity. At the same time, the Christians are accused of unfaithful atheism! (See footnote on p. 178.) In those days, it was the opinion of educated Greeks that the Christian faith was unreasonable and unproven, an opinion that is not far from Mendelssohn's enlightened understanding (see the next footnote).

[behaving on the ground of reliability] or *Treue* [faithfulness].* In the Hebrew Bible, therefore, this is not the most accurate expression for the Jews' type of faith,—this it became only later, although it still happened prior to the days of Jesus and Paul. Language, and this is true not only in our

*See footnote ‡ on p. 182. In his interpretation of Gen. 15:6, in which Buber writes that Abraham 'continued to trust' God and that God 'deemed this as the proving true of him' (p. 44), Buber has eminent forerunners. Moses Mendelssohn writes, for example, in his 'Jerusalem': 'Ja, das Wort in der Grundsprache, das man durch Glauben zu übersetzen pflegt, heißt an den mehrsten Stellen eigentlich *Vertrauen, Zuversicht,* getroste Versicherung auf Zusage und Versheißung. *Abraham vertraute dem Ewigen, und es ward ihm zur Gottseligkeit gerechnet* (1 B. M. 15:6): Die Israeliten *sahen, und hatten Zutrauen zu dem Ewigen und zu Moses, seinem Diener* (2 B. M. 14, 31). Wo von den ewigen Vernunftwahrheiten die Rede ist, heiß es nicht, glauben, sondern *erkennen* und *wissen*' ['In fact, the original Hebrew term [*Emuna*] that is usually translated as "faith" means, in most cases, merely "trust", confidence, or firm reliance on pledge and promise: "Abraham trusted in the Lord, and He counted it to him for righteousness" [Gen. 15:6]; "And Israel saw . . . and trusted the Lord and Moses, His servant" [Exod. 14:31]. Whenever the text refers to eternal verities, it does not use the term "believe" but "understand" and "know"'. Translation from: Moses Mendelssohn, *Jerusalem, and Other Jewish Writings,* translated and edited by Alfred Jospe (New York: Schocken Books, 1969, p. 71.) Mendelssohn thus understands, much as Buber does so later, the Hebrew verb *ha'amin (glauben),* to believe, to have faith] in the simple meaning of having trust. In medieval Jewish philosophy of religion, faith is equated with rational conviction. See Moses Mendelssohn, *Schriften zum Judentum,* vol. 2 (Jubiläumsausgabe), edited by Alexander Altmann (Stuttgart, 1983), pp. 166–68 and the footnote on pp. 344–45. By the way, Mendelssohn was very consistent in his view that in Judaism one does not speak of *glauben* [believing or having faith in] regarding matters of eternal truth of reason, but rather of *erkennen und wissen* [understanding and knowing]. In the year 1779, Mendelssohn translated D. Friedländer's *Lehrbuch für jüdische Kinder* [Schoolbook for Jewish children], the Hebrew version of the thirteen *Grundartikel des Judenthums nach R. Moshe Maimonssohn* [Basic articles of Judaism according to R. Moshe ben Maimon]. Translated literally from the Hebrew, the sentence reads, 'Ich glaube mit vollem Glauben' [truly faithfully I have faith], whereas Mendelssohn translates it into German as,

184

case and not only in Hebrew, in its prereflexive state may satisfactorily confine itself to the use of a verb. Thus, it is common usage to speak of *glauben* [believing] or of *zu Gott umkehren* [returning to God], but abstract thought alone uses concepts [terms][11] and cannot do without a fitting noun. Here one wishes to say not only that one should return to God; here one speaks of the *Teshuva,* of return. Biblical Hebrew does not have a noun with this meaning. In the Biblical text, the word *Teshuva* means only 'das zurückgebracht werden' [being brought back] and nothing else.* The post-Biblical search for a concept hence 'borrowed' a Hebrew noun of the same stem, though carrying different meaning. And the same happened to the concept of faith. As we have already seen, there is a verb in the Hebrew Bible for *glauben* [to have faith], but the word *Emuna,* which is built from the same stem, does not actually mean *der Glaube* [the faith]. In later times, as one looked for a well-fitting expression for a religious concept that can express the concept *der Glaube* [the faith], one took up the noun *Emuna.* That, by the way, is built according to the same grammatical structure as *Teshuva,* the return. Thus, though the notation *Emuna* does not entirely match the Biblical application of the word, it developed and became the precise description of the Jewish type of faith. As we shall see later, Rabbinical sources indicate that the word *Emuna* as used in Biblical

---

'Ich erkenne für wahr und gewiss' [I acknowledge as true and certain]. See Friedrich Niewöhner, 'Jüdisch-christliche Religionsgespräch', in *Das jüdisch-christliche Religionsgespräch* (Stuttgart, 1988), p. 32. It would be possible to follow these traces further, but I ask only *one* question: Is everything just a matter of semantic differences, or is it not rather the work of the subliminal striving to distinguish oneself from Christianity, which, right at that time, came to confront [Jewish faith]?

*See Buber here, p. 26, footnote 2.

verses was understood and transformed in the same sense of the later *abstractum* [abstract word] *der Glaube* [the faith].

A word, then, receives its basic meaning as a response to the needs of a thinking human being [*des denkenden Menschen*]. Nevertheless and at the same time, this meaning will be determined as well through the speaking community [*die sprechende Gemeinde*] and its perception of the world [*Weltanschauung*]. And furthermore, it will be determined as much by the word's grammatical stem, which gives it its basis. This, too, is of relevance here. In Judaism, the Hebrew words for 'having faith in' and 'faith' are rooted much more deeply in the meaning of *Treue und Vertrauen* [loyalty and trust] than in common Christian usage (and in many European languages)*—and on this, Buber is perfectly right. On the other hand, most of the time it is acknowledged that faith in its religious dimension is a Jewish invention—from the two Greek examples we were able to understand that pagan polytheism can hardly offer much space for the concept of *'Glauben an Gott'* [believing in God].

A classical summary of the old Rabbinical perception of faith is a homily referring to Moses [Exod.] 14:31–15:1.†
There it is written:'And Israel (at the Sea of Reeds) saw that great work which the Lord did upon the Egyptians: and the people feared the Lord, and believed the Lord, and his servant Moses'.[12] Hence the faith *in* God and Moses! And immediately afterwards we read: Then sang Moses and the Israelites this song unto the Lord, and Israel's great song of praise follows directly thereafter. In the ancient Rabbinical

---

*Nevertheless, in Greek, the Slavic languages, and Hebrew, *treu* [loyal] and *Glauben* [faith] have a common stem. And in Latin, there is *fides* and *fidelis*.

†See also Ps. 106:12.

homily,* the inspired hymn at the Sea of Reeds is under-stood as a gift for Israel's faith. 'Great is the faith of Israel, that she had in God, for as her reward for her faith in God, the Holy spirit rested on them, so that they sang the song'. Paul apparently knew this old Jewish exegesis, and he ap-plied its enclosed postulate in ways specific to him; the pos-tulate saying that the *Geistesgabe*[13] [intellectual capacity, also gift of the spirit, being presented with spirit][14] has its cause in faith. He writes to the Galatians (3:2–3): 'This only thing would I learn of you, Received ye the Spirit by the works of the law or hearing of faith? Are ye so foolish? Having begun in the spirit, are ye now made perfect by the flesh?'[15] Hence with Paul, there is a tension between the spirit, which comes forth from faith, and the works of the law.

Still, let us return to the ancient Jewish homily on the faith! After relating to Israel's faith at the Sea of Reeds, which is bestowing her with spirit, the homily continues, 'And you also find that Abraham, our father, inherited this and the coming world only because of his faith in God, as is said in Gen. 15:6: And he believed in the Lord; and he counted it to him for righteousness'.[16]† Our homily proves also with Biblical reference that God rewards faith with sal-vation. About them, those who keep the faith, it indeed

*See *Mechilta d'Rabbi Ismael,* edited by H. S. Horovitz and I. A. Rabin (Jerusalem, 1970), pp. 114–15 (for Exod. 14:31–15:1), and the same Rab-binical work with an English translation, edited by Jacob S. Lauterbach (Philadelphia, 1933), vol. 1, pp. 252–55. For a German translation, see: J. Winter und August Wünsche, trans., *Mechilta* (Leipzig, 1909), pp. 110–11. A parallel passage is in the other version of the work: *Mechilta d'Rabbi Simon b. Jochai,* edited by J. N. Epstein und E. Z. Melamed (Jerusalem, 1955), p. 70. [The quotation from Lauterbach reads as follows: 'Great indeed is faith be-fore Him who spoke and the world came into being. For as a reward for the faith with which Israel believed in God, the Holy Spirit rested upon them and they uttered the song' (p. 199).]

†On this Biblical verse, see Buber, pp. 43–50.

says: 'Open ye the gates, that the righteous nation which keepeth the truth (or, the faith) may enter in' (Isa. 26:2).[17] Through this gate, then, will pass those who have faith. And still in another old Rabbinical book (Sifra to Lev. 18:5), this verse from Isaiah finds application to the believers among non-Jews as well. 'It is then not written: Open the gates that priests, Levites, and Israelites may enter in; but: Open the gates that a righteous non-Jew *(goj)*, who has faith, may come in'.[18]

As we turn our attention again to the ancient Jewish homily on the faith, we learn from it also that when Israel might[19] *am Ende* [in or at the end, but against all odds certainly] gather in again from her dispersion, this, too, will be a reward for her faith. And as proof, a verse from Song of Songs (4:8) is brought up truly with a bold interpretation. No less bold, but much deeper, is its conclusion on the grace of the last days from a word of Psalms (92:2–5): 'It is a good thing to give thanks unto the Lord, and to sing praises unto thy name, O most High: To show forth thy loving-kindness in the morning, and thy faithfulness every night. . . . For thou, Lord, hast made me glad through thy work: I will triumph in the works of thy hands'.[20] There, the psalmist says 'your *Emuna*' and means God's loyalty, whereas the author of the homily understands *Emuna* in this place as faith, as the faith in God, and the term *Nächte* [every night] he understands as the eclipse of God, which is the world's present condition. He writes: 'What made it possible for us to reach this joy? The reward for the faith, which our fathers had believed in this world, which indeed is wholesomely night. It is because of this that we became worthy of the world to come, which indeed is wholesomely morning. This is the meaning of the Scripture's word: ". . . to bring tidings of your grace in the morning, and of your faith every night." ' One's courage to keep the faith in this aeon, dark as night, shall be blessed with God's grace and serene happiness on the bright-shining morning at the time of salvation.

Buber says: 'To draw attention to . . . connections is a fundamental aim of this book. The apparent digressions also serve this aim' (p. 12). One may hope that the reader took notice already that this afterword to Buber's book, with all its deviations, also pursues a fundamental aim. Hence, I may have permission here to ask how far the roots of the ancient homily on faith may reach back[21] into even earlier times. Another passage of the Rabbinical work containing our homily says: 'Shema'yah says: "The faith with which their father Abraham believed in Me is deserving that I should divide the sea for them"* For it is said: "and he believed in the Lord; and he counted it to him righteousness" (Gen. 15:6).[22] Avtalion says: "The faith with which they believed in Me is deserving that I should divide the sea for them." For it is said: "And the people believed, when they heard"' (Exod. 4:31).[23] The question, then, is whose faith caused the parting of the Sea of Reeds: Was it Israel's faith while in Egypt or possibly even already the faith of Abraham? Thus is the question upon which the two wise men, Shema'yah and Avtalion, dwell in reflection, and they were older than the famous Hillel. Thence, they lived in the first century B.C. This homily, the subject of our closer

---

*Regarding Exod. 14:15, see *Mechilta,* edited by Horovitz and Rabin, pp. 98–99; edited by Lauterbach, vol. 1, pp. 218–20; translated by Winter and Wünsche, pp. 94–95. [Flusser: 'lesen wir: "Schemaja sagt: Wert ist der Glaube, den an Mich euer Vater Abraham geglaubt hat, daß Ich ihnen (Israel) das Meer spalte, denn es steht geschrieben (1 Moses 15:6). O Und er glaubte an den Herrn, und das rechnete er ihm als Gerechtigkeit an. —Awtalion sagte: Wert ist der Glaube, den sie (Israel) an mich (damals) geglaubt haben, daß Ich ihnen das Meer spalte, denn es steht geschrieben (2 Moses 4:31). O Und das Volk glaubte und sie hörten."']

examination, also mentions Israel's faith during the exodus from Egypt and Abraham's faith as well. From this, it follows that it is very likely that the homily developed from a conversation between Shema'yah and Avtalion. At any rate, this concept of faith, which constitutes a precondition for the Christian concept of faith, was substantiated from pre-Christian times. Not only differences, but common grounds, too, are just as important.

Together with other sayings from Scripture, the Rabbinical homily on faith brings up the famous Biblical quotation in Habakkuk. 2:4.* Buber gave a correct interpretation:' "But the man proved true will live in his trust" ' [p. 48].[24] So according to the prophet's original intention. However, concurring with the later understanding, we translate it as: 'The righteous man will live in his faith'.[25] The weight that this verse had in Judaism becomes obvious from a Talmudic passage (Maccot 24a). There the objective is the reduction of the great number of laws in Judaism to a small denominator. In the various attempts to reduce it, one refers to singular Biblical verses. In the end, it is Rabbi Nachman bar Isaac who succeeds in reducing the laws to a single one:'Habakkuk then came and reduced them to one, as it is said: The righteous man lives in his faith'.[26] Here, too, there is no tension, but harmony between faith and conduct.

Still, how shall we understand Habakkuk's (2:4) ambivalent words? As we shall see soon, the ambivalence of this sentence made history. Whereto, then, belongs the faithfulness in the sentence? Maybe it is a closer description of the righteous man: the man proved true righteously is marked out by his faithfulness, and he will live. The other percep-

*On Hab. 2:4, see Buber, pp. 48–50. The Biblical verse is cited in Rom. 1:17; Gal. 3:11, and Heb. 10:38.

tion, the more common one, relates faith to life: faith is the condition upon which man is presented with life. This is, already, the understanding of a very early interpolator of Jesus Sirach (15:15), when he writes: 'When you will have faith in him (God), then you will also live'.* But the proposal to link life to faith does not yet solve the problem: what kind of life this will be, of which faith is its condition. Is it eternal life? Nonetheless, this was the understanding of the Essene author of the commentary on Habakkuk, as we read in a scroll from the Dead Sea (Hab. 8:1–3): 'The righteous man lives in his faith (Hab. 2:4). This relates to those in the house of Judah who act according to the law, and these He (God) will free from the place of condemnation (i.e., from hell) owing to their labor and to their faith in the teacher of righteousness'. The house of Judah marks typologically the Essene unification [*Einung*],[27] and the teacher of righteousness is its founder. Hence, the word *the righteous man* in Habakkuk is interpreted with regard to the Essenes chosen by God. Maybe it is at the same time an allusion to the description 'the teacher of righteousness'. Those who have faith in him will then inherit eternal bliss. Certainly, the faith of the Essenes had a greater meaning than simple faithfulness, but then it also did not mean

*The interpolation is very old; it appears in the Hebrew version as in the Syrian versions, but the Greek translator—a nephew of the author—did not know of it yet. Prior to the interpolation, the text speaks of the loyalty *(Emuna)* to act according to God's will. From this, the editor, who is to be taken responsible for the interpolation, derived the idea to add his verse. The creative interpretation of Heb. 2:4, which is a very old amendment to Ben Sira 15:15, became subject to new changes in the Gospel of John. The faith in God, which gives life, is now related to Jesus. As, according to John, Jesus is resurrection and life, he [Jesus] can say: 'he that believeth in me, though he were dead, yet shall he live' (John 11:25 [*KJV*]). Here too, then, the history of ideas becomes exemplified in the changes of meaning in the word of a prophet.

much beyond the faith in Moses as in Exod. 14:31—but, still, the passage points to the New Testament's faith in Jesus.

Now we shall follow the lead of Hab. 2:4 via the Greek Bible on to Paul. We do so by following in Buber's footsteps.* In the Hebrew text, it is written: 'The righteous man lives in his faith'.[28] The Greek translator thought, according to custom, of Habakkuk's intention as saying life is the child of faith. That faith he furthermore tried to emphasize; as to prevent misunderstandings, he said, now in Greek: 'The righteous man lives *by* [*out of*] faith'.[29]† The Greek translator of Habakkuk could not have imagined the far-reaching consequences of his clarification for Paul's type of faith. In the Hebrew text as well as in the Greek text, thereafter, these words are put into the following order: 'The righteous man, by [out of] faith (he) lives'. Hence, Paul was able to interpret this passage from Scripture as follows: he who becomes righteous by [out of] the faith lives. And hence originated the Pauline justification out of faith,‡ based not only on the Pauline understanding of Hab. 2:4, but also on the verse in Gen. 15:6 mentioned previously: 'And he (Abra-

*See footnote on p. 190.

†The Greek version of Hab. 2:4 actually reads, 'The righteous man will live by [out of] my faith', and so accordingly the words in Heb. 10:38 are cited. The passage does not address the righteous man, who lives by his faith, but instead it is God who is now perceived as the subject. As Japsen, *Theologisches Wörterbuch* (cited in footnote‡ on p. 182) rightly assumes, the Greek translator took this from his Hebrew source. Hence, *emmunati* and not *emmunato*. For this passage, see also: *Biblia Hebraica Stuttgartensia* (Stuttgart, 1984), p. 1051. However, some Greek manuscripts omitted the word *my* and thus read only: 'The righteous man will live by faith'; the verse is cited in Rom. 1:17 and Gal. 3:11.

‡It is quite common that a semantic change evokes a powerful idiom. — One such change, which turned into a bone of contention among denominations of profession, has a history of its own. Luther translates Rom. 3:28:

192

ham) believed in the Lord; and he counted it to him for · righteousness'.[30] In this passage, Paul found faith as well as righteousness.

Galatians 3:11 sheds light on how much Paul wanted to read out of Hab. 2:4: 'But that no man is justified by the law in the sight of God, *it is* evident: for, The just shall live by faith'.[31] It becomes clear, for example, from Gal. 2:16, whereto Paul's justification is directed, that: 'Knowing that a man is not justified by the works of the law, but by the faith of Jesus Christ, even we have believed in Jesus Christ, that we might be justified by the faith of Christ, and not by the works of the law: for by the works of the law shall no flesh be justified'.[32] The same word of Psalms (143:2)[33] to which this passage refers is also used, and in this very meaning, in the Epistle to the Romans (Rom. 3:20).[34]

The word of Psalms, to which the reference relates, may

'So halten wir es nun, dass der Mensch gerecht werde ohne des Gesetzes Werke, *allein* durch den Glauben' ['Hence we hold that man is justified without the work of the law, *solely* by faith'. The English translation *(KJV)* does not follow Luther: 'Therefore we conclude that a man is justified by faith, without the deeds of the law' (Rom. 3:28)]. The word *allein* is not in Paul, and this Luther knows. He thought that he inserted it [the word *allein*] according to the meaning of the verse, but he missed the fact that there had been precursors in previous times, including Thomas Aquinas (see Ulrich Wilckens, *Der Brief an die Römer,* EKK [Neukirchen-Vluyn, 1978], vol. 1, p. 247, fn. 771). The first witness to this understanding is Origines. Therefore, I suppose that the text's term *allein* and its interpretation, as it influenced future interpretations, came up no later than during the second century, a time during which the canonization had not yet come to an end. In those days, it was still possible to confront Rom. 3:28 with James 2:24. Here it reads as follows: 'Ye see then how that by works a man is justified, *and not by faith only*' ['so seht ihr, daß der Mensch durch Werke gerecht wird, *nicht durch Glauben allein*']. On may hope this finding will help to undo the theological grounding of ideologies, which I would consider highly rewarding.

also be translated as: 'for in thy sight no man living* shall be justified'. Paul puts new weight [*Gewicht*] on the word of Scripture because for him the two Hebrew terms *righteousness* and *to become righteous* mean something else, something in principle more profound than in the Hebrew Bible. Paul did not invent the fresh meaning of these two terms.

In the aftermath of the discovery of the Dead Sea Scrolls, it became evident that this modification or new meaning of the terms did not originate with Paul, but that the anthropology of justification had already been an essential component of the religious system of the Essenes.[†] No wonder that Psalm 143:3 of the Essene hymnbook is varied in four places (7:28; 9:14–15; 13:16–17; 16:11). The last two passages read as follows: 'I know that no man will be justified without you'[35] and 'only in your grace can man be justified'.[36] A passage in the same Essene hymnbook (4:30–33) sheds light on the Essene background of Paul's teachings on justification: 'I understood that righteousness is not with man, and perfect conduct not with the *Menschenkind* [literally, child of man]. With God Almighty only shall be all works of justice. But the path of man will not persist, lest through the spirit that God created to mend man's path, so that all creatures and all of creation may recognize the might of his power and the abundance of his grace with all sons in appreciation'. Other passages in the Epistles of Paul certainly come to the mind of the attentive reader.

According to the Essene view, therefore, man cannot achieve righteousness out of himself without God's grace. From this and in sharp contrast to the sect of Essenes, who rigidly abide by the law, Paul derives the understanding not

---

*In Paul, both passages read 'no flesh'.

†See D. Flusser, 'Die jüdische und griechische Bildung des Paulus', in *Paulus* (Freiburg im Breisgau, 1980), pp. 18–26.

only that the works of the law cannot help man but moreover that they are obstacles to God's grace. And here Paul puts faith into its place: not through the works of law, but through faith will man be justified. Thus, Paul sets up the polarity between the 'pure' faith and the works of the Jewish law. Surely this does not correspond with the Jewish type of faith (see Buber, pp. 51–58).

From a Jewish perspective, faith is closely tied to the works: 'A man, taking up *one single* commandment with faith, appreciates that the Holy Spirit shall rest on him'.[37]* And the faith by which man shall find justice is in Paul, not simply the faith in God, but exclusively the faith in Jesus Christ.

Paul maintains many times that 'no man is justified by the law' (Gal. 3:11), and one must agree with him, though not with the meaning that he places on it. Already according to the Essene religious system, there is no justification for man but by God's grace. In saying so, one actually assumes that one will attain salvation by it. Paul adopted this view and, furthermore, heightened its religious anthropology through the polarity between the works of the law and the redeeming faith in Jesus. But, for a Jew, there is no true sense in the idea that Paul rejected: that there is justification by the law. According to the Jewish type of faith—and this applies also to Essenism—it is hardly perceivable how anyone might consider that life according to the law is the path to one's salvation, to one's redemption. For, in Judaism, this indeed is not the original intention of the works of the law. Through God, the works are an obligation directed unto Him. By conduct, the Jew wishes to fulfill the will of the Heavenly Father. And, on occasion, there appears salvation for Israel during her history of well-being and disaster,

*See the passages mentioned in the footnote on p. 187.

though only on the messianic morn will salvation truly light up. And as far as this concerns faith, in Judaism one may claim that no other way but faith leads to salvation. The distinction of the Jewish type of faith from the other, which is common to most Christians, originated most probably when the idea came into being that, as already pointed out, the concern is not the faith in God but in particular the faith in Jesus.—And the nature of this faith is such as to enable man here and now to reach salvation through Jesus. Owing to this shift in the type of faith, salvation, too, develops a particular content that cannot be found either in Judaism or in Islam. Therefore, we again have come to consider Buber's two types of faith.

The Jewish *Emuna,* faith, living and weaving, hardly has any place with the Essenes. And its concept is, as far as I can see it, of little significance in Hellenistic Judaism. In contrast, we can see the importance of faith already in Rabbinical Judaism, and this before the times of Jesus and Paul. As is well known, faith is a cornerstone of Jesus' piety, and it is from the Jesus-tradition that Paul understood the significance of faith. From here he took the concept and integrated it into his own religious system. Buber (p. 55) thinks that Old Testament faith and, along with it, the living faith of post-Biblical Judaism oppose Paul's thought, whereas the faith of Jesus finds its place within the Jewish type of faith. The following observation, to my view, seems to be relevant: the historical Jesus spoke only about the faith in God,* but he never asked that one should believe in him.† Jesus was strictly opposed to any cult of personality for his person: 'not every one that saith unto me, Lord, Lord,

*He spoke only about faith in general; he never mentioned God explicitly!

†According to the first three Gospels. An exception, which only proves the rule, is Matthew (18:6). Here, the words *in me* are Matthew's addition in comparison with Mark 9:42. According to Matt. 27:42, the enemies

shall enter the kingdom of heaven; but he that doeth the will of my Father, which is in heaven' (Matt. 7:21–23, Luke 6:40, and see Luke 11:27–28!).[38] The radical change from the faith of Jesus to the faith in Jesus occurred only later, very shortly after his crucifixion. It is not only with Paul, but also with John that the faith in Jesus can be found.

As we have already seen,* according to Rabbinical understanding, not only will Israel, abiding by the law, be rewarded for her faith, but also the truthful non-Jews will be rewarded for their faith, though they are not bound to Moses' law. This is already in accordance with Old Testament universalism. Following Jonah's preaching, the men of Niniveh believed in God (Jon. 3:5), and their repentance was accepted. According to the words of Jesus (Matt. 12:41; Luke 11:32), the men of Nineveh will therefore 'rise in judgment with this generation, and shall condemn it'.[39] Two times Jesus emphasized the willingness of the non-Jews to believe (Luke 7:9, Matt. 8:10 and Matt. 15:28). In both cases, this event took place during one of his miraculous works of healing. In these [works], faith is active. Particularly expressive are Jesus' words while healing the woman who was suffering with hemorrhage (Matt. 9:21–22): 'Daughter, be of good comfort; thy faith hath made thee whole'.[40] Jesus perceives faith always as a force, which is active alongside his healing; but even in other instances, faith can change everything. 'If ye had faith as a grain of mustard seed, ye might say unto this sycamine tree, Be thou plucked up by the root, and be thou planted in the sea; and it should obey you' (Luke 17:6).[41] Jesus' view here is relevant for his

---

mocked the crucified Jesus: 'If he be the King of Israel, let him now come down from the cross, and we shall believe him'.

*The passage is Sifra to Lev. 18:5.

entire understanding of the world. Not only in relation to faith, but also elsewhere, Jesus takes up such terms that are of central importance for Judaism, in particular Rabbinical Judaism, though without conceiving them as static perceptions; on the contrary, he understands that they are dynamic, moving powers, capable of changing the world decisively. In Jesus' view, such power is not only in faith, but also in the notion of the return to God, in forgiveness, in the love for the neighbor, and in the kingdom of heaven. In order to start the motion of these powers, Jesus did not address God, but men. Hence—in sharp contrast to the Essenes—he avoided speaking of grace and God's mercy (Mark 5:19b is of secondary importance). Jesus, on the other hand, i.e., in contrast to the Essenes, demands that man act with mercy toward the neighbor. An exception to the rule, thus stressing it, is Matt. 5:7: 'Blessed are the merciful: for they shall obtain mercy' (see Matt. 18:33).[42] An important conversation with Buber will perhaps shed some light on this strange behavior of Jesus. I asked Buber why God's grace finds hardly any place in his work. He explained:'I write theology for men, not for God'. In regard to the only correct understanding of some particularly important doctrines of Jesus, Buber's *Two Types of Faith* could have been a decisive contribution to research and to the two living religions, Christianity and Judaism, if Buber had not been such a brilliant author. Nothing could have been further from his mind than scholarly jargon. In particular, this concerns the rather grotesque dispute about Jesus and the Pharisees. A forced attempt to construct a polarity between the preaching of Jesus and matters Jewish was undertaken many times and, after an intermission of understandably long duration, again makes itself heard, almost noisily. On the other hand, the voices of those who claim Jesus entirely for Rabbinical Judaism grow stronger. Surely it is right to understand Jesus, from the

198

point of his Judaism, as a personality of distinctive spiritual creativity. 'I am more than ever certain that a great place belongs to him in Israel's history of faith and that this place cannot be described by any of the usual categories' (Buber, p. 13). Hence, it is futile to raise the question to which extent Jesus considered himself as one of the Pharisees. Buber rightly presupposes more or less identical positions for the Pharisees and the trend of Rabbinical Judaism. After the discovery of the Dead Sea Scrolls, it became evident, though, that the Essene motifs are recognizable in the sermon of Jesus. But it continues to be true that the religious and ethical tidings of Jesus grew out of the fertile grounds of Rabbinical Judaism. It is Buber's invaluable merit to account for Jesus an independent point of view, which differed from the current teachings of the Pharisees but did not collide with them.* Do Jewish and Christian theologians have sufficient bravery to join Buber in his venture, this flight of an eagle?

We want to turn our attention to Buber's exegesis on Matt. 5:17.† According to Buber's understanding, Jesus intended to say here 'that he has not come to dissolve the Torah but to "fulfil" it, and this means indeed to make it manifest in its full original meaning and to bring it into life' [Buber, pp. 62–63]. In two passages, Buber explains Jesus' understanding of this issue. The first example concerns the commandment of love for the enemy (Matt 5:43, 45):‡ 'In

---

*Buber says with beautiful words in regard to Jesus: 'It is to be emphasized that among the rabbis of the period other views of the subject are to be found, for the inner dialectic continues within Pharisaism itself; but the great and vital lineage of this doctrine is unmistakable' (p. 63).

†See Buber, pp. 62–63. I came to similar conclusions, albeit through other ways. See D. Flusser, *Entdeckungen im Neuen Testament,* vol. 1 (Neukirchen-Vluyn, 1987), pp. 21–31.

‡See Buber, pp. 68–78.

its fundamental meaning it is so deeply bound up with Jewish faith and at the same time transcends it in so particular a way that it must be especially discussed at this point' (Buber, pp. 68–69). What then is the meaning of the word 'neighbor,' whom, according to Lev. 19:18, one must love? Literally—but not in the true meaning of the word—it was possible to relate the Hebrew verb, used in this passage, 'preferably to the personal friend'. But, rightly, Jesus sets against 'love of a friend, love of a person who loves me, love toward a person who hates me'. It is also important that Jesus has no intention to force upon men the love for the enemy, but rather one must meet with a loving attitude the person who hates one. In other words, one should respond to the hate with love. In my view, understood this way, not only is the law possible, but it is also desirable to fulfill it.

In the case of the love for an enemy, Jesus' interpretation is surely daring; but the position of freedom that Jesus took here responds to Rabbinical exegesis. In Rabbinical thought, too, exists casuism with the purpose to humanize the Holy Scripture. Maybe, here, Buber's understanding is correct when he says, 'All in all, the saying of Jesus about love for the enemy derives its light from the world of Judaism in which he stands and which he seems to contest: and he outshines it' (p. 75).

The second example, Jesus' view toward divorce, might help us with our quest for the distinctive direction of Jesus' preaching. By the way, the saying about divorce is preserved in two versions. According to Matthew (5:32 and 19:9), divorce is permitted only in the case of 'sexual offense'— which corresponds, as Buber notices, 'with the strict view of the school of Shammai' (p. 66). According to the other version (1 Cor. 7:10–11; see also Mark 10:9), any divorce is forbidden. After the discovery of the Dead Sea Scrolls, it became evident that this second version mirrors the Essene custom.* Buber correctly notes Jesus' view about divorce: 'How this is to be understood becomes clear when we refer to the narrative (Mark 10, Matt 19, Luke 16) in which Jesus actually says this against divorce, according to which the remarriage of a divorced person shall reckon as adultery. In both instances, the "Pharisees" appeal to Moses, who (Deut. 24:1) instituted the form of divorce. Thereupon Jesus makes a significant doubled reply. In the first place, Moses wrote down this commandment "because of the hardness of your hearts"; . . . In the second place, Jesus refers to God's word in Paradise (Gen. 2:24) that a man shall leave his father and mother and cleave to his wife, and they shall become one flesh.† Jesus understands this word as a commandment: he appeals from the Mosaic revelation to that of creation' (Buber, pp. 66–67). In addition, it has to be noted that the Biblical word about the letter of divorce (Deut. 24:19) starts out as follows: 'When a man has taken a wife, and married her, and it comes to pass that she finds no favor in his eyes. . .'[43] This, then, clearly is a conditional sentence. The woman may not displease the husband, but as he may begin to hate his wife, Moses agreed to divorce 'For the hardness of your heart' (Mark 10:5).[44]

With regard to love for the enemy, Jesus broadens the meaning of the Biblical word by breaking down, so to speak, the barriers of love for the neighbor. Regarding divorce, Jesus plays two sayings, which he understood as one

---

*It is important that Jesus quotes the same verse against divorce from Moses [Gen.] 1:27 in Matt. 19:4 and Mark 10:6, the same verse that is quoted in the Essene text from Damascus (4:19–5:1). The relationship of the two passages is far greater!

†For the other Biblical word (Gen. 1:27) that Buber brings up here, see the previous footnote. For Matt. 5:31–32 and about the divorce with Jesus, see U. Luz, *Das Evangelium nach Matthäus*, vol. 1, EKK (Zürich, 1985), pp. 268–79.

unconditioned commandment, off against the saying on the letter of divorce, which, as noted, in its form is a conditional sentence. Compared to the case of love for the enemy, this is more of a daring procedure. But this method, too, was then common usage in Judaism. In order to lift up the true and valid meaning of Scripture, it was considered necessary to use, so to speak, the freedom of manipulating individual words of Scripture. Jesus did so, too, and still one has the inevitable impression that the world of imagination of Jesus' preaching does not correspond completely to the sphere of Pharisaic-Rabbinical Judaism. In *The Two Types of Faith*, Buber tries seriously to emphasize the particularity of Jesus' attempts compared to those of the Pharisees. In one passage, Buber reduces the particularity of Jesus to a short formula: the true revolution of Jesus had been the return 'to return to the original purity of the revelation' (p. 99). And in another passage, Buber describes the distancing range between the faith of Jesus and the imperative of the Pharisees as follows: 'The life-problem of the man who comes from the world of the "law" is therefore for the Pharisees and Jesus: how do I get from a way of life seemingly according to the revealed will of God to a true life in it, his will which leads to eternal life? The difference is this that "revealed" means for the Pharisees: through the historical revelation in the Word brought into the tradition of Israel and manifest in it; for Jesus however the tradition of Israel has not adequately preserved the historical revelation in the Word, but now it is adequately disclosed in its meaning and purpose' (p. 92). Or, in other words, 'It has become evident that Jesus . . . considers the Thorah capable of fulfilment, not merely in accordance with its wording, but in the original intention of its revelation' (p. 79). And in order not to tire the reader too much, the last quotation: 'The Jewish position may be summarized in the sentence: fulfilment of the divine commandment is valid when it takes place in conformity with the full capacity of the person and from the whole intention of faith. If we want to give a parallel formulation for Jesus' demand that is transcending that position, the sentence may run like this: fulfilment of the divine commandment is valid if it takes place in conformity with the full intention of the revelation and from the whole intention of faith' (p. 56).*

There can be no doubt about the issue that Buber understood the essence of Jesus' type of faith: Jesus starts out from the wording of the Scripture in order to reach beyond it the original purpose of the revelation, the full intention of revelation. The Word of Scripture became for him transparent in a peculiar way; but the question remains as to what he perceived looking through the 'iotas and dots' of Scripture (Matt. 5:18). It has been said that the place that belongs to Jesus in Israel's history of faith 'cannot be described by any of the usual categories' (Buber, p. 13), but does this end all further investigations? And didn't small and great teachers and rabbis in the long chain of previous Jewish generations serve the cause of necessary preparations for the great breakthrough of Jesus? In particular, men of the Rabbinical-Pharisaic school, who in all fields of conduct and thought had taken trouble, according to their capacities, to remove the old Oriental slag clinging to the Jewish faith since times long gone in order to let the true human kernel of Judaism light up brightly. In the sources, the name 'Pharisees of love' is given to them. On his part, Jesus pursued consequently

---

*Buber closes this sentence as follows: '—in which however the conception of the intention of faith receives an eschatological character'. Here he shows the influence of Albert Schweizer's 'konsequenten Eschatologie' [consequent eschatology]. I could not discover in any passage of the Gospels an eschatological intention in his [Jesus'] conception of faith.

the paths of these thoughts in the same direction and derived from them the necessary conclusions that his prede-
cessors, compelling, had not passed. Thus, he succeeded in
reaching out to the intention of revelation. In my view,
Jesus' preaching is characterized by his attempt to regard as
null and void all of those regulations and imaginations of the
oral and written tradition that might cause suffering and sinful evil. In his understanding, such regulations and notions
oppose the original intention of revelation, for, really, the
Heavenly Father cannot demand any wrong. I believe that
my assumptions can be attested from the Gospel itself, but I
know as well that this is not all of the truth. However, I shall
be satisfied if, following Buber's insight, I succeeded in ad-
vancing our understanding of the truth one small step.

Hence, it is significant that Buber does not reduce apolo-
getically the particularity of Jesus' preaching. He once told
me: if one is able to listen attentively, one can hear Jesus
speaking out of the later reports of the Gospels. And, just as
Buber looks at Jesus' tidings of faith with fresh understanding, so does he likewise approach Jesus' 'self-understanding'
with caution, not wishing to diminish Jesus' high consciousness with petty 'enlightening' fantasy. It is characteristic for
Buber's liberty from today's common prejudices that, in
contrast to most New Testament scholars, he takes the synoptic story of temptation very seriously. He characterizes it
as irremovable, and it is for Buber a 'legendary elaboration of
the encounter with the demoniacal which determines a
definite stage in the life of the "holy" man'.* Buber's precise
sense for true religious experiences does not forsake him
even when he, in contrast to popular critical research, does
not denounce Jesus' question in Caesarea Philippi (Mark
8:27–33 and Parr.) as 'a "faith-legend", transmitted presum-

*Buber here, p. 32, fn. 1.

ably in a fragmentary form. . . . My impression is that the narrative may well contain the preserved nucleus of an authentic tradition of a conversation which once took place 'on the way'. . . . Whatever may be the case with the much-debated problem of the 'Messianic consciousness' of Jesus, if it is to be understood as human, we must admit lapses in the history of this consciousness, as must have been the case on the occasion which was followed by the conversation with the disciples—assuming that one is inclined to take this conversation seriously, as I do' (Buber, pp. 30–32).

Today it is a truism that one cannot comprehend an irrational event simply with mere reason, and yet throughout the research on Jesus' life the temptation is particularly great to interpret the supernatural in natural ways. We have already seen that Buber's nature saved him from this danger. On the other hand, one may not close one's eyes to the legendary tendency of religious records. Even the sincere scholar, truly faithful, cannot evade the use of his critical reason while looking at the holy texts of the congregation of his own denomination. How, then, is it possible to establish a picture, made halfway safe, if one wishes neither to falsify the facts in a simple enlightening manner nor, led astray by naïve belief in miracles, to construct a implausible reality? A scholar who wishes to set himself to the issue of religions is to my understanding hardly capable of safeguarding himself against the contradiction between critical realism and an objective description of the 'supernatural'. This almost unavoidable inadequacy discloses itself especially in the scholarly diagnosis of Jesus' high self-esteem. The surrealistic painter Salvador Dali calls his method 'paranoid-critical', and in modern art one speaks of 'fantastic realism'. It must be hoped that we are not so bad off, and surely Buber is not when he deals with Jesus' messianic consciousness. But with him, too, one cannot entirely put off the impression that, all in all, the figure of Jesus appears a little unreal; at the same time, however, Buber brings to light some correct and valid aspects of Jesus' messianism that scholars unfortunately have overlooked.

Thus, it is very difficult to imagine that at any time a man of flesh and blood responded to the servant of God in Isaiah and related to him in ways such as Buber supposes for Jesus (pp. 105–8).* The same is true for the original purpose of Jesus' sayings, which Buber considers to be genuine (pp. 117–26) and which [45] allegedly shines through the discourse of Jesus with Nicodemos, as handed down in John 3:1–8. The discourse itself deals with the issue of birth out of the spirit. Buber thinks that the true nucleus of the tradition of baptism is hidden behind this record in the Gospel of John. With this, Buber wants to say 'that in the oldest tradition of the baptism of Jesus in the Jordan [46] the heavenly voice chose and raised him to be the Son of God' (p. 116). Buber's hint here is quite important and should be pursued further.

According to the correct version† in Luke 3:22, the voice

---

*On p. 107, Buber mentions Bultmann's argument, important in itself '. . . that in none of the words of Jesus is there a certain reference to the suffering of the servant of God'. Other scholars could be mentioned in support of Bultmann, such as Morna D. Hooker, *Jesus and the Servant* (London, 1959). Buber, on the other hand, thinks that Jesus wished not to speak overtly about this matter. The question whether Jesus related himself to Isaiah, chap. 53, depends on the answer to the question whether or not he [Jesus] had foreseen his future suffering and death and had approved of it as God's demand. In my volume of articles *Entdeckungen* (see the footnote† on p. 199), I consider it as confirmed that the 'historical' Jesus related himself to Isaiah (Isa. 53:12) in two passages in Luke (11:21–22 and 23:37). Unfortunately, I cannot repeat my argument here.

†The wording of the heavenly voice during the baptism of Jesus (Luke 3:22 and Parr.) as well as during his beatification (Luke 9:35 and Parr.) wavers in the different Gospels and in the manuscripts. See also the other early Christian witnesses.

from heaven announces on Jesus' baptism: 'Thou art my Son; this day I have begotten thee'.[47] This is a word of Psalms (2:7), and in this passage its meaning can be no other than that during baptism Jesus became the Son of God. And then Luke (3:23) * goes on, following the same meaning:'And Jesus himself began to be about thirty years of age, being (as was supposed) the son of Joseph'.[48] † I suppose that the evangelist Luke inserted into his source the weakening term 'Jesus being (as was supposed)' ['so galt er (Jesus)'] in order to adjust the text to common perception. According to that source, the descendant of David ‡ was just the son of Joseph—until, upon baptism, the voice from heaven proclaimed him as Son of God. Hence, Luke precluded two chapters to his source, which speak mainly about the heavenly birth of Jesus. Their narratives do not stem from the same tradition as the parallel two first chapters of the Gospel of Matthew. From a similar date given at the beginning of the Judeo-Christian Gospel of the Ebionites (Epiphanius, haer. 13:6),§ it becomes evident that the

---

*Luke 3:21–23 is actually one single sentence!

†According to an old source, the Arab author Abd al-Dschabar (tenth century C.E.), Jesus was considered the son of Joseph until his baptism and the voice from heaven. See S. Pines, *The Jewish Christians of the Early Centuries,* the Israel Academy of Sciences and Humanities, vol. 1, no. 13 (Jerusalem, 1966), p. 63.

‡An archeological finding has proved that during the days of Jesus there were descendants of King David in Palestine. See D. Flusser, ' "The House of David" on an Ossuary', *Israel Museum Journal* 5 (spring 1986), pp. 37–40.

§'The start of their [the Ebiones'] Gospel says: It occurred in the days of Herod, the king of Juda, under the high priest Kaiphas, that then came one, named John'; quoted from Wilhelm Schneemelcher, *Neutestamentliche Apokryphen,* 5th ed., vol. 1 of *Evangelien* (Tübingen, 1987), pp. 140–41; Kerinthos (around 100 C.E.) thought as well that 'Jesus had not been born out of a virgin but, like all other human beings, had been begotten, and namely by Joseph and Mary. . . . After baptism Christ had . . . descended

source of Luke started out with 3:1. Strangely, the assumption that Jesus became the Son of God through baptism had once been so dominant that it caused the repression of the memory of the youth of the human being Jesus.* And, most certainly, because of the theory of adoption, at times very influential, the records on Jesus were started only with his baptism rather than with the first thirty years of his life. Thus is the case with Mark and John, and so it had been with the source of Luke. But it is quite likely that even Buber would agree with me that the baptism-tradition— according to which at the baptism in the Jordan the voice from heaven chose and raised Jesus to be the Son of God— although important for the history of early Christian dogmatics and the literary side of the Gospels, states little of relevance about what really happened. Not even the divine birth of Jesus is completely called into question by this old dogmatic view. And one would fall victim to fantastic realism, the danger in wait, if one wished to evaluate the adoptianism of baptism so as to conclude from it that Jesus, through a supernatural experience, had become conscious of his raised Sonship during his baptism.

As has been said, no one, not even Buber, can ban this danger entirely while analyzing critically Jesus' self-understanding. In this tricky venture, one must strive to accomplish smaller or bigger partial success. And it is the same with Buber's analysis of the strange statement in front of the high priest:'Hereafter shall the Son of Man sit on the right hand of the power of God' (Luke 22:69 and Parr.).[49]

---

onto him in a dove's features' (Hypolytos, *Die Widerlegung alter Häresien* vol. 7, p. 33, and vol. 10, p. 21). The witnesses on Kerinthos are contained in Adolf Helgenfeld, *Die Ketzergeschichte des Urchristentums* (Leipzig, 1884; Darmstadt, 1983), pp. 411–21.

*We learn something about his youth in Luke 2:22–52.

Personally, I would not alter this statement as much as Buber did, but he, too, says that these words 'may be derived from the content of a genuine statement' (p. 108).*
And Buber continues: 'then the biographical fact is given, around which after the death of Jesus and the visions of the disciples the crystallizing of the mythical element lying ready in the hearts of those influenced by Hellenism took place, until the new binitarian[50] God-image was present. Not merely new symbols but actually new images of God grow up from human biography, and precisely from its most unpremeditated moments' [p. 109].

Here, Buber points his finger to one of the transitions from one to the other type of faith. As it seems, one cannot overemphasize Buber's merit in not allowing himself to be led astray by his pronounced commitment to Judaism to diminish the high self-esteem of Jesus to the anonymous, colorless banality of a 'common' Jew. By the way, spoken frankly: Is there a 'common Jew' after all? And during the hectic times of Jesus, compared to our days, there has been even less of the kind. In those days, there were in Judaism charismatic miracle workers, messianic pretenders, prophetic dreamers, and ecstatic mystics. Jesus was not the only one to believe that he played a key role in God's economy; so did the founders of Essenism, the Teachers of Justice, and the poet of the Essene hymnbook. And Buber says as well that Jesus perceived himself as the Messiah, the Son of God and the raised Son of Man. Today, as it seems, one can back up Jesus' high self-esteem with additional arguments but without falling into phantasmagoric blindness. And yet, as Buber understood rightly, Jesus' high self-esteem is one of the bridges to the other type of faith.

*See also D. Flusser, 'At the Right Hand of the Power', in *Immanuel 14* (Jerusalem, 1982), pp. 42–46.

'The work of deification was a process, a compulsion, not arbitrariness. Only in this way indeed do new images of God ever originate' (Buber, p. 130). I am not convinced of such processes of irrefutable compulsion, for which there cannot be any proof either. Perhaps one can speak of certain driving forces, which are immanent in all ideologies and which move toward realization. Here, I am not thinking of theological impulses, but rather of psychological impulses, and they are the ones of which Buber was probably thinking. He also intimates that in the *Vergottung* [deification] of Jesus other internal Jewish ideas were involved, apart from Jesus' high self-esteem itself. Thus, the mainly Rabbinical theory of hypostasis was used for Jesus. Now he represents the imminence of God—in other words, His glory, His power, His wisdom and greatness, His spirit, and His word. The Jewish faith in creation through the word of God was united with the perception of a prehistoric existence of the Messiah and transferred onto Jesus: the preexistent Christ is the Word, through which the world was created.* Likewise, apparently, early Christians of Jewish origin composed the ancient prehistory of Jesus, but its composition definitely generated from Jewish pre-Christian motifs. As far as the posthistory of the cross is concerned, doubtlessly the faith in resurrection is Jewish, as the hope in the Second Coming of Christ at the end of the days is established in the Jewish eschatological messianic faith; and, indeed, the 'historic' Jesus himself reported about the Last Judgment, when the 'Son of Man' will be the judge (Matt. 25:31–49; see Luke 17:22–37).

Before our eyes, a cosmic history thus rose up, which started out with the creation of the world and will find its

---

*According to Buber (p. 139, fn. 2), Paul had never in his proven letters asked for the *Gottescharakter* [God-appearance] for the preexistent Christ.

closure at the end of all times—and its hero is a Jewish man who lived approximately two thousand years ago and was crucified under Pontius Pilatus. Up to now, however, we have retained the main point of all events—that is, the atoning power of Jesus' tragic death of sacrifice—because it is exactly this perception that provided the characteristic meaning for the entire metahistorical drama: basically, through it the other type of faith was born. The belief that the death of a martyr has an atoning effect is essentially Jewish;* however, I am not quite sure that Jesus himself understood his death in that way. Here, I can hint only that none of Jesus' sayings about the atoning character of his threatening death is grounded philologically. It perhaps should be considered that although it may be common practice to have faith in the atoning powers of a stranger's self-sacrifice, still it is almost beyond anyone's imagination to perceive his own future forcible death as an atoning sacrifice—maybe except during the last hours before his decease, and on that exist no records in Jesus' case. The faith in the atoning power of the blood witnesses' death arose during the times of the Maccabees, a result of the forced religious affiliation by the king of the Greeks, Antiochos Epiphanes, as an outcome of a cognitive dissonance in the Jewish consciousness. Although in those days the martyrs were compelled by force to participate in the worship of idols, they preferred rather the religious death, and hence arose the belief that they softened the scorn of God by their martyrdom (2 Macc. 7:38). From then until today, from blood-tried Ju-

*See also D. Flusser, 'Das jüdische Martyrium im Zeitalter des zweiten Tempels und die Christologie', *Freiburger Rundbrief* 25 (1973): 187–94, and Eduard Lohse, *Märtyrer und Gottesknecht* (Göttingen, 1955). See also, in comparison, Klaus Berger, *Die Auferstehung des Propheten und die Erhöhug des Menschensohns* (Göttingen, 1976).

211

daism into the whole of mankind, the hope that the sacrificing death of the blood witnesses may not have been suffered in vain is a comfort and a source of strength for all men who have to prove themselves in moral constraints.

This is equally true for the martyrs of Christianity, except for one significant distinction: it is true that Christian martyrs die in imitation of Christ's passion, but the atoning power of martyrdom in Christianity is basically limited to the cross alone. The blood of the killed witnesses of faith does not atone and reconcile with God—this happened already on the cross because 'Christ died for our sins' (1 Cor. 15:3).[51] The restriction of the representative atoning death of martyrdom from a general conception to Jesus alone was inevitable through the cosmic extent of history and through Christ's singular divine essence. The exclusiveness of salvation, which can be obtained only through the faith in Christ Jesus, dictates essentially the other, second type of faith to which Buber points. Never in the long history of Jewish faith did I ever come across such exclusiveness of the path of salvation expressed so sharply.* To prevent any possible errors it must be emphasized that the other type of faith developed only after the death on the cross and only gradually. As it has been said, the 'historical' Jesus held an

---

*One may bring up the Jewish messianic movement of Sabbatai Zvi in the seventeenth century as proof of the contrary position insofar as in this case an indirect Christian influence must be assumed. With regard to Chassidism, it is known now that R. Nachman of Brazlav, for example, perceived himself as mediating between men and God, but neither he himself nor any of his disciples thought that a man who would not have faith in him would fall prey to condemnation. And with regard to the Essene *Einung* [community], members of the community indeed believed that 'all of them who do not know His (i.e., the Essene covenant) are idle' (1 QS 5:13), but at the same time the Essenes were certain that in the end Israel would adopt their truth.

exalted self-esteem and was aware of his key role in the economy of God, but at the same time he objected to all personal cults and never said that one should have faith in him. And surely, when he suffered the martyr death, many of the Jews who never became Christians still believed that the blood of Jesus, killed by the Romans, had been spilled for the atonement of the sins of Israel. When the disciples saw the risen Christ, then, too, the form [*Gestalt*] of their faith was not altered fundamentally. The other type of faith began to unfold itself in the midst of Christianity, when Jesus' death on the cross became the central point of a cosmic drama.

In another context, in his commemorative word for the great Christian theologian Leonhard Ragaz,* an essay not accorded due recognition, Buber, truly in classical fashion, announces his reservations against Christology: 'But I strongly believe that we shall never acknowledge Jesus as Messiah who has come, for that would oppose the innermost sense of our messianic passion, which truly is what Ragaz considers in us so very essential for the coming of the Kingdom of God. There is no knot beaten into the mighty rope of our messianic faith, which, tightened to a rock at Sinai, stretches to a standard, which is yet invisible, but rammed into the grounds of the world. . . . For us, there exists no cause of Jesus; for us, there is only the one cause of God'.

Thus the weighty words of Martin Buber. The reader should have taken notice when he read about the 'Messiah who has come' and noted Buber's Jewish confrontation of the 'cause of God' and the 'Christian' cause of Jesus. And, truly, in the living faith of most Christians the cause of

---

*M. Buber, 'Ragaz und "Israel" ', in *Pfade in Utopia,* new ed. (Heidelberg, 1985), p. 378.

Christ is henceforth further in the forefront than the cause of God. And henceforth again they are hit by the past happenings of salvation such as to make the scales tip in favor of the *Gekommenen*, i.e., who came, and the *Kommenden*, i.e., who will come, thus almost became some kind of supplement, so to speak. To how many ordinary Christians is it unknown that [the name] Christ is simply a Greek translation of the Hebrew *Messiah*? Already in the New Testament, the name Christos, going off on its own, parts from the Hebrew original meaning* and, finally, the word becomes a surname and indication of the Jesus. Today the messianic dignity of Jesus is emphasized mainly in the 'dialog' with the Jews, in the conversion of Jews, and in the Jewish-Christian congregations that came into existence through these conversions. Besides, today, the messianic character of Jesus is, of course, important for the Christian chiliastical movements, which are convinced of the near dawning of the messianic age. It is true within the present-day ideology of these groups that the Christological orientation toward the past grew weak in favoring acute expectations toward the Messiah. However, in this respect, Jesus' Good Tidings do not gain much by this structural shift because chiliastical fury does not reconcile easily with the commandment of the love for the enemy.

In my view, the two types of faith cannot be explained as a dichotomy between Judaism and Christianity or as an ontological opposition between the trust and the *Glauben, dass* [belief, that]. Also, I would not dare to state along with Buber that the one type of faith is characteristic for the ar-

---

*See D. Flusser, 'Die jüdischen Heilsgestalten im Urchristentum' (in Hebrew), in *Messianismus und Eschatologie* (Jerusalem, 1984), pp. 125–26. See also Fr. Hahn, *Christologische Hoheitstitel* (Göttingen, 1964), pp. 133–230.

chaic experience of Judaism, whereas the second came out of the premises of the Greek type of thought. To me, it seems that the two types of faith represent a tragic internal Christian problem, one whose scope Christians may be beginning to understand only today. The first type of faith really is originally Jewish, for it sprang off from the religious needs of monotheism, and therefore it is common to the three great monotheistic religions, Judaism, Christianity, and Islam. The faith of Jesus, too, belonged to this first type of faith. The second type of faith is typical for Christianity because it came forth from within it [Christianity] after the cross and joined the first type of faith there. Its objective is the Christ-event, an immense world theater, which begins solemnly with the Word of creation and, at the end of times, comes to its closure with the Last Judgment. The cosmic construction has been erected from Jewish motifs; let it be those that stem from Jesus' elevated self-esteem or others that the Jewish body of thought has supplied at other times. The focus of the event, however, is atonement through the hero's death and his resurrection.

We observe this historic-metahistoric history with an almost holy shyness and do not dare to ask about its outward factual reality because this concerns many men and because so many imagine wrongly that if they do not have faith in this event, they might get lost. But, still, we may ask one question: Is, possibly, the story as it related itself, although its subject is Jewish, rather not a late antique pseudomorphosis and, therefore, appealing to heathen peoples, or did it develop independently as Jewish and without heathen assistance at birth? Anyhow, the epic essence of the tale about Jesus is suitable to break through to the roots hidden in the fertile dark of man's soul and to present the recipient with a new life. Through these salvation-bringing tidings, both the essence of salvation and the essence of faith have changed.

Faith now is no longer a familiar intimacy or the knowledge of the truth of a fact. Now it has become the only path leading to salvation. And salvation is no longer the rescue from danger or the reward for right behavior, but mainly an existential occurrence, a purifying, liberating, and delivering changing of the believer. Faith is now chained to the crucified and resurrected hero, and it is from him, the God-like one, that faith shines backward. In an ecumenical service in honor of the New Year, I heard Catholic and Protestant Christians sing, 'He (Christ) is the path that we tread, the truth that we trust. / He wants to stand with us like a brother, until we shall see him in glory'. In his book, Buber points to the central omnipotence of the Christ-faith for his Christian friends (pp. 132–33). I, too, met the same experience in almost all Christians questioned on this matter. The starting point and the certain nucleus of their faithfulness is not the Jewish root of Christianity, about which they want to learn more from me, not the knowledge of the guiding God of the worlds, and certainly not the love for God and neighbor, which moves mountains. All this they took along as something good and doubtlessly important, but the focal point and the *Urerlebnis* [original knowledge] of their religious experience is Christ. If my Christian readers will examine themselves without prejudice, they too will realize that the supernatural Christ, who died and rose for them, is the rock of their personal faith. That is the second type of faith, and Buber recognizes it as the one that is typical for Christianity. This is true as far as such a religious experience was granted only to someone Christian by Providence. For him, this type of faith is self-evident, but for someone born a Jew or a Muslim this kind of belief is, according to its nature, alien—else he experiences it by conversion. This form of believing, however, has been inculcated into a Christian.

216

We have stated previously that the distinction between the two types of faith has effected a gulf amidst Christianity, which can be bridged only with great difficulties. The first type of faith—which, as said, is common to Christianity, Judaism, and Islam—cannot deprive itself of the Christian religion not only because it was the faith of Jesus, but also because Christian monotheism is built on this type of faith. The second, 'Christological' type of faith is typical only for Christianity. Actually, the conditions for a symbiosis between the two types of faith should be inherent in Christianity, and this has been true because the 'Christological' type of faith is supported by the older one, but unfortunately there exists between the two types of faith an ontological distinction in essence. Or should one rather speak of perhaps a psychological opposition between the two structures?

This finding renders it self-understood why within Christianity, almost since its first steps, a rivalry erupted between the two types of faith. Yet the fascination of the 'Christological' type of faith is overwhelmingly strong: in most cases, the Christian believer tends to surrender to faith in the, for him, solely redeeming Christ-event. Therewith, nothing else is left to the older type of faith than to become the serving maid of the younger sister. Basically this a terrible pity, for during the course of the Christian ages to this day the voice of the 'historical' Jesus has thereby been removed and has almost been silenced, a voice that could have effected the breakthrough to the kingdom of heaven and the all-encompassing love, indeed the love for the enemy. However, compassion for Jesus' suffering can move the heart to active sympathy for the troubled fellow man; it is true that the redeeming faith effects the reformation of the believer's soul, but its power does not suffice to reform the community of men. And as the history of the great churches unfortunately has shown, individual or collective egoistic salvation has blinded Christians' inner eyes and thereby has enabled them to pass passively by bloody wrongs or even to commit such deadly sins themselves. It may be said for comfort, however, that since the times of the Reformation or perhaps even since the Waldensers, small Christian congregations have existed on the fringes of the great churches—such as the Bohemian Brothers, the peace lovers among the Anabaptists, the Mennonites, and other groups who heard the voice of Jesus out of the Gospels. Buber's friend Leonhard Ragaz from Switzerland was a great man among them. And, at present, Jesus' particular type of faith is making its way step by step through the great churches as well.

I believe that I was right when I said that the rivalry between the two types of faith within Christianity has been not only a result of a historical process, but also a gestalt-psychological problem. Namely, it has become evident that the second 'Christological' type of faith cannot be simply added as supplement to the first one. I repeat: the faith in the atoning power of the cross was certainly unfolded probably right after Jesus' death, so that his sacrificing death alone was perceived as atonement for the world, and the appearance of the resurrection unfolded its full meaning at that time. The elevated self-esteem of the 'pre-Easter' Jesus and his God's Sonship were heightened into divinity, and Christ became the immanence of God, His glory. Hereby the *Christusdrama* [drama of Christ] was extended, turning backward to the beginning of the creation of the world by equating Jesus with the Word of creation. The end was already established by the 'historic' Jesus, who, as said, spoke about the Son of Man judging at the Last Judgment. This short review was necessary in order to show that, in the face of Jesus' faith, the 'Christological' type of faith was nothing entirely new. We do not wish to trivialize the new orientation and its supplementary elements, but at the same time we must admit that it did not come out of the blue; we should not forget that the later type of faith developed out of the earlier attempts, out of Jesus' self-understanding, and out of his real biography. However, we must admit that, as may be known, Jesus' elevated self-esteem and his knowledge about the key role which he played in the economy of God did not belong to the type of faith that Jesus offered to men. As far as we may know, he never demanded that one should believe in him, in his messianism and his God's Sonhood. And it is apparently absurd to imagine that he wished one should *believe in* the kingdom of heaven.

Thus, Buber's basic position is correct, and one should not call it into question out of bias. There are really, and this is true within Christianity, two different types of faith—one, the first one, common to the three monotheistic religions, and the other one belonging solely to Christianity. That is, as is said today, a phenomenological fact. Besides, in historical view, the second type of faith immediately followed the first one in time. Also, it is true that owing to this structural distinction between the two types of faith within Christianity, rivalry has erupted almost from its starting point. It is true that the two types of faith are entirely different, but not opposed, and therefore it is most advisable, as it is also dangerous, not to separate radically the two types of faith from each other through a deep cut. The consequence of this radical cut would be the separation of things belonging to each other, for therewith one would cut off the 'Christological' type of faith from its roots, which feed on the first phase of Christianity. And something else: the type of faith represented by Jesus gives a more rationalistic impression than the cosmic-Christological path of faith, which, moreover, is typical only for the Christian. Henceforth, the spontaneous Jewish reaction, in most instances, is therefore an instinctive feeling of strangeness toward the second Christian type of faith. That which for the multitude of Christians signifies the most intense experience of faith and the soul's precious treasure seems to most Jews to be an incomprehensible and unreasonable construction. Characteristic for that point of view is the thinker Rabbi Leo Baeck, who is rightly well known among Jews. He undertook a separation into two parts [*Zweiteilung*] that is different from Buber's: for Baeck, Judaism is the classical religion and Christianity the romantic religion. Buber, on the other hand, did not succumb to a danger that is quite widespread among Jews, but traits of a specific rationalism can be found within Buber as well.

Again we mention the position toward Christianity that is common among Jews with regard to that problem for the sole reason that in it the separate structure of thought combines with a misapplied rationalism. What we actually should be concerned with here is not the Jewish-Christian controversy, but the fact that a pseudoscientific and a pseudorationalistic criticism proved to be damaging for the correct evaluation of the situation, as in the case of the real, existing two types of faith. These [damaging consequences] become evident mainly with regard to Jesus' elevated self-understanding. Many scholars and theologians tend to deny Jesus this trait of character and tend to add it as something irrational to the second type of faith. As the misunderstanding rationalism tends to dismiss the irrational as unhistorical and untrue,* this kind of evaluation sheds a problematic light on Jesus' self-understanding as well as on the entire

*The reader should not come to think hereby that I am unaware of the fact that there is an entire theological school that considers those issues to be contents of faith under the assumption that the intellectual confirmation of these issues is untrue. In the introduction to his *Drei Gespräche* [Three discourses], Solowjew already mocked those, as we may put it, 'fides in quam creditur'.

'Christological' type of faith. And so many well-educated Jews agree with uninspired 'enlightening' Christians in falsely assuming that if it could be demonstrated that Jesus was an ordinary sensible Jew, then Judaism could bring him back home completely.

Hence, the assumption that there are two types of faith is correct, but their mutual delineation is very difficult; if, in addition, denominational and other forces play a role, then the delineation becomes even more questionable. Julius Wellhausen, for one example, said angrily that Jesus was no Christian, but a Jew. With some justification, Rudolf Bultmann* draws a theological borderline to Jesus: 'The preaching of Jesus belongs to the prepositions of the theology of the New Testament and is, itself, not part of it. . . . Christian faith occurs only since there is a Christian kerygma [message], i.e., a kerygma that proclaims Jesus Christ to be the eschatological act of salvation and, meaning Jesus, the one who died on the cross and was resurrected'. However, most sharp-witted was the first explorer of the two types of faith within Christianity. In a fragment titled 'Die Religion Christi' [The religion of Christ],† from the year 1780, which rightly became famous, G. E. Lessing draws sharp lines between the two types of faith, and it can only be recommended that the reader read the entire short fragment. According to Lessing, 'the religion of Christ and the Christian religion are two entirely different things. That one, the religion of Christ, is the one that he, Jesus, knew himself and practiced . . . as a man. This one, the Christian religion, is the religion that considers it as true that he had been more than man and makes him as such an object of

---

*Rudolf Bultmann, *Theologie des Neuen Testaments,* 7th ed. (Tübingen, 1977), pp. 1–2.

†G. E. Lessing, *Werke,* vol. 7 (München, 1976), pp. 711–12.

adoration. It is incomprehensible how both these religions, the religion of Christ as well as the Christian one, can exist in Christ as in one and the very same person . . . that, namely, the religion of Christ is contained in the Evangelists [Gospels] quite differently from the Christian one. In them, the religion of Christ is contained by words most clear and precise. The Christian one, on the contrary, is so uncertain and so ambivalent that there is hardly one single passage to which two different persons, as long as the world stands, have attached the same thought'.

On purpose, I quoted a great deal from the fragment, so that the contemporary reader may distinguish more easily between Lessing's weaknesses and his stronger qualities. There can be no doubt that one has to explain Lessing's weakness in light of the *Zeitgeist der Aufklärung* [the spirit of the time of the Enlightenment]. It is true that meanwhile and until today the *Licht der Aufklärung* [Enlightenment's light] has been darkened by a thick cover of profundity, but the weakness did not disappear therewith. Until today and in certain circles even more than previously, if I should not be mistaken, Jesus is denied any higher self-understanding than a strictly human self-understanding. Because Lessing does the same, there is nothing in his way in separating razor-sharp the faith of the man Jesus from the faith in the superhuman Christ. However, as can be assumed with poets and writers, Lessing's strength is on the philological–literary field. He is completely right in saying, 'The teachings and foundations of both (types of faith) can hardly be found in one and the same book (of the New Testament)'. From his view, 'the religion of Christ'—i.e., the faith of the 'historical' Jesus—is contained in the Gospels 'with words most clear and precise', whereas the 'Christian' type of faith is contained in the Gospels (the fragment refers to them only at its end) in words 'so uncertain and ambivalent' that there is hardly one single passage 'to which two different persons, as long as the world stands, have attached the same thought'. What Lessing writes here is true for the first three Gospels, which are characterized as synoptic. What a pity that he did not proceed with his fragment! If my understanding of his thought is right, he would have continued writing: within all the other books of the New Testament, however, the Christian religion is indeed founded 'with words most clear and precise', whereas in these same books the faith of Jesus is contained 'so uncertain and so ambivalent' that about its essence two persons cannot come to an agreement.

For a long time now, it has been understood that 'Die Religion Christi' belongs among the most eminent theological contributions to come from Lessing's distinguished pen. At the time when the correct consequences are derived from his findings, then it will be possible to learn more about the historical background of the two types of faith in early Christianity. Today, however, it is true that one can no longer agree with Lessing without some reservations about his statement that in the Gospels the religion of Christ is contained by 'words most clear and precise'. On the other hand, it is to be hoped that there are still enough Gottesgelehrte [theologians] who, in harmony with Lessing, are convinced that 'the religion of Christ is contained in the Evangelists [Gospels] quite differently from the Christian one'. The accuracy of Lessing's observation finds full confirmation in an additional analysis:* 'As we analyze the different texts of the New Testament, we will find a fundamental difference between the Gospels and the Epistles of the Apostles, on the one hand, and the rest of the New Testament, on the other hand. If only the second part of the

*See D. Flusser, 'Das Schisma zwischen Judentum und Christentum', in Evangelische Theologie 40. Jahrgang (München, Mai-Juni 1980), pp. 218–23.

New Testament had come down to us, our information about the personality and the life of Jesus would have remained quite fragmentary, and we would know hardly anything about his teaching. Only very few of Jesus' sayings are contained herein. And these sayings are neither theological nor dogmatic, but "halachic." However, if only the synoptic Gospels had been preserved, then we would have only little knowledge about the Christological drama. And I hope to demonstrate somewhere else that passages in the synoptic Gospels, where significant Christian motifs appear, were introduced into the texts during the Greek stage of development, sometimes by the evangelists themselves.* This is also true for those two passages on the atoning function of Jesus' death (Matt. 10:45 and Parr., and Mark 14:24 and Parr.); it is only from the Gospels that we know about Jesus' faith, and the faith in Jesus was developed mainly outside the synoptical Gospels.†

A clue to the genesis of the two types of faith in early Christianity is the fact that actually all records of the customary 'Christian' faith were not conceptualized in Hebrew (or Aramaic), but in Greek only.‡ And on attentive reading, one cannot avoid these editorial remarks and has to admit that they are basically shallow and by themselves of little theological productiveness: they are—not in the best sense of the word—ecclesiastical.§ If we were in the posses-

*See, for Matthew, preliminary D. Flusser, 'Zwei Beispiele antijüdischer Redaktion bei Matthäus,' in *Entdeckungen*, vol. 1 (cited in full in footnote† on p. 199), p. 87, fn. 10.

†Ibid., pp. 218–19.

‡This is true also for the indeed anti-Judaistic passages in the synoptic Gospels!

§In the Gospels, the point is 'an interpreting summary of the Jesus-tradition with the purpose of safeguarding and transmission of the Good Tidings' (Schneemelcher, *Neutestamentliche Apokryphen*, p. 10 [cited in full in footnote§ on p. 207].

sion of other, more profound and distinguished records for the second type of faith in Christianity or, as Lessing puts it, for the 'Christian religion' in the New Testament, these editorial changes of the old material would really be 'uncertain and ambivalent'. If, then, one evaluates without bias the Greek editor's type of work on the Jesuanian material, one comes to the conclusion that this editorial activity took place in a period characterized by a temporary relative religious standstill within the Greek-speaking community of early Christianity.* The way things stand now may be explained best by the hypothesis that the second type of faith, so called according to Buber or in Bultmann's words the kerygma of the Hellenistic community, came into being fairly soon and developed fairly soon. The faith *in* Jesus won these circles over for Christianity, but in order to satisfy the needs of those who wanted to learn more about Jesus, one turned to the records about the sayings and actions of the 'historical' Jesus. These original sources originated in totally different circles—namely, among the disciples of Jesus and through them we know today about the faith of Jesus. One may assume that in these original sources the faith of Jesus was contained 'in words most clear and precise', but unfortunately the original wording in the first three Gospels has been adapted in different ways to the faith of the early church. Already the New Testament, hence, contained the two types of faith. Buber, too, has understood that correctly.

Should one imagine that the two types of faith struggled in the womb of Christianity? Christians themselves may not

---

*These observations were generated from many years of philological studies of the Gospels. The Jesuanian material was at the hands of the editors in literary Greek translations. I think mainly of the editorial work that must have preceded the synoptic Gospels.

be aware of it. And we do not wish, by any means [*beileibe nicht*], to broaden or deepen further the ugly rift between these two essences of the faith. We do not wish to do so because we ourselves perceive faith as an optional path toward the goal and do not consider it right to confuse the type of faith with the goal. We truly take the issue seriously—that the divine truth is visible to us only through a veil. Therefore, we are barred from Buber's statement that 'The faith of Judaism and the faith of Christendom are by nature different in kind, each in conformity with its human basis' (pp. 173–74). Certainly it is true that the first type of faith is, as also Jesus understood it, the eminent Jewish one. But it is also that of Islam. And in observing matters from a higher position [*höheren Standpunkt*], one must agree on almost all points with Lessing when he writes: 'The religion of Christ is the religion that he [Jesus] as a human being recognized and practiced; [the one] that any man can have in common with him; [the one] that any man must wish to have in common with him; [and this ever and ever more so] as he imagines the sublimity and kindness of the character of Christ as a human being only'.* If we take a broader view, even the perception of God in philosophy, from Greek onward, belongs, among others, to the first type of faith. The second type of faith, as has been said previously, belongs only to Christianity. Its *Objekt* [subject, topic] is Jesus Christ, whereas, from a different point of view, Jesus constitutes the *Subjekt* [subject, actor] of the first type of faith.

On pure historical examination, the second type of faith originated later, but here we must not forget that it is not accidental at all that Jesus became its focus. It unfolded not only the cross and the resurrection, but, as we think, also the high self-understanding of the 'historical' Jesus to a tremen-

*See footnote† on p. 221.

dous cosmic drama. As has been said previously, Jesus, however, on his part never demanded that one should believe in him, and he repudiated any personal cult toward him.* Jesus' elevated self-esteem, then, does not belong to his tidings of faith. After Easter, as is known, things changed.

In the realm of thought, supplements do not have less value than the earlier tradition, even when the old is transformed by the new or even superceded. The unexpected novelty, by itself, is neither the right version nor the better one nor the inferior or morally suspect one. From this point of view, little can be said, as it seems, in opposition to the added one, the one typical only for Christianity. Historical judgments should never automatically be value judgments, anyway. But independent even from all value judgments, there exists in our case an unsolved serious problem with regard to the structure of the Christian religious system, and there can be no doubt that one—from Lessing to Buber—had to take notice of the two different kinds of faith. The existence of the two types of faith within Christianity can be explained not only historically, but psychologically as well. The internal tension between and the contest of the two types of faith throughout the long history of Christianity should be examined; thereby a gap in our knowledge would be filled. The separation certainly had originated already in the first decades of the church,† and as far as we may know, the multitude of Christians were won over almost immediately by the 'Christological', the second type of faith, because this path of faith assured the convert of redemption. Jesus' type of faith, on

---

*In my view, it is easy to prove that Jesus wished to be addressed by his disciples as 'Herr' [Master] and not as 'Rabbi'. See Flusser, *Entdeckungen* (cited in full in footnote† on p. 199), p. 106, and the list [of references] in R. Riessner, *Jesus als Lehrer* (Tübingen, 1981), p. 247.

†See footnote* on p. 224.

the other hand, was transmitted to the future generations only through the first three Gospels.*

The true fundamental religious experience of almost any believing Christian is founded until today on his Christ-experience, although in it, naturally, Jesus' tidings of faith are considered seriously. Already in the Middle Ages, there were men living in those days whose conduct was decisively determined by the Good Tidings of Jesus. But since the days of the Reformation, the scales within the High Churches were also tipped in favor of *Glauben an* [faith in] Christ. However, not only such groups as the Bohemian Brothers took, already in those days, the social heritage of Jesus and his disciples seriously. In contrast to Luther's type of faith, the humanist Erasmus of Rotterdam also acknowledged in the 'Philosophy of the Christ' the real essence of the Christian religion—and his view would influence liberal Christianity in future days. Nowadays and in all Christian churches and groups, the importance of Jesus is coming more and more to everyone's mind, although there is at times quite a bit of confusion.

The gulf between the two types of faith within Christianity has not been bridged until today. Such as it was, Christianity brought much good. But evil consequences came out of the extent of the repression that this other type of faith was holding toward Jesus' understanding of God and men so that the latter was hardly known even to some clergymen or, even worse, was regarded almost with suspicion. Anyhow, it effected little good that Jesus' type of faith was not admitted on terms other than those of a servant to the redeeming faith in Christ. The faithful compassion for the Son of God, who suffered an unjustified death regard-

*From the apocryphical Gospels (see footnote§ on p. 207), one learns nothing about Jesus' type of faith. Unfortunately, in most cases, no one pays attention to this [fact].

228

less of his innocence, affects some in ways that it arouses their helpful empathy for suffering and rejected human beings. This compassion, however, could not prevent the terrible evil deeds in the Christian worlds, deeds of inhumanity that, not seldom, were committed out of zealous faith. I can hardly imagine that Jesus' type of faith would have permitted acts of the kind if his type of faith had been adopted throughout Christianity on terms of unconditional commitment. Today one cannot avoid acknowledging the binding authority of Jesus' tidings of faith for the Christian faith. Will the time draw nearer when 'mankind is gathered in from the exiles of the "religions" into the Kingship of God' (Buber, p. 174)?

Buber's *Two Types of Faith* is a study of genius that today is as valid as in the hour when this great Jewish thinker laid out its concept and wrote it down. Buber has put his finger on an acute problem, the question about Jewish and Christian identity. The dualism of faith in Christianity, which Buber diagnosed, could not be bridged until today. For a Jew who has faith in God, Buber's essay is a proven signpost to the Christian sister religion. And referring to the Christian reader, I hope that it might become easier than ever for Christians to profess to their two types of faith simultaneously—to the original Jewish and to the new, the genuine Christian one. Thus, with the help of Buber's essay, they might look into the face of their Jewish brothers with love and understanding.*

*By providential matching, just when I finished writing this last page, a loving friend put into my hands the *Festschrift for W. Strolz, 17. November 1987*, and inside it (pp. 103–20) was R. J. Z. Werblowsky's essay 'Überlegungen zu Martin Bubers "Zwei Glaubensweisen"'. His reflections impressed me greatly. Meanwhile, something new came out of this exercise: R. J. Z. Werblowsky, 'Reflections on Martin Buber's 'Two Types of Faith', *Journal of Jewish Studies* 39, no. 1 (1988): 92–101. A brilliant drawing!

Translator's Notes to the Afterword

1. In the text, quotations from Scripture come from *The Holy Bible: Authorized King James Version (KJV)* (Nashville, Tenn.: Cornerstone, 1999) and sometimes from the German translation as used or offered by David Flusser. In the footnotes, they come from (a) *The New Jerusalem Bible, Standard Edition (NJB)* (New York and London: Doubleday, 1989); (b) *The Jerusalem Bible: The Holy Scriptures (JB)* (Jerusalem: Koren, 1980); and (c) the German translation as used or offered by David Flusser when it is not in the main text body.

2. Martin Buber, *Zwei Glaubensweisen,* mit einem Nachwort von David Flusser (Gerlingen: Lambert Schneider, 1994).

3. Martin Buber, *Two Types of Faith,* translated by Norman P. Goldhawk (London: Routledge and Kegan Paul, 1951), reprinted in this volume.

4. Not italized at this point in either Buber's or Flusser's text.

5. Flusser: 'intensive Kenntnisnahme eine(s) Soseins'.

6. James 2:19, *NJB:* 'You believe in the one God'; Flusser: 'Du glaubst, daß Gott einer ist'.

7. 'Hie ist zu merken, daß zweierlei Weis glaubt wird. Zum ersten von Gott, das ist wenn ich glaub, daß wahr sei, was man vom Türken, Teufel, Hell sagt. Dieser Glaub ist mehr ein Wissenschaft oder Merkung, denn (als) ein Glaub. Zum andern wird in Gott geglaubt, das ist, wenn ich nit allein glaub, daß wahr sei, was von Gott gesagt wird, sondern setze mein Trau (Vertrauen) in ihn, begeb und erwege mich mit ihm zu handeln und glaub ohn allen Zweifel, er werd mir also sein und tun, wie man von ihm sagt, auf wilch Weis ich nit glaubte dem Türken oder Menschen, wie hoch man sein Lob preisete, denn ich glaub leichtlich, daß ein Mann frumm sei, ich wags drum nicht auf ihn zu bauen. Solcher Glaub, der es wagt auf Gott, wie von ihm gesagt wird, es sei im Leben oder Sterben, der macht allein einen Christen-Menschen und erlanget von Gott alles, was er will, der mag kein böse falsches Herz haben, denn das ist ein lebendiger Glaub, und der wird geboten in dem ersten Gebot, daß do (da) sagt: Ich bin dein Gott, du sollt (sollst) kein ander Götter haben. Drum ist das Wörtlein *in* fast (sehr) wohl gesetzt und mit Fleiß wahr zu nehmen, daß wir nit sagen: Ich glaub Gott dem Vater oder von dem Vater, sondern *in* Gott den Vater, *in* Jesum Christum, *in* den heiligen Geist'.

8. Note Flusser's sophisticated wording in German: 'daß der Mensch ein Wort für das Glauben einfach benötigt'.

9. Prov. 14:15, *NJB:* 'The simpleton believes any message'; *JB:* 'The sim-

230

ple man believes everything'; Flusser: 'Der Einfältige glaubt jedem Wort'. Prov. 26:25, *NJB:* 'do not trust such a person's pretty speeches'; *JB:* 'when he speaks fair, do not believe him'; Flusser: 'Wenn er (der Mann) freundlich redet, glaube ihm nicht!'

10. Flusser: 'Das glaube der Jude Apella, nicht ich'. Or, translated in the present terminology: 'In this the Jew Apella may have faith, not I'.

11. Flusser uses the German word *Begriff. Begriff* is 'concept', but also *'terminus technicus,' 'abstractum'*—all of them nouns. He distinguishes between *Glaubensbegriff* (concept of faith) and *Glaubensweise* (type of faith); both words are nouns, concepts, *termini.* Later Flusser speaks of the Hebrew concept of (and the Hebrew term for) *Gerechtigkeit* (justice), avoiding the application of *Begriff* for the phrase *gerecht werden* (to become just). The latter is not a noun in English or German, but, as Flusser puts it delicately, it became a Hebrew concept, a Hebrew term. In this passage, Flusser explains *Emuna* and *Teshuva* and thereby the adoption of a Biblical phrase as a noun in post-Biblical times. He later indirectly refers to the explanation that he gives here.

12. Exod. 14:31, *NJB:* 'when Israel saw the mighty deed that Yahweh had performed against the Egyptians, the people revered Yahweh and put their faith in Yahweh and in Moses, his servant'; *JB:* 'And Israel saw that great work which the Lord did upon Mizrayim: and the people feared the Lord, and believed in the Lord, and in his servant Moshe'; Flusser: 'Als Israel (am Schilfmeer) sah, wie gewaltig sich die Hand des Herrn an den Ägyptern erwiesen hatte, da fürchtete das Volk den Herrn, und sie glaubten an den Herrn und an seinen Knecht Mose'.

13. The use of the word *Geistesgabe* is a very fine example of Flusser's sensitivity in writing and understanding the many-folded history of words in all realms of their application, even in colloquial speech. This word in particular, herein similar to a word such as *Geistesgegenwart,* has a quite sober meaning, simply "reason, intellectual capacity." But reason and intellectual capacities—in particular if related to great men of literature, theology, philosophy, or other fields of scholarship, sciences, and art, and if related to works of original, creative, even genius understanding or achievements—are extraordinary gifts for which man has no answer or no merit. In the way Flusser uses the German word *Geistesgabe,* one should note the distinction from the classical and romantic idea of 'genius', which inspired—not only—the German word *Genie.* Nevertheless, the term *Geistesgabe* may be used in very ordinary contexts, but, on the other hand, it may also hint at spiritual spheres of religion and other practices as well. *Begabt sein* means to be talented; to some extent, this term already calls for the implied moral

obligation to use the gift and to be responsible for the achievements undertaken.

Hence, Flusser, by using the term *Geistesgabe,* avoids doing what he described earlier: parting with any side or any historical interpretation, especially historical religious views. As Flusser uses it, the term is inclusive, not exclusive.

14. In cases like this one, I leave Flusser's German wording in the text and place a translation in brackets. Many of Flusser's terms already deal with the subject matter of his essay on the semantic level.

15. Gal. 3:2–3, *NJB:* 'There is only thing I should like you to tell me: How was it that you received the Spirit—was it practice of the Law, or by believing of the message you heard? Having begun in the Spirit, can you be so stupid as to end in the flesh'? Flusser: 'nur da möchte ich von euch wissen: habt ihr den Geist empfangen aus Werken des Gesetzes, oder aus des Glaubens Kunde? So töricht seid ihr? Im Geist habt ihr begonnen, um im Fleisch zu enden'?

16. Gen. 15:6, *NJB:* 'Abram put his faith in Yahweh and this was reckoned to him as uprightness'; Gen. 15:6, *JB:* 'And he had faith in the Lord, and this he [God] accounted to him for justice'; Flusser: 'Und er glaubte an den Herrn, und das rechnete er ihm als Gerechtigkeit an'.

17. Isa. 26:2, *NJB:* 'Open the gates! Let the upright nation come in, the nation that keeps faith'! *JB:* 'Open the gates that the righteous nation that keeps faithfulness may enter in'; Flusser: 'Tut auf die Tore, daß einziehe das gerechte Volk, welches die Treue (oder: Glauben) bewahrt'.

18. Flusser: 'Es steht ja nicht geschrieben: Tut auf die Toere, daß einziehen Priester, Leviten und Israeliten; vielmehr: Tut auf die Tore, daß ein gerechter Nichtjude *(goj),* welcher Glauben besitzt, einziehe'.

19. Or *will.* Both translations are possible, but for this little word the difference in connotation is great.

20. Ps. 92:2–5, *NJB:* 'It is good to give thanks to Yahweh, to make music for your name, Most High, to proclaim your faithful love at daybreak, and your constancy all through the night, you have brought me joy, Yahweh, immensely deep your thoughts'; *JB:* 'It is a good thing to give thanks to the Lord, and to sing and to praise thy name, O most High: to relate thy steadfast love in the morning, and thy faithfulness every night. . . . For thou Lord hast made me glad through thy work'; Flusser: 'Köstlich ist es, den Herrn zu preisen, deinen Namen, o Höchster zu singen, des Morgens deine Gnade zu verkünden und deine Treue in den Nächten. . . . denn du hast mich erfreut, o Herr, durch dein Walten, ich frohlocke über das Werk deiner Hände'.

21. The German word *zurückgreifen* also means 'to fall' or 'to go back'. However, in this context it implies a notion of recovery.

22. Gen. 15:6, *NJB:* 'Abram put his faith in Yahweh and this was reckoned to him as uprightness'; *JB:* 'And he believed in the Lord; and he counted it him for righteousness'; Flusser: 'Und er glaubte an den Herrn, und das rechnete er ihm als Gerechtigkeit an'.

23. Exod. 4:31, *NJB:* 'The people were convinced, and they rejoiced'; *JB:* 'And the people believed: and when they heard'; Flusser: 'Und das Volk glaubte, und sie hörten'.

24. Hab. 2:4, *KJV:* 'but the just shall live by his faith'; *JB:* 'but the just shall live by his faith'; *NJB:* 'but the upright will live through faithfulness'; Flusser: 'Der Bewährte aber wird in seinem Vertrauen leben'.

25. Flusser: 'Der Gerechte wird in seinem Glauben leben'.

26. Flusser: 'Da kam Habakuk und brachte sie (die Gebote) auf eines, denn es heißt: der Gerechte wird in seinem Glauben leben'.

27. 'Unification' comes too close to *Vereinigung:* the act of establishing a community, gathering individuals to a union that by way of uniting them dissolves individual particularities under and into a common behavior and spiritual state of mind. *Einung* is more than 'union', more than 'community'; it is also more than *Einigkeit* because it contains the act of achieving *Einheit*, a transcendent moment. This passage, of course, provides another example of Flusser's literary responses and implicit analytic approach to the subject of his essay.

28. Flusser: 'Der Gerechte wird in seinem Glauben leben'.

29. Flusser: 'Der Gerechte wird *aus* dem Glauben leben'. Literally translated, *aus* is 'out', which is different from the English *by*. However, as the English translation of Rom. 1:17 says 'The just will live by faith', this is used here as well with *out of* in brackets. The quotations from Paul concerning the law have in English *by*, but in German *durch*. There is a significant difference in the two German words *aus* and *durch* (through, with). The quotation from Gal. 3:11 (see note 31) always has in English *by*, in German *aus* and *durch*.

30. Gen. 15:6, *KJV* and *JB:* 'And he [Abraham] believed in the Lord; and he counted it to him for righteousness'; *NJB:* 'Abram put his faith in Yahweh and this was reckoned to him as uprightness'; Flusser: 'Und er [Abraham] glaubte an den Herrn, und das rechnete er ihm als Gerechtigkeit an'.

31. Gal. 3:11, *NJB:* 'Now it is obvious that nobody is reckoned as upright in God's sight by the Law, since *the upright will live through faith*'; Flusser: 'Daß aber durchs Gesetz niemand gerechtfertigt wird vor Gott, ist offenbar, denn der Gerechte aus dem Glauben wird er leben'.

32. Gal. 2:16, *NJB:* 'have nevertheless learned that someone is reckoned as upright not by practicing the Law but by faith in Jesus Christ; and we too came to believe in Jesus Christ so as to be reckoned as upright by faith in Christ and not by practicing the Law: since no human being *can be found* upright by keeping the Law'; Flusser: 'In der Erkenntnis, daß der Mensch nicht gerechtfertigt wird, aus den Werken des Gesetzes, sondern durch den Glauben an Jesus Christus, haben wir glaichfalls an Jesus Christus geglaubt, damit wir durch den Glauben an Jesus Christus gerechtfertigt werden uns nicht aus den Werken des Gesetzes, denn aus den Werken des Gesetzes wird kein Fleisch gerechtfertigt'.

33. Ps. 143:2, *KJV:* 'And enter not into judgment with thy servant: for in thy sight shall no man living be justified'.

34. Rom. 3:20, *KJV:* 'Therefore by the deeds of the law there shall no flesh be justified in his sight: for the law is the knowledge of sins'.

35. Flusser: 'ich weiss, daß kein Mensch ohne dich gerechtfertigt wird'.

36. Flusser: 'nur in deiner Güte kann ein Mensch gerechtfertigt werden'.

37. Flusser: 'Ein jeder, der auf sich *ein* Gebot im Glauben nimmt, der ist wert, daß auf ihm der heilige Geist ruhe'.

38. Matt. 7:21, *NJB:* 'it is not anyone who says to me, "Lord, Lord," who will enter the kingdom of Heaven, but the person who does the will of my Father in heaven'; Flusser: 'Nicht jeder, der zu mir sagt: Herr, Herr, wird in das Reich der Himmel eingehen, sondern wer den Willen meines Vaters im Himmel tut'.

39. Matt. 12:41, *NJB:* 'On Judgment Day the men of Nineveh will appear against this generation and they will be its condemnation'; Flusser: 'im Gericht mit diesem Geschlecht auftreten und es verurteilen'.

40. Matt. 9:21–22, *NJB:* 'Courage, my daughter, your faith has saved you'; Flusser: 'Sei getrost, meine Tochter, dein Glaube hat dich gerettet'.

41. Luke 17:6, *NJB:* 'The Lord replied, 'If you had faith like a mustard seed you could say to this mulberry tree, "Be uprooted and planted in the sea," and it would obey you'; Flusser: 'Hättet ihr Glauben wie ein Senfkorn, so könntet ihr zu diesem Maulbeerbaum sagen: entwurzele dich und verpflanze dich ins Meer, und er würde euch gehorchen'.

42. Matt. 5:7, *NJB:* 'Blessed are the merciful: they shall have mercy shown them'; Flusser: 'Selig sind die Barmherzigen, denn sie werden Barmherzigkeit erfahren'.

43. Deut. 24:19, *NJB:* 'Suppose a man has taken a wife and consummated the marriage; but she has not pleased him and he has found some impropriety of which to accuse her'; Flusser: 'Wenn jemand ein Weib zur Frau nimmt und sie ihm dann nicht gefällt'.

44. Mark 10:5, *NJB:* 'It was because you were so hard hearted'; Flusser: 'mit Rücksicht auf die Härte eurer Herzen'.

45. The structure of Flusser's sentence allows us to relate the implicit and undecided reference both to the *Urabsicht* (original purpose) and to the *Aussage* (saying), but not to both because the verb is put in the singular form.

46. 'In the Jordan' is Flusser's addition.

47. Ps. 2:7, *NJB:* 'You are my son, today I have fathered you'; Flusser: 'Mein Sohn bist du: ich habe dich heute gezeugt'.

48. Here quoted from *NJB,* Luke 3:23, *KJV:* 'and Jesus himself began to be about thirty years of age, being (as was supposed) the son of Joseph'; Flusser: 'und er Jesus war bei seinem Anfange etwa dreißig Jahre alt und war—so galt er—der Sohn des Joseph'.

49. Luke 22:69, *NJB:* 'But from now on, the *Son of Man* will be *seated at the* right hand of the Power *of God*'; Flusser: 'von nun an wird der Menschensohn zur rechten der Kraft sitzen'.

50. Flusser: 'binitarische' (derived from Latin: *binatim/bini,* 'two-folded'.

51. 1 Cor. 15:3, *NJB:* 'that Christ died for our sins'; Flusser: 'Christus ist für unsere Sünden gestorben'.

INDEX TO THE PRINCIPAL
SUBJECTS AND NAMES

Abraham, 44, 46ff., 54, 88, 120, 184, 187, 189
Adam, 73, 119, 158–59
Akibah, 76, 151, 154
Amenophis IV, 126
Anthropomorphism, 129, 153
Apocalypse of Baruch, 159
Augustine, 135
Avtalion, 89–90

Baptism tradition, 206–9
Bergmann, 176
Binitarianism, 128f.
Brunner's doctrine of God, 163f.
Bultmann, 117, 206, 221, 225

Conversion, 10
Cyrus, 110

Daniel, 109, 112, 144
David, 64, 73, 106, 166, 207
Dead sea scrolls, 194, 199, 200

Deutero-Isaiah, 107, 111–12, 120, 206
Dostoevski, 132

Elenchos, 37
Eliah, 99, 104
Emunah, 26, 28–29, 63, 116, 128, 131, 154, 169, 170ff., 176, 178, 184–85, 188
Enoch, 43, 99, 104, 112
Epicurus, 41
Erasmus, 228
Eschatology, 210
Essenes, 191, 194–95, 201, 209, 212
Eternal life, 41, 129, 133
Existence of God, 38–41, 43
Ezekiel, 86ff., 144
Ezra-Apocalypse, 145ff.

Faith
— in Epistle to the Hebrews, 36ff., 43
— in John's Gospel, 39ff.

Faith (*cont.*)
— in Synoptic and John's
   Gospel, 32–35
— its twofold meaning, 7–12
Fate and providence, 150ff.
Feeling, 8
Francis of Assisi, 131

Gamliel II, 73
Goliath, 73

Habakkuk, 48f., 190–92
'Hardening of the Heart',
   83–90
Hassidism, 59, 61, 77
Hegel, 90
Hosea, 138

Images in the conception of
   God, 129–32
Immediacy towards God, 130f.,
   140, 150, 154, 157, 159ff.,
   164, 169

Jabne, 64
Jannai, 62
Jeremiah, 144
Jesus
— Ascension from the cross and
   resurrection, 99,
   133
— Deification, 112, 115f.,
   130
— Faith in Christ, 96f.
— Following Jesus, 94ff. 115,
   124
— Jesus and Israel, 89f.
— Messianic office, 30ff.
— Messianic secret, 107f.
— Nicodemus, 117–25, 206

— Prayer, 155ff., 159ff.
— Preaching 24ff., 29, 94f.
— Self-consciousness, 31,
   102ff., 208
— Suffering and Death, 102–5,
   112f., 211–12,
— Teaching on belief and
   unbelief, 17–18, 39f.,
   191
— Teaching in Sermon on
   Mount, 59–76
— Thomas, 127
Job, 40, 57, 144, 146
John the Baptist, 24, 26, 105,
   156
Josephus, 34, 145, 151
Josiah, 143, 145
Jubilees, Book of, 76
Judaism and Christendom,
   176–77, 180–81, 209–11,
   214–17, 220–21, 226

Kafka, 163, 165f., 167ff.
Kierkegaard, 167, 173, 180
Kingship of God, 27f., 118

Leibnitz, 180
Lessing, 180, 221–23, 226–27
Lishmah doctrine, 92ff.
Love in Old Testament, 68–72,
   136
Luther, 122, 180–81, 193

Maccabees, Second Book of,
   144, 211
Maccabees, Fourth Book of,
   152
Maimonides, 184
Marcion, 141, 167
Mediator, 150, 152ff., 164

238

Megiddo, 143
Mendelssohn, 184
Messiah, 30–31, 51, 105–13, 116, 121, 152
Middah, Middot, 152ff.
Mishnah, 41–43
Monotheism, 133f.
Moses, 45, 66–67, 75, 99, 184–86, 192, 201

Nachman, 190, 212
Nicodemus, 117–25, 206

Paul
— Faith and law, 44, 46–50
— Faith and works, 51–55
— Faith in Christ, 96ff.
— Gnosticism, 83, 148, 166
— Government of the world, 81f.
— 'Hardening of the heart', 85f.
— Love of God, 135f., 137ff.
— Monotheism, 133f.
— Prayer, 161
— Redemption, 82f., 88f., 91, 96f., 98
— Resurrection of Christ, 98
— Romans vii, 147ff.
— Torah, 80ff., 83ff., 91f.
— Wrath of God, 139ff.
Paulinism, 162ff., 166, 168f., 173
Pharaoh, 83, 86, 144
Pharisees, 58, 61ff., 65–68, 151, 159f., 198, 199, 201–3
— 'Direction of the heart', 63ff., 79

— Doctrine of the *Middot* of God, 152ff.
— *Lishmah* doctrine, 92ff.
— Love to God, 136ff.
— Love to man, 73f., 79
— Torah, 91–94
Philo, 34, 119, 152
Pistis, 26, 43, 97, 169, 170–73, 176–78
Pneuma, 121ff.
Prayer, 155–61
Problem of suffering, 143–50, 152
Psalms, 188, 193–94

Rang, 132
Re'ah, 69ff., 72
Resurrection, 9, 99ff.
Ruach, 122f.

Sabbatai Zvi, 212
Satan, 161
Schlatter, 124
Septuagint, 47, 52, 69
Sermon on the Mount, 59f., 62f., 65f., 67ff., 75f., 160
Servant of JHVH, 105, 110f.
Simon Magus, 19
Sin, 64f., 81f.
— Jewish doctrine of sin and forgiveness, 157ff.
Soederblom, 132
Solomon, 61, 64
Son of God, 75, 125f.
Son of Man, 103, 112f.
Spinoza, 136

Talmud, 41, 47, 61, 158
Thomas, 127f.

239

Torah, 41, 53, 56ff., 61, 63–67,
    73, 79f., 92f., 97, 114

Usener, 116

Wellhausen, 221
Wisdom, Book of, 164f.

Wisdom of Solomon, 144
Wrath of God, 139f.

Zaddikim, 77, 144
Zealots, 68
Zedek, Zedakah, 45